# CHINESE-ENGLISH DICTIONARY OF POLYPHONIC CHARACTERS

# 多音多义字汉英字典

Compiled by
Roderick S. Bucknell and Yang Mu

白瑞德、杨沐编

SINOLINGUA  BEIJING
华语教学出版社　北京

First Edition    1999

ISBN 7-80052-634-8

Copyright 1999 by Sinolingua

Published by Sinolingua

24 Baiwanzhuang Road, Beijing 100037, China

Tel: 86 – 010 – 68326333 / 68994599

Fax: 86 – 010 – 68326642

E-mail: sinolingua@ihw.com.cn

Printed by Beijing Foreign Languages Printing House

Distributed by China International

Book Trading Corporation

35 Chegongzhuang Xilu, P.O. Box 399

Beijing 100044, China

*Printed in the People's Republic of China*

# TABLE OF CONTENTS

# INTRODUCTION

This dictionary is designed to provide students of modern standard Chinese with essential information on polyphonic characters.

The term "polyphonic character" is used here to refer to a Chinese character that has more than one reading or pronunciation, each with its particular associated meaning and/or area of usage. A typical example is the character 重. Depending on the context, this character is read either as zhòng, in which case it means "heavy, important", or as chóng, in which case it means "to repeat; again; layers". For example,

zhòng : 很重 hěn zhòng (very) heavy
　　　　重量 zhòngliàng weight
　　　　重视 zhòngshì to regard as important
chóng : 重新 chóngxīn again, anew, afresh
　　　　重叠 chóngdié piled layer on layer

Another common example is 没. This character is read either as méi, signifying a negative, or as mò, meaning to sink; to disappear; for example:

méi :    没有钱 méiyǒu qián to have no money

mò :    沉没 chénmò to sink, drown


These relationships can be represented graphically as follows:

重 {
  zhòng — heavy, important

  chóng — to repeat; again; layers
}

没 {
  méi — not

  mò — to sink; to disappear
}


This situation contrasts with the simplest, ideal case, in which a given written character is associated with a single reading or pronunciation and with a single meaning, as in the following example:


高— gāo —tall, high


The Chinese term for a character exhibiting this associated ambivalence in the sound and meaning dimensions is 多音多义字 duōyīn duōyì zì, "multi-sound multi-meaning character", or, more loosely, 破音字 pòyīn zì, "split-sound character". A convenient English equivalent is "polyphonic character", or simply "polyphone".

As can be discovered by consulting a character dictionary, polyphonic characters account for about five per cent of all Chinese

2

characters. However, their importance is much greater than that figure would suggest, because they include some of the most commonly used characters in the language; for example, 还, 没, 好, 长, 少, 得, 的, 了 are all polyphones.

The phenomenon of polyphony adds considerably to the difficulty of mastering written Chinese. In the case of a polyphonic character, the student not only has to learn the two (or more) different readings, but also must learn to recognise which of them is required in each particular situation. To provide assistance in coping with such difficulties is the principal aim of the present dictionary.

The problems posed by polyphony in Chinese have long been recognised, and consequently many dictionaries of polyphonic characters have been compiled. However, almost all such dictionaries are monolingual and designed for use by the Chinese themselves. Chinese-English dictionaries of polyphonic characters are rare. The present one is, as far as the compilers are aware, the first such bilingual dictionary based on the simplified characters and providing full information on pronunciation and usage in the written form of the modern standard Chinese language (普通话 pǔtōnghuà).

The simplification of the characters, together with certain other aspects of the language reforms that were implemented in the 1960s and '70s, had many repercussions on the phenomenon of polyphony. The reforms eliminated some former cases of polyphony (e.g., 徵, 乾); and they also, paradoxically, brought some new cases of polyphony into existence (e.g., 干, 斗). All such recent developments have been taken into account in compiling the present dictionary, in order to provide a completely up-to-date guide to usage with respect to polyphony in modern standard Chinese.

Despite the care taken in its preparation, this dictionary will no doubt be found to be marred by errors, omissions, and other defects. The compilers will welcome any comments from readers in this regard and will seek to take them into account when preparing future editions.

# DESIGN AND USE OF THE DICTIONARY

## 1. Reference standard and criteria for inclusion

On questions of pronunciation and orthographic usage in modern standard Chinese, one of the most widely accepted standard references is the *Xiandai Hanyu Cidian* 现代汉语词典〔*Modern Chinese Dictionary*〕(Beijing: Commercial Press, revised edition 1996). The present dictionary follows that standard closely in all matters relating to polyphony, while differing from it substantially as regards specific content and arrangement (e.g., criteria for inclusion, layout of entries, example phrases and sentences, and provision of English renderings).

For the present purpose a character is recognised as a polyphone, and therefore as eligible to be considered for inclusion in this dictionary, if, according to the *Xiandai Hanyu Cidian*, the following two conditions are satisfied:

    a) the character has two (or more) readings, *and*

    b) each of those readings has its own distinctive associated range of meaning and/or area of usage.

On these criteria, the characters 重 and 没, cited above, clearly qualify as polyphones.

On the other hand, the character 谁, despite having two readings, shéi and shuí, does not qualify. This is because these two readings do not correspond to any distinction in meaning or usage; whichever of the two readings one uses, the meaning remains "who?". The phonetic ambivalence of 谁 is a case of free variation rather than of polyphony. To qualify it as a polyphone, a character's two readings must be associated with different meanings, or at least with different areas of usage. This situation can be clarified by citing parallel examples from English. Free variation is seen in the word *economic*, pronounced either [ˌi:kə'nomik] or [ˌekə'nomik] with no distinction in meaning. Polyphony is seen in *read*, pronounced either [ri:d] (present tense) or [red] (past tense); also in *sow*, pronounced either [sou] "to plant" or [sau] "adult female pig".

There are a few borderline cases. An example is the character 血. It has the two readings xiě and xuè, both of which mean "blood". But despite this identity in meaning, the two readings are not freely interchangeable; the speaker/reader has little freedom to choose between them. The reading xiě is the appropriate one in 一滴血 yì dī xiě "a drop of blood", 流血 liú xiě "to bleed", and 血淋淋 xiělínlín "dripping with blood". The reading xuè is required in 血球 xuèqiú "blood corpuscles", 血统 xuètǒng "a blood lineage", and 血汗 xuèhàn "blood and sweat" (signifying "hard toil"). Generally, xiě is used in more straightforward, colloquial, non-technical words and contexts, while xuè is used in more formal, technical words and contexts, and in cases where the reference is figurative or poetic. This is, therefore, not a case of free variation; although the two readings of 血 have the same meaning, they correspond to different areas of usage. Consequently, 血 does qualify as a polyphone.

Rather different is the case of the character 一, which is read yì, yí, or yī, all with the same meaning ("one, unity, single"). As with 血, the speaker or reader does not have free choice among the possible readings. However, in this case the choice is determined by purely phonological factors: the character is pronounced yí before a following tone 4, yì before tone 1, 2, or 3, and yī before a pause. Knowledge of this simple rule is all that is needed to ensure the correct pronunciation. Consequently, the character 一 is not regarded as a polyphone. Similar remarks apply for 不, whose two readings, bù and bú, are similarly determined by the phonological context.

Not all of the polyphones attested in modern standard Chinese are included in the present dictionary. Some are judged to be too rare, specialised, or archaic to deserve inclusion in a dictionary having a mainly practical objective. An example is the character 镐. It satisfies the primary defining criteria: when read gǎo, it refers to a kind of hoe or pickaxe; read hào, it is the name of the first capital of the Western Zhou Dynasty (11th century B.C.). This character is nevertheless excluded from the dictionary on the grounds that the latter reading, hào, is too rare and specialised. Although 镐 is indeed a polyphone according to *Xiandai Hanyu Cidian*, it fails to meet the further criterion of practical usefulness.

A polyphonic character may also be excluded if either of its readings is limited to a regional dialect or to non-standard speech

7

that lacks wide currency, or if one of its two readings is exclusively classical or literary and therefore unfamiliar to most Chinese native speakers. An example of the latter situation is the character 噱, read both xué ("a joke") and jué ("to laugh"). The second reading/meaning is limited to literary usage, and that suffices to disqualify the character from inclusion.

On the other hand, even though one of the readings of a polyphonic character is exclusively dialect or exclusively literary, that character may still qualify for inclusion if the reading in question is sufficiently well known. For example, the character 约, normally read yuē, also has the dialect reading yāo when the meaning is "to weigh". The latter pronunciation is widely enough known and used to justify this character's inclusion in the dictionary. Again, the character 蛇, in addition to its usual reading shé ("snake"), has a second, literary reading yí. This literary reading is fairly well known because of its occurrence in a fixed four-character expression (成语 chéngyǔ), namely: 虚与委蛇 xūyǔ-wēiyí, meaning "to treat courteously but without sincerity". This justifies the character's inclusion in the dictionary.

Such judgements admittedly involve an element of arbitrariness, but this is largely unavoidable. Most dictionary compilers face the same problem of striking a balance between the competing ideals of comprehensiveness and practical usefulness. As a result of applying the above principles, the present dictionary contains a total of 386 polyphonic characters.

## 2. Format of the entries

Each of the dictionary entries conforms to a standard format, whose principal features are illustrated in the following example:

堡　　**bǎo bǔ pù**

　bǎo　a fortress, walled village

　　　堡垒 **bǎolěi** a fortress, bastion

　　　堡寨 **bǎozhài** a fort, camp

　bǔ　〔a component of certain place-names〕

　　　堡子 **bǔzi** 〈dial.〉a town or village surrounded by an earth
　　　　wall; a village

　　　吴堡 **Wúbǔ** a place in Shaanxi Province

　pù　〔a component of certain place-names〕

　　　马家堡 **Mǎjiāpù** a town in Hebei Province

The entry heading (in larger type) consists of the polyphonic character in question, in this case 堡, followed by its two (or more) readings, in this case **bǎo, bǔ** and **pù**. The reading judged to be the more familiar, common, or useful is listed first; in this case the relatively well-known **bǎo** precedes the rarer **bǔ** and **pù**. (Less clear-cut cases are discussed below.)

The remainder of the entry then treats the different readings in turn. For each reading (repeated as a subheading at the left), the relevant information is presented in two sections. The first section sets out the meaning(s) associated with the reading — in the case of **bǎo**, "a fortress, walled village". The second section presents a selection of "compounds", or multi-character words, in which the character has the reading/meaning in question—in this case the words 堡垒 bǎolěi and 堡寨 bǎozhài. Such words are listed in alphabetical order of their *pinyin* spelling. For clarity, the two languages are printed in different fonts. While English is in regular roman font, *pinyin* transcription of Chinese is in sans serif font, with the readings of the polyphonic character in **bold**.

The following is an example of a more complicated entry:

# 都　dōu　dū

dōu　① all, altogether: 他们都走了。Tāmen **dōu** zǒu le. They have all left.// 他都知道。Tā **dōu** zhīdao. He knows it all.// 都是你，我们才误了火车。**Dōu** shì nǐ, wǒmen cái wù le huǒchē. It's all because of you that we missed the train.

② even: 他待她比亲爹都好。Tā dài tā bǐ qīn diē **dōu** hǎo. He treats her even better than her own father.

③ already: 都十点了，你还不走。**Dōu** shí diǎn le, nǐ hái bù zǒu. It's already ten o'clock and you still haven't left.

dū　① a capital city

② a large city

③ 〔a surname〕

都市 **dū**shì a metropolis

首都 shǒu**dū** a national capital

Here, each reading of the head character, 都, represents three more or less distinct meanings, distinguished by the use of circled numbers. The sequence in which these meanings are listed under each reading has no particular significance; nor does it have any bearing on the sequence of the compounds that follow, these being simply in alphabetical order.

For the first reading, dōu , each of the three meanings is provided with one or more illustrative sentences. These are designed to illustrate how 都, when read dōu , can serve as a single-character word in a phrase or sentence. Such example phrases or sentences (in a variety of written styles ranging from colloquial to formal) are provided for any words, other than nouns and adjectives, for which clarification of usage seems called for. They are provided not only for single-character words (as in the above sample entry) but often for compounds as well. As the entry shows, such illustrative material is preceded by a colon; and where two or more examples are given, they are separated from each other by the sign "//".

In some cases, one of the readings of a polyphonic character is attested only in a compound, which makes it pointless (or even impossible) to assign a corresponding meaning to the character alone. An example is the character 卜 when read bo: this is found only in the word luóbo, "radish". In such cases the dictionary entry shows the reading followed directly by the compound in question, thus:

bo    萝卜 luóbo the radish

Some entries include a section headed *Polyphonic compound*. A typical example of a polyphonic compound is the combination 重犯. Here both readings of the character 重 are possible, so that the combination represents two different words, namely zhòngfàn "a person guilty of a serious crime" and chóngfàn "to repeat a crime or mistake". Normally the ambiguity of a polyphonic character is resolved as soon as one recognises the compound in which it occurs. However, in a polyphonic compound the ambiguity remains and can be resolved only by examining the wider context. For this reason, polyphonic compounds are usually provided with illustrative phrases or sentences.

## 3. Further notational conventions

Except in the cases of 一 and 不, the *pinyin* transcriptions show underlying forms. It is assumed the reader will apply the familiar rules relating to a succession of third-tone syllables, and to suffixation of 儿 ér. Thus, 我得去 is transcribed as Wǒ děi qù, which is to be read as Wó děi qù; and 一点儿 appears as yìdiǎnr, to be read as yìdiǎr.

Where an alternative reading is allowable (i.e., where there is phonetic free variation), this is indicated in parentheses; for example,

暖和 nuǎnhé (or -huo )

Alternative character forms are similarly noted. For example, the entry for 扁 gives the second meaning under the reading biǎn thus:

② ( = 匾) a horizontal name-plate

This signifies that 扁 may be replaced by 匾 in cases where it is read **biǎn** and means "a horizontal name-plate".

A meaning is often specified by giving a series of two or more near-synonyms separated by commas; e.g., "to exhaust, use up". A meaning's area of application is sometimes clarified by extra words in parentheses; e.g., "to raise (livestock)" and "(of earth, skin, etc.) cracked in a tortoise-shell pattern".

Occasionally, slightly divergent but closely related meanings are given within a single definition, separated by a semicolon; examples are "from; since" and "foul smelling; undesirable, unwelcome".

The sign " = " leads from a literal meaning to its corresponding figurative or extended meaning; e.g., "blood and sweat = hard toil". The second meaning is a figurative extension of the first.

As noted above, a circled number marks the beginning of a new and distinct meaning definition, thus:

① to take part in

② to consult

A colon indicates that what follows is an illustration of what precedes; for example:

to pour boiling water on: 冲茶 **chōng chá** to brew tea

Words in square brackets explain the function of a character or compound, usually in terms of linguistic categories, rather than defining its meaning. For example, "〔a surname〕" signifies that the character in question can serve as a surname, rather than having the

meaning "surname". Similar cases are: [a place-name], [onomato-
poeia for ... ], [a particle signifying ... ], [used in transcribing
foreign words].

Notations in angle brackets indicate the particular area of usage
of the character or word in question; e.g., ⟨lit.⟩ signifies "literary
or classical usage", and ⟨dial.⟩ "restricted to a certain regional dialect" (see the section, Abbreviations).

As mentioned earlier, the sequence in which the two (or more)
readings of a character are listed within an entry is based on an as-
sessment of their relative frequency in the language; e.g., for 堡,
the familiar reading bǎo is listed before the rarer bǔ and pù. This
decision is not easily made in cases where the two readings are almost equally familiar and frequent; e.g., 长 cháng long zhǎng to
grow. In such cases the readings are usually given in alphabetical
sequence: in the entry for 长, cháng precedes zhǎng . There is,
however, an exception to these general principles: in keeping with
Chinese practice, a reading in neutral tone is never placed first,
even if it is the more common and familiar reading. For example, for
the character 了, the more common neutral-tone reading le is placed
second after the less common toned reading liǎo .

## 4. Sequence of the entries

The "principal" reading of any particular character, i.e. the
first reading that appears in the heading of its dictionary entry, de-
termines the location of that entry in the dictionary as a whole. In
other words, the entries are sequenced alphabetically according to

*14*

the *pinyin* spelling of the first or principal reading. (The spelling includes the tone, and the neutral tone is sequenced after tone 4.) Thus, the entry for 堡 bǎo is located after the entry for 薄 báo and before that for 背 bèi. Where two entries have the same principal reading, the character with the smaller number of strokes precedes; e.g., 地 dì (6 strokes) precedes 的 dì (8 strokes).

It may happen that a user of the dictionary, when seeking a certain character, knows only one of its two readings, or is uncertain which would be regarded as the principal reading. Such problems have been taken into account by providing cross-references. For example, the entry for the character 堡 bǎo bǔ pù is located under bǎo; if one were to seek it instead under pù, one would be directed to bǎo by the following cross-reference:

堡 　 pù → bǎo

Such a cross-reference from secondary reading to principal reading is provided for every character, except where the two readings differ only in tone. For example, for the character 挨 āi ái, the second reading, ái, is not cross-referenced to the first, since the two items would then be adjacent; a search for ái would in any case lead one to āi.

Finally, as a further aid in locating entries, a Stroke-Count Index is provided at the end of the dictionary.

# 前　言

本书是一部小型语言工具书,旨在为英语国家学习现代汉语的学生提供多音多义字的基础知识。

"多音多义字"(俗称"破音字")是指有两个或更多读音的汉字,而每一读音又有其独立的意义或惯用法。倘以"字形"、"字音"、"字义"三个概念来表述,"多音多义字"就是每字一形多音多义,比如"重"字:在"很重"、"重量"、"重视"等词里读音为zhòng,表示"分量大、不轻、要紧"等意思;而在"重新"、"重叠"等词里读音为chóng,表示"再一次、重复、层"等意思。又如"没"字:读作méi表示否定,例如"没有钱";读作mò则表示"淹入水中、隐灭、消失"等意思,例如"沉没"。单音字的情况则较简单,比如"高"字:它只有一个读音gāo,也只表达同一类的字义,用以形容从下往上的距离大、位置在上或年龄较大等。

从现有的汉语字典来看,多音多义字约占汉字总数的百分之五。然而,它们的重要性却不容忽视。不少多音多义字是最常用字,例如"还"、"没"、"好"、"长"、"少"、"得"、"的"、"了"等等。这些字的存在为许多外国人学习汉语增加了困难。学生碰到一个多音多义字的时候,不仅要知道它的不同读音,而且还得掌握每种读音的不同用法。本字典的主要目的,即在于帮助这些学生克服这些方面的困难。

*17*

中国学者早就注意到了多音多义字问题，编了不少多音多义字典。然而那些字典几乎全是为中国人编写的汉语字典，同类的汉英字典则极少。据本字典编者所知，本字典是至今为止唯一的使用简体字、以中国大陆的普通话惯用法为标准、针对外国学生的需要而编写的多音多义字汉英字典。

从二十世纪六十年代以来推行的汉字简化以及其他的文字改革措施，对多音多义字的存在产生了影响。在简化字中，汉字原有的一些多音多义字读音字义均比以前少了，或是成了单音字，例如"徵"、"乾"；而一些原有的单音字却成了多音多义字，例如"干"、"斗"。在本字典的编撰过程中，编者充分考虑了这些因素，以使本字典成为一本符合现代规范的最新工具书。

对本字典可能存在的错误及不足之处，编者热切希望读者批评指正，以便将来再版时予以订正。

# 凡 例

## 一、规范及收字准则

在中国大陆普通话的发音及用法等方面,《现代汉语词典》(商务印书馆北京 1996 年版修订本)是一部公认的标准辞书。本字典所收各字的读音及用法,即遵循《现代汉语词典》的规范。当然,在收字准则、英文释义、例词选择、例句创作以及编排体例等方面,本字典有自己的特色与内容,与《现代汉语词典》并不雷同。

本字典所依据的收字准则有两条,即所收的字首先必须是多音多义字,其次必须是现代汉语中较为通用的字。

一个多音多义字必须同时符合下列两个条件:

(1)该字至少有两种不同的读音;

(2)每一种读音都有自己的意义范围或惯用法。

《前言》中所举的"重"、"没"二例,就都符合这两个条件。相反,例如"谁"字,它虽有两种不同的读音shéi 和shuí,但后者只是前者的又读,其字义并无不同,因而不是多音多义字。

但有些汉字的情形似乎介于二者之间,较难归类,例如"血"字。它有xiě 与xuè 两种读音。这两种读音的意义虽然一样,但却有各自的惯用法。一般而言,xiě 多用于口语或较具体、非专业的词中,如"一滴血"、"流血"、"血淋淋";而xuè 则多用于较正式、较专业或带有抽象、引申意义的词中,例如

"血球"、"血小板"、"血统"。因此,"血"字是多音多义字。与此不同的例子是"一"字。该字有三种读法yì、yí、yī,但不论哪一种读法,意义都一样。它的不同读音变化是一种与字义无关的语音现象:在第一、二、三声前读作yì,例如"一天"、"一年"、"一点";在第四声前读作yí,例如"一个";单用或在停顿前读作yī。因此,它不算多音多义字。"不"字(读作bù或bú)的情况与此相同。

本字典未将汉语中所有的多音多义字全都收入,而只收入了较为通用的字汇及音义。不通俗的专门术语音义、现代语中未见或极少见的古汉语音义、地区局限性太强的口语或方言音义、以及冷僻的姓名或地名读法,均不予收录。例如"镐",它虽是多音多义字(gǎo:刨土工具;hào:周朝初年的国都名),但hào在现代汉语中极少用到,而倘排除hào这一音义,"镐"就只是个单音字了,因而本字典未收此字。又如"噱"字虽有xué(如"噱头")与jué(大笑)两种音义,但jué只见于文言文,倘排除jué这一个音义,"噱"字就不是多音多义字了,故本字典亦未收此字。已收入本字典的字汇,也不包括其可能还有的但在现代语中却不常用的音义(例如古汉语音义)。另一方面,有些多音多义字的部分音义虽属于方言但已流行较广,或虽多见于文言文但在现代语中亦不冷僻,则仍予以收录。例如"约"(yuē)的另一音义yāo(称量)虽为方言,但流传已较为广泛,故仍收入。又如"蛇"shé在"委蛇"中读作yí,这虽是文言文,但"虚与委蛇"一语在现代汉语中并不冷僻,故亦收入。当然,判断一种音义是否常用,并无绝对精确的界定可作依据。在一部篇幅有限的字典中,如何最大限度地兼顾所收条目的广泛性与实用性,在相当大的程度上只能依赖编纂者的判断与取舍,因而可能多少带些主观性,但这大概是任何类型的字典都难免会有的局限性。

## 二、条目编排体例

本字典共收单字条目 386 个,按其读音的顺序排列。每一单字之下按该字所含的不同音义分项,取该字在现代汉语中最常用的那一音义为其首项。例如"堡"字有三种读音 bǎo,bǔ 和 pù,前者较常用,故取为该字条目的首项,按拼音查字时宜根据这一常用读音 bǎo 查"堡"字:

**堡**　bǎo bǔ pù

bǎo　a fortress, walled village

　　　堡垒 bǎolěi a fortress, bastion

　　　堡寨 bǎozhài a fort, camp

bǔ　〔a component of certain place-names〕

　　　堡子 bǔzi 〈dial.〉 a town or village surrounded by an earth wall; a village

　　　吴堡 Wúbǔ a place in Shaanxi Province

pù　〔a component of certain place-names〕

　　　马家堡 Mǎjiāpù a town in Hebei Province

为了避免将中文拼音与英文混同,我们采用了两种不同的印刷字体:中文拼音以商社李字体印刷,而英文则以常见的罗马字体印刷。为醒目起见,该单字的拼音均用黑体印刷,比如上例中的"堡垒"和"马家堡",其拼音就印刷成 bǎolěi 和 Mǎjiāpù。

在上例中，每种读音只包括一个义项。但在许多条目中，一种读音包括两个或更多的义项，分列于该读音之后并以阿拉伯数字标示区分，最后则按拼音顺序列出一些例词或成语，有的还附有例句。如下例：

# 都　dōu　dū

dōu　① all, altogether: 他们都走了。Tāmen dōu zǒu le. They have all left.// 他都知道。Tā dōu zhīdao. He knows it all.// 都是你，我们才误了火车。Dōu shì nǐ, wǒmen cái wùle huǒchē. It's all because of you that we missed the train.

② even: 他待她比亲爹都好。Tā dài tā bǐ qīn diē dōu hǎo. He treats her even better than her own father.

③ already: 都十点了，你还不走。Dōu shí diǎn le, nǐ hái bù zǒu. It's already ten o'clock and you still haven't left.

dū　① a capital city

② a large city

③〔a surname〕

都市 dūshì a metropolis

首都 shǒudū a national capital

如上例所示，在某一义项中，倘若该字可以作为一个单字词使用，一般也附有例句或词组。倘在同一义项中所给的例句或词组不止一个，则以"//"号将这些例子分开。

以下是几种需要加以说明的情形：

22

（1）首项读音同音同调的单字条目，笔画较少的排在前面。如"地"(dì 六画)就排在"的"(dì 八画)的前面。

（2）有些字的几项音义都较常用，则按其读音拼写顺序排列，顺序最前者取为首项。例如"长"字（cháng：距离大；zhǎng 年纪大），按拼音顺序取 cháng 为其首项。

（3）某些字的最常用音义是轻读虚义，则一般不用作该字条目的首项，而取其可能有的重读实词音义为首项。例如"了"字，取 liǎo（完成；明白）而不取 le 为该字首项。

（4）除了首项读音以外，每一单字的其他读音也都各自作为独立的单字条目分别列出，但都只在其拼音旁边以"→"号标示该字在本字典中的首项读音，以便读者查检。例如上述堡字，在拼音 pù 项下也作为独立的单字条目列出，但只包括如下内容：

堡　　pù → bǎo

读者可循此指示，查阅"bǎo"条目。

（5）有些字的多种读音只是同音异调，例如"挨"(āi, ái)，就没有必要按上述（4）的做法将第二种读音 ái 再以单字条目的形式独立列出了，因为显而易见它已直接列在 āi 的后面了。

## 三、注音及拼写

本字典编者设定读者已经掌握汉语拼音的基本拼读规则，因此除了"一"(yī、yí、yì)与"不"(bú、bù)两字以外，例词例句中各字都只注原调，不注变调。例如"我得去"，处于第三声 děi 之前的 wǒ，实际上读作第二声 wó，但字典中的注音仍按拼写惯例注为 Wǒ děi qù。儿化音的拼音书写，也只按惯例在基本形式后面加 r，而不标出语音的实际变化，例如"一点儿"拼写为yìdiǎnr，却不写为yìdiǎr。对于可以轻读的字，则视具体情况，在应当轻读的实例中就只标示注音而不标示调号，例如"卡子"就拼写为qiǎzi。

## 四、释义及其他

（1）各条目的每一义项都有英文释义，其后是词例解释及用法，以冒号隔开。如

to pour boiling water on：冲茶 chōng chá to brew tea

（2）在同一英语释义中，同义词以逗号分开，如"to exhaust, use up"，涵义或用法差别较大的部分则以分号隔开，如"from; since"及"foul smelling; undesirable, unwelcome"。有时在圆括弧中标出该义的使用范围，如"to raise（livestock）"及"（of earth, skin, etc.）cracked in a tortoise-shell pattern"，或以等号标出引申义，如"blood and sweat ＝ hard toil"。

（3）英文释义中有关语法特征及使用范围等方面的说明置于方括弧内。如"〔a surname〕"（姓），标示该字可用为姓，并不表示该字是"姓"的意思。其他如"〔a place-name〕"（地名）、"〔onomatopoeia for...〕"（象声字）、"〔a particle signifying ...〕"（虚词）、"〔used in transcribing foreign words〕"（音译字）等，情况与此类似。

（4）某些条目的释义中注明了有关的修辞或文体范围，所用略语放在尖括弧内。如〈lit.〉（书）表示该字或该词为书面语，〈dial.〉（方）表示"方言"。

（5）有时某一单字的某一读音本身并无单独涵义，而只在与别的字联用时才有意义。例如"卜"字只在"萝卜"一词中才读为bo，倘单独一个"卜（bo）"字，则无实际意义。在这种情

况下,该条目的"bo"项下就没有"卜(bo)"本身的释义,而是列出"萝卜"一词并加以解释。

(6)在某些词例中有的字可有又读,则将又读音标在圆括弧内并加注英文"or",如"暖和 nuǎnhé(or -huo)"。对于异体字或通假字,则以圆括弧标出并加一等号。如"扁"字条下有"(=匾)",表示在这一义项中"扁"为"匾"的异体字或两字通假。

(7)在绝大多数情况下,一个多音多义字的读法与意思,只要看它用在哪一个词里就能知道,但在少数情况下必须根据上下文才能判断。例如"重犯"一词中的"重"字(zhòngfàn:犯了大罪的人;chóngfàn:再次犯罪),其音义即取决于上下文。此类词例我们也尽可能列出并附以例句,以帮助读者理解。

(8)为便利查字,本字典附有《笔画检字表》。

# ABBREVIATIONS

| | |
|---|---|
| approx. | approximately |
| arch. | archaic |
| cf. | compare |
| coll. | colloquial |
| dial. | restricted to a certain regional dialect |
| esp. | especially |
| fig. | figurative |
| hon. | honorific |
| lit. | literary or classical |

# A

**阿**　ā　ē

ā　①〔a prefix to people's pet names or titles〕：阿妹 Ā Mèi
〔used when addressing one's younger sister, or a younger female〕// 阿毛 Ā Máo〔used when addressing someone named Mao or as a term of endearment〕
②〔used in transcribing foreign words〕

阿拉伯 Ā lābó Arab; Arabia

阿门 ā mén Amen!

阿姨 ā yí a nursemaid, nanny; auntie, aunt

ē　①to play up to, pander to
②〔used in transcribing foreign words〕

阿弥陀佛 Ē mítuó Fó Amitābha Buddha

阿谀 ē yú to fawn on, flatter：他专会阿谀拍马，讨好上
司。Tā zhuān huì ē yú pāi mǎ, tǎohǎo shàngsi. He's
especially good at flattering people and ingratiating himself with the boss.

**嘎**　á → shà

**挨**　āi　ái

āi　①in sequence, by turns：别等了，反正挨不到你了。
Bié děng le, fǎnzhèng āi bú dào nǐ le. Don't wait

any longer. In any case you won't get a turn.

②to get/be close to, to be next to: 我挨着他坐。Wǒ āizhe tā zuò. I sat next to him. // 路边的小树一棵挨一棵。Lù biān de xiǎo shù yì kē āi yì kē. The small trees lining the road were right next to one another.

挨次 āicì one after another, one by one, in turn: 组长把全组的人挨次叫去个别谈话。Zǔzhǎng bǎ quán zǔ de rén āicì jiào qu gèbié tánhuà. The group leader called out everyone in the group and talked to them one by one.

挨个儿 āigèr 〈coll.〉one by one, in turn: 门卫把他们挨个儿搜查了一遍。Ménwèi bǎ tāmen āigèr sōuchále yíbiàn. The gatekeeper checked each of them in turn.

挨户 āihù from door to door: 挨家挨户分发传单 āijiā āihù fēnfā chuándān to distribute leaflets from door to door

挨近 āijìn to get close to; to be near to: 他慢慢挨近入口处。Tā mànmàn āijìn rùkǒuchù. He gradually got closer to the entrance. // 学校挨近工厂。Xuéxiào āijìn gōngchǎng. The school is near the factory.

ái ①( = 捱 ) to suffer, endure: 挨饿 ái è to suffer from hunger // 挨打 ái dǎ to receive a beating, be spanked // 这日子太苦，我真没法子挨下去。Zhè rìzi tài kǔ, wǒ zhēn méi fǎzi ái xiàqù. Life is too hard these

days; I really can't endure it any longer. // 他忍着腿
上的伤痛，一步一步地挨到门口。Tā rěnzhe tuǐ
shang de shāngtòng, yí bù yí bù de ái dào
ménkǒu. Despite the pain of his leg wound, he made
it, step by step, to the door.

②to delay, play for time: 挨时间 ái shíjiān to stall, delay, play for time

## 艾　ài　yì

ài　①the Chinese mugwort (*Artemisia argyi*)

②⟨lit.⟩ to stop

③[a surname]

艾炷 àizhù a moxa torch for cauterising

方兴未艾 fāngxīng-wèi'ài just unfolding, in the ascend-
ant: 那地区的独立运动方兴未艾。Nà dìqū de dúlì
yùndòng fāngxīng-wèi'ài. The independence movement in that region is just getting under way.

yì　怨艾 yuànyì ⟨lit.⟩ resentment, a grudge: 她苦干了一
年，毫无怨艾。Tā kǔgànle yì nián, háo wú yuànyì.
She endured a year of hard toil without any resentment.

## 凹　āo　wā

āo　concave, depressed, indented: 路面凹凸不平。Lùmiàn
āo tū bù píng. The road surface is bumpy and uneven.

凹面 āomiàn concave

凹透镜 āotòujìng a concave lens

wā　a concavity, depression [sometimes used in descriptive

place-names〕

核桃凹 Hétāowā a place in Shanxi Province

## 拗  ǎo  ào  niù

ǎo  〈dial.〉 to break off, snap off: 把树枝拗下来 bǎ shùzhī ào xiàlai to break off a tree branch // 他拗断了几根竹竿。Tā ǎoduànle jǐ gēn zhúgān. He broke off a few sticks of bamboo.

ào  ①difficult to pronounce; to "twist" the tongue

②to disobey

拗口令 àokǒulìng a tongue-twister

违拗 wéi'ào to disobey

niù  ①stubborn, recalcitrant: 我哥哥的脾气拗得很。Wǒ gēge de píqi niù de hěn. My brother is very stubborn by nature.

②to dissuade: 他决心已定，我拗不过他。Tā juéxīn yǐ dìng, wǒ niù bu guò tā. He's already made up his mind, and I can't dissuade him.

执拗 zhíniù stubborn, wilful: 这个老头儿脾气十分执拗。Zhège lǎotóur píqì shífēn zhíniù. This old fellow is really stubborn.

# B

## 扒  bā  pá

**bā** ①to grasp, cling to：扒着窗台 **bā**zhe chuāngtái clinging to the window-sill // 扒在栏杆上 **bā** zài lángān shàng clinging to the railing

②to dig up：在地上扒出一个浅坑 zài dì shàng **bā** chū yí ge qiǎn kēng to dig out a shallow hole in the ground // 扒开河堤 **bā** kāi hédī to dig through a dike

③to pull down：他们把那座破房给扒了。Tāmen bǎ nà zuò pò fáng gěi **bā**·le. They pulled down that dilapidated house.

④to push/pull aside：把土扒在一边 bǎ tǔ **bā** zài yìbiān to push earth to one side

⑤to strip off, peel away：把他的衣服扒下！Bǎ tā de yīfu **bā** xià! Take his clothes off! // 老张把兔子的皮扒了。Lǎo Zhāng bǎ tùzi de pí **bā** le. Lao Zhang stripped off the rabbit's skin.

扒拉 **bā**la to push lightly：把灰扒拉一下 bǎ huī **bā**la yíxià to push ashes aside

**pá** ①to rake up, rake together：扒拢散落的树叶 **pá** lǒng sànluò de shùyè to rake fallen leaves together

②stewing, braising：扒羊肉 **pá** yángròu stewed mutton // 扒鸡 **pá** jī braised chicken

③〈dial.〉to scratch：扒痒 **pá** yǎng to scratch an itch

④to steal, pickpocket：我的钱包被人扒了。Wǒ de qiánbāo bèi rén **pá** le. My wallet was stolen by a pickpocket.

扒犁 **pá**li〈dial.〉a sledge

扒窃 páqiè to steal, to pickpocket：那人因在市上扒窃而被捕。Nà rén yīn zài shì shàng páqiè ér bèi bǔ. That person was arrested for stealing in the market.

扒手 páshǒu a pickpocket

## 把　bǎ　bà

bǎ

①〔a measure word for objects with handles〕：一把伞 yì bǎ sǎn an umbrella // 三把刀子 sān bǎ dāozi three knives

②〔a preposition that transposes the object before the verb〕：请把门关上。Qǐng bǎ mén guān shàng. Please shut the door. // 把油灯吹灭 bǎ yóudēng chuī miè to blow out an oil lamp

③a handful：一把米 yì bǎ mǐ a handful of rice

④〈coll.〉to keep guard：他是个把门的。Tā shì ge bǎ mén de. He is a gatekeeper.

⑤to grasp：你可得把牢了，别松手。Nǐ kě děi bǎ láo le, bié sōng shǒu. You have to hold tight. Don't let go.

⑥〈coll.〉a few, a good number, approximately：加把劲 jiā bǎ jìn to put in a final effort (to complete a nearly finished task) // 老张有一把年纪了。Lǎo Zhāng yǒu yì bǎ niánjì le. Lao Zhang is getting on in years. // 百把人 bǎi bǎ rén a hundred or so people // 个把月 gè bǎ yuè about a month

⑦a handle：自行车把 zìxíngchē bǎ handlebars of a bicycle

把柄 bǎbǐng a handle

把持 bǎchí to control, monopolise

把关 bǎguān to guard a pass; to check on

把手 bǎshǒu a handle, grip, knob, handlebar

把守 bǎshǒu to guard: 把守边关 bǎshǒu biānguān to guard a border pass

把握 bǎwò to hold, grasp; assurance, certainty: 你应当把握这个好机会。Nǐ yīngdāng bǎwò zhège hǎo jīhui. You should grasp this good opportunity. // 他相当有把握。Tā xiāngdāng yǒu bǎwò. He is fairly confident.

bà　〈coll.〉〔usually with suffixed 子 -zi or 儿 -r〕a handle; a stalk

把儿 bàr a handle or stem: 刀把儿 dāo bàr a knife handle // 话把儿 huà bàr an occasion for scandal // 花把儿 huā bàr the stalk of a flower

把子 bàzi a handle

**耙** bà → pá

**伯** bǎi → bó

**膀** bǎng　pāng　páng

bǎng the upper arm

膀臂 bǎngbì the upper arm; a "right-hand man"

膀子 bǎngzi the upper arm; the shoulder

翅膀 chìbǎng birds' wings

pāng a swelling

膀肿 pāngzhǒng swollen (of muscles)

páng 膀胱 pángguāng the bladder

## 磅　bàng　páng

bàng ①the pound (weight)：三磅 sān bàng three pounds

②a scales：这批货过磅了没有？Zhè pī huò guò bàng le méiyǒu? Has this batch of goods been weighed?

③〈coll.〉to weigh：请把那个箱子磅一下。Qǐng bǎ nàge xiāngzi bàng yíxià. Please weigh that suitcase.

磅秤 bàngchèng a platform scales

páng 磅礴 pángbó boundless, majestic

## 炮　bāo → pào

## 薄　báo　bó　bò

báo ①thin：这本书很薄。Zhè běn shū hěn báo. This book is very thin.

②(of taste, flavour) weak, light：酒味很薄。Jiǔ wèi hěn báo. It is a light wine.

③(of feeling, emotion) cold, lacking warmth：他待我不薄。Tā dài wǒ bù báo. He treats me quite well.

④(of land) poor, infertile：这儿土薄，庄稼长不好。Zhèr tǔ báo, zhuāngjia zhǎng bù hǎo. The land here is infertile, so the crops don't grow well.

薄饼 báobǐng a kind of thin pancake (also báo bǐng a thin cake)

薄田 báotián infertile land

bó ①thin, weak; mean

②⟨lit.⟩ to approach, be close to

③⟨lit.⟩ to despise

④frivolous

鄙薄 bǐbó to despise: 我一向鄙薄那种人。Wǒ yíxiàng bǐbó nà zhǒng rén. I have always despised that sort of person.

薄待 bódài to treat shabbily: 王老板从未薄待过他的雇员。Wáng Lǎobǎn cóngwèi bódàiguo tā de gùyuán. Wang has never treated his employees shabbily.

薄暮 bómù ⟨lit.⟩ dusk, twilight

薄弱 bóruò weak, fragile: 薄弱环节 bóruò huánjié a weak link

淡薄 dànbó thin, light, faint, hazy: 她留给我的印象已经很淡薄了。Tā liú gěi wǒ de yìnxiàng yǐjīng hěn dànbó le. The impression she left on me is already faint.

厚此薄彼 hòucǐ-bóbǐ prejudiced in favour of one rather than the other

轻薄 qīngbó frivolous, skittish: 他在那几位女人面前的举止相当轻薄。Tā zài nà jǐ wèi nǚrén miànqián de jǔzhǐ xiāngdāng qīngbó. His bearing in the presence of those women was rather skittish.

日薄西山 rìbó-xīshān near sunset = moribund

如履薄冰 rúlǚ-bóbīng like walking on thin ice = a precarious situation: 在那个暴君的统治下过日子真是

如履薄冰。Zài nàge bàojūn de tǒngzhì xià guò rìzi,
zhēn shì rúlǚ-bóbīng. Living under that tyrant's rule
was really like walking on thin ice.

bò    薄荷 bòhe peppermint

## 堡    bǎo    bǔ    pù

bǎo   a fortress, walled village

堡垒 bǎolěi a fortress, bastion

堡寨 bǎozhài a fort, camp

bǔ    [a component of certain place-names]

堡子 bǔzi 〈dial.〉 a town or village surrounded by an earth
wall; a village

吴堡 Wúbǔ a place in Shaanxi Province

pù    [a component of certain place-names]

马家堡 Mǎjiāpù a town in Hebei Province

## 刨    bào → páo

## 背    bèi    bēi

bèi   ①the back, the reverse side: 手背 shǒubèi the back of
the hand // 刀背 dāobèi the back of a knife blade // 那
块砖头打在我的背上。Nà kuài zhuāntou dǎ zài wǒ
de bèi shàng. That piece of brick hit me on the back.

②to memorise: 背一首诗 bèi yì shǒu shī to memorise a
poem // 他把整本书背下来了。Tā bǎ zhěng běn
shū bèi xiàlai le. He memorised the whole book.

③to hide something from, do something behind someone's
back: 那些事都是背着我干的。Nàxiē shì dōu shi

bèizhe wǒ gàn de. All those things were done behind my back.

④with the back towards, backing on to: 背山面海 bèi shān miàn hǎi with hills behind and the sea in front

⑤〈coll.〉hard of hearing: 那老人耳朵有点儿背。Nà lǎorén ěrduo yǒu diǎnr bèi. That old man is a little hard of hearing.

⑥to act contrary to, violate, break (e.g. a promise, contract)

⑦to turn away from, leave: 背过脸去 bèi guò liǎn qù to turn one's face away

⑧unlucky, inauspicious

背部 bèibù the back

背地里 bèidìli behind someone's back; on the sly: 背地里说坏话 bèidìli shuō huàihuà to backbite

背光 bèiguāng shaded from the light

背后 bèihòu behind; behind someone's back

背景 bèijǐng background

背叛 bèipàn to betray, forsake: 背叛共产主义 bèipàn gòngchǎn zhǔyì to betray communism

背时 bèishí untimely, unfortunate

背诵 bèisòng to recite from memory

背心 bèixīn a sleeveless pullover

背信弃义 bèixìn-qìyì to break faith with someone

背约 bèiyuē to renege on a treaty: 那家公司无理背约，使我们受到很大损失。Nà jiā gōngsī wúlǐ bèiyuē, shǐ wǒmen shòudào hěn dà sǔnshī. That company reneged on the agreement without justification, and caused us big losses.

背运 bèiyùn out of luck, unfortunate

离乡背井 líxiāng-bèijǐng to leave one's native place (esp. against one's will)

bēi　to carry, esp. on the back: 背东西 bēi dōngxi to carry things

## 奔　bēn　bèn

bēn　to run, flee: 马儿向前急奔。Mǎr xiàng qián jí bēn. The horse raced ahead.

奔波 bēnbō to hurry about busily: 为了那笔生意，他奔波了整整一个月。Wèile nà bǐ shēngyi, tā bēnbō le zhěngzhěng yí ge yuè. On account of that deal he was rushing around for a whole month.

奔窜 bēncuàn to flee: 敌军向东城门奔窜。Díjūn xiàng dōng chéngmén bēncuàn. The enemy troops fled toward the eastern gate.

bèn　to strive or hurry toward some goal

奔头儿 bèntour something to strive for, a prospect

投奔 tóubèn to go to (someone) for support or shelter: 投奔亲友 tóubèn qīnyǒu to seek refuge with relatives and friends

## 绷　bēng　běng　bèng

bēng　①to pull tight, bind: 绳子绷得很紧。Shéngzi bēng de

hěn jǐn. The rope was stretched taut.

②to spring, bounce: 弹簧绷出来了。Tánhuáng bēng chulai le. The spring jumped out.

③(in sewing) to baste, tack

绷带 bēngdài bandages

绷骗 bēngpiàn 〈dial.〉 to cheat

绷子 bēngzi an embroidery frame; bed springing made of split cane or coir rope

běng ①to stretch: 绷着脸 běngzhe liǎn pulling a grim face

②to endure with difficulty: 绷不住 běng bu zhù unable to endure

bèng to break open

绷裂 bèngliè to split or crack: 帐篷顶上绷裂了一道大口子。Zhàngpeng dǐng shàng bèngliè le yí dào dà kǒuzi. The roof of the tent split wide open.

# 裨 bì pí·

bì 〈lit.〉 to supplement

裨益 bìyì benefit

无裨于事 wú bì yú shì of no help, not helping matters: 他们采取的补救措施全都无裨于事。Tāmen cǎiqǔ de bǔjiù cuòshī quán dōu wú bì yú shì. The measures they took to redress the situation did not help at all.

pí ①〈arch.〉 secondary

②[a surname]

裨将 píjiàng a lower ranking general in ancient China

**扁**  biǎn  piān

biǎn  ①flat：那个足球被人踩扁了。Nàge zúqiú bèi rén cǎi
bǐan le. The football was trampled flat.

②( = 匾 ) a horizontal name-plate

扁虫 biǎnchóng tapeworm（also biǎn chóng a flat-
shaped worm）

扁担 biǎndan a carrying-pole

扁额 biǎn'é a horizontal inscribed board

piān  〈lit.〉small in appearance：一叶扁舟 yí yè piān zhōu a
small（leaf-like）boat

**泌**  bì → mì

**秘**  bì → mì

**辟**  bì → pì

**便**  biàn  pián

biàn  ①convenient：今天下大雨，不便走远路。Jīntiān xià
dà yǔ, bú biàn zǒu yuǎn lù. It's raining hard today,
so it's not convenient to walk far.

②ordinary, casual, simple

③to excrete; excreta

④then：这机器只要半天便可修好。Zhè jīqi zhǐ yào
bàn tiān biàn kě xiū hǎo. This machine will take only
half a day to fix. // 向前走，一拐弯便是。Xiàng
qián zǒu, yì guǎi wān biàn shì. Go straight ahead,
and as soon as you turn the corner, that's it.

便饭 biànfàn ordinary everyday food

便衣 biànyī plainclothes (police etc.); ordinary dress

方便 fāngbiàn convenient

小便 xiǎobiàn to urinate; urine

pián 大腹便便 dà fù piánpián fat, pot-bellied

便宜 piányi cheap; advantage unfairly taken: 这家店里的东西相当便宜。Zhè jiā diàn lǐ de dōngxi xiāngdāng piányi. In this shop things are fairly cheap. // 小王喜欢占人家的便宜。Xiǎo Wáng xǐhuān zhàn rénjia de piányi. Young Wang likes taking advantage of people.

# 别 bié biè

bié ①to leave, part

②to differentiate, distinguish

③difference, distinction: 男女有别。Nán nǚ yǒu bié. Men and women are different.

④other, another: 别的东西 bié de dōngxi other things

⑤different, distinct, special

⑥inserted, stuck in: 腰里别着手枪 yāo lǐ biézhe shǒuqiāng with a pistol stuck in one's belt

⑦fastened (with a pin etc.): 胸前别着一朵花 xiōng qián biézhe yì duǒ huā with a flower pinned on one's chest

⑧Don't: 别说话! Bié shuō huà! Don't talk!

别人 biérén other people

别针 biézhēn a safety pin; a brooch

告别 gàobié to say good-bye

区别 qūbié to differentiate; distinction

特别 tèbié special; particular

性别 xìngbié sex distinction, gender

biè　别扭 bièniu awkward, uncomfortable, difficult; unable to see eye to eye: 这件衣服很别扭。Zhè jiàn yīfu hěn bièniu. This garment is quite uncomfortable. // 他们俩正闹别扭呢。Tāmen liǎ zhèng nào bièniu ne. Those two are on really bad terms right now.

# 屏
bǐng → píng

# 伯
bó    bǎi

bó　①father's elder brother

②a senior (male)

伯伯 bóbo uncle (father's elder brother)

伯父 bófù uncle (father's elder brother)

伯劳 bóláo ⟨lit.⟩ the shrike

伯母 bómǔ aunt (wife of father's elder brother)

bǎi　大伯(子) dà bǎi (zi) ⟨dial.⟩ husband's elder brother

# 泊
bó    pō

bó　①to moor, berth: 泊岸 bó àn to anchor alongside the shore

②quiet, unexcited, unambitious

泊位 bówèi a berth (for boats)

淡泊 dànbó uninterested in fame, wealth, etc.

停泊 tíngbó to moor, berth: 那船停泊在离岸不远处。

Nà chuán tíngbó zài lí àn bù yuǎn chù. The ship moored at a spot not far from the shore.

pō　a lake: 梁山泊 Liángshān Pō Liangshan Lake (in Shandong Province)

湖泊 húpō lakes (in general)

血泊 xuèpō a pool of blood

**薄** bó bò → báo

**簸** bò　bǒ

bò　a winnowing basket

簸箕 bòji a winnowing basket; a dustpan

bǒ　①to winnow: 簸米 bǒ mǐ to winnow rice

②to rock

簸荡 bǒdàng to rock (as a boat): 江心浪大，小船簸荡得厉害。Jiāngxīn làng dà, xiǎo chuán bǒdàng de lìhài. The waves in the river were big, and the small boat rocked violently.

**卜** bǔ　bo

bǔ　①to divine: 卜卦 bǔ guà to divine using the Eight Trigrams

②divination: 求签问卜 qiú qiān wèn bǔ to divine using bamboo sticks // 占卜 zhān bǔ to divine

③to foretell, predict: 生死未卜 shēng sǐ wèi bǔ hard to know whether (someone) is alive or dead

④[a surname]

卜辞 bǔcí oracle inscriptions on tortoise-shells or animal

bones of the Shang Dynasty (16th-11th century B.C.)

卜筮 bǔshì to divine using tortoise-shell and milfoil

bo 萝卜 luóbo the radish

堡 bǔ → bǎo

# C

采 cǎi　cài

cǎi

①to collect, gather, select: 采药 cǎi yào to collect medicinal herbs

②to mine, extract: 采矿 cǎi kuàng mining // 采煤 cǎi méi coal mining // 采油 cǎi yóu oil drilling

③spirit, facial expression

④( = 彩 )〈lit.〉variegated, colourful

采办 cǎibàn to select and purchase: 采办货物 cǎibàn huòwù to purchase goods

采集 cǎijí to gather, collect: 采集标本 cǎijí biāoběn to collect specimens or samples

文采 wéncǎi〈lit.〉literary grace

兴高采烈 xìnggāo-cǎiliè in high spirits, very happy: 过年了，孩子们兴高采烈。Guò nián le, háizimen xìnggāo-cǎiliè. It was New Year, and the children were in high spirits.

cài 采地 càidì a fiefdom, vassalage

采邑 càiyì a fiefdom, vassalage

# 参 cān shēn cēn

cān ①to take part in

②to consult

参加 cānjiā to participate：你为什么没参加昨天的会？ Nǐ wèi shénme méi cānjiā zuótiān de huì? Why didn't you take part in yesterday's meeting?

参考 cānkǎo to examine and compare (in order to consult or learn something)：他们的方法值得参考。Tāmen de fāngfǎ zhíde cānkǎo. Their methods are worth consulting. // 参考资料 cānkǎo zīliào reference materials

参议院 cānyìyuàn the Senate

参与 cānyù to take part：参与制定规划 cānyù zhìdìng guīhuà to take part in the formulation of a plan

shēn ①ginseng：这种参是人工栽培的还是野生的？ Zhè zhǒng shēn shi réngōng zāipéi de háishi yěshēng de? Is this type of ginseng cultivated or does it grow in the wild?

②one of the twenty-eight zodiac constellations

人参 rénshēn ginseng

参商 shēnshāng Orion and Lucifer = long separation; enemies

cēn 参差不齐 cēncī bù qí uneven, irregular：这田里的麦苗长得参差不齐。Zhè tián lǐ de màimiáo zhǎng de cēncī bù qí. The wheat seedlings in this field have grown unevenly.

**孱** càn → chán

**藏** cáng   zàng

cáng to conceal, store, hoard: 把它藏在家里吧! Bǎ tā cáng zài jiā li ba! Hide it at home!

藏量 cángliàng stock, the amount held in storage; a reserve

藏匿 cángnì to hide, harbour: 藏匿罪人也算重罪。Cángnì zuìrén yě suàn zhòngzuì. Harbouring a criminal is itself a serious crime.

藏书 cángshū a book collection (also cáng shū to collect books): 他的藏书很丰富。Tāde cángshū hěn fēngfù. He has an extensive library.

矿藏 kuàngcáng mineral resources

zàng ①a storehouse, repository

②a body of scripture (Buddhist or Daoist)

③〔abbreviated name of〕Tibet

宝藏 bǎozàng precious (mineral) deposits

道藏 Dàozàng the Daoist scriptures

库藏 kùzàng a storehouse

西藏 Xīzàng Tibet

**参** cēn → cān

**曾** céng   zēng

céng once, ever, already 〔indicating past tense〕: 我曾学过五年英文。Wǒ céng xuéguo wǔ nián Yīngwén. I have

studied five years of English. // 未曾耳闻 wèi **céng** ěr
**wén** to have never heard of before

曾经 **céng**jīng to have ever (done a certain thing); already: 他曾经来过此地。Tā **céng**jīng lái guo cǐ dì.
He has been here before.

zēng ①great-grand-

②〔a surname〕

曾祖父 **zēng**zǔfù great-grandfather

叉　　chā　chá　chǎ　chà

chā ①a fork, cross: 请你在每个错字上头打个叉。Qǐng nǐ
zài měi ge cuò zì shàngtou dǎ ge **chā**. Please put a
cross above each incorrect character.

②to interlace, cross: 她的双手叉着腰。Tā de shuāng
shǒu **chā**zhe yāo. She had her hands on her hips.

③to pierce or stab with a fork or similar implement: 叉鱼
**chā** yú to spear fish

叉车 **chā**chē a fork-lift truck

叉子 **chā**zi a fork

chá 〈dial.〉to block up, jam, become stuck: 叉在喉咙里
**chá** zài hóulóng li stuck in one's throat // 路口被车辆叉
住了。Lùkǒu bèi chēliàng **chá** zhù le. The intersection
was jammed with traffic.

chǎ to part forming a fork: 叉着腿站着 **chǎ**zhe tuǐ zhànzhe
standing with legs apart

chà 劈叉 pǐ**chà** to do the splits

# 杈　chā　chà

chà　　an implement resembling a pitchfork

chà　　a tree branch：打杈 dǎ chà to prune

树杈 shùchà the crotch of a tree

# 差　chā　chà　chāi　cī

chā　　①a difference, discrepancy, mistake

②the difference（remainder when one number is subtracted from another）

差别 chābié a discrepancy, difference

差强人意 chāqiáng-rényì just passable：这个施工方案说不上怎么好，差强人意而已。Zhège shīgōng fāng'àn shuō bú shàng zěnme hǎo, chāqiáng-rényì éryǐ. This construction plan can't be said to be so good, just passable.

误差 wùchā an error：误差很小。Wùchā hěn xiǎo. The error was small.

chà　　①inadequate, unsatisfactory, lacking:他英语口语很差。Tā Yīngyǔ kǒuyǔ hěn chà. His spoken English is unsatisfactory.

②to differ from, fall short of：差不多 chà bu duō almost, differing only a little // 还差多少钱才够买车？Hái chà duōshao qián cái gòu mǎi chē? How much is it short of the purchase price of a car?

差点儿 chàdiǎnr ① not quite good enough：这双鞋的质量差点儿。Zhè shuāng xié de zhìliàng chàdiǎnr.

The quality of this pair of shoes is not quite good enough. ② almost: 他差点儿死了。Tā chàdiǎnr sǐ le. He almost died.

差劲 chàjìn substandard, disappointingly poor: 这台机器太差劲了! Zhè tái jīqì tài chàjìn le! This machine is so poor!

chāi ①to dispatch, send on a mission: 差她去办。Chāi tā qù bàn. Send her to do it.

②an errand, job

差遣 chāiqiǎn to assign, post (an employee etc.): 他被差遣到边疆去了。Tā bèi chāiqiǎn dào biānjiāng qù le. He was posted to the border region.

出差 chūchāi away on official business: 我上星期出差了。Wǒ shàng xīngqī chūchāi le. Last week I was away on official business.

苦差 kǔchāi hard work

美差 měichāi a cushy job

邮差 yóuchāi a postman

cī 参差不齐 cēncī bù qí uneven, irregular: 他的头发剪得参差不齐。Tā de tóufa jiǎn de cēncī bù qí. His hair was cut unevenly.

*Polyphonic compound:*

公差 gōngchā common difference (in mathematics); tolerance (in machinery)

　　gōngchāi a public errand

查　chá　zhā

chá to investigate, check, look up: 查账 chá zhàng to audit accounts // 查字典 chá zìdiǎn to look up in a dictionary

查看 chákàn to investigate, look into: 查看一处新房址 chákàn yí chù xīn fángzhǐ to look into a new house site

检查 jiǎnchá to inspect; an inspection: 检查卫生 jiǎnchá wèishēng to inspect sanitation // 卫生检查 wèishēng jiǎnchá a sanitation inspection

zhā ①( = 楂 ) the hawthorn

②〔a surname〕

山查 shānzhā a species of hawthorn

# 楂　chá　zhā

chá ①( = 槎 ) short bristly hair or beard: 胡子楂 húzi chá a stubbly beard

②( = 茬 ) stubble left after harvesting: 麦楂 mài chá wheat stubble

zhā the hawthorn

山楂 shānzhā a species of hawthorn

# 衩　chà　chǎ

chà side-slits (in a gown to give freedom of movement): 这衣服衩开得太大了。Zhè yīfu chà kāi de tài dà le. The side-slits in this dress have been made too wide.

衩口 chàkǒu side-slits (in a gown)

chǎ 裤衩 kùchǎ underpants

**差** chāi → chā

**屏** chán càn

chán 〈lit.〉 weak, feeble, unfit

屏弱 chánruò feeble in health：这孩子十分屏弱。Zhè háizi shífēn chánruò. This child is really feeble in health.

càn 屏头 càntou 〈dial., abusive〉 a coward

**禅** chán shàn

chán Buddhist concentration, meditation；Zen

禅定 chándìng a state of deep concentration attained in Buddhist meditation

禅堂 chántáng a Buddhist monastic hall

禅宗 Chánzōng the Chan or Zen school of Buddhism

shàn ①to abdicate in favour of another

②to worship the earth

封禅 fēngshàn an ancient ritual in which the emperor worshipped heaven and earth

禅让 shànràng to hand over the throne to another

**单** chán → dān

**长** cháng zhǎng

cháng ①long：很长的绳子 hěn cháng de shéngzi a long rope

②length：这段公路全长一百公里。Zhè duàn gōnglù quán cháng yì bǎi gōnglǐ. This stretch of highway has a total length of one hundred kilometres.

③a strength, strong point: 取人之长，补己之短 qǔ rén zhī cháng，bǔ jǐ zhī duǎn to overcome one's weaknesses by learning from the strengths of others

长度 chángdù length

长久 chángjiǔ a long time

长寿 chángshòu long life

长于 chángyú to be particularly good at: 他长于绘画。 Tā chángyú huìhuà. His forte is painting.

专长 zhuāncháng a strong point, a special ability

zhǎng ①an elder, chief

②senior: 我长她一辈。Wǒ zhǎng tā yí bèi. I am a generation older than she is.

③to grow: 长高 zhǎng gāo to grow tall // 庄稼长得很好。Zhuāngjia zhǎng de hěn hǎo. The crops are growing well.

校长 xiàozhǎng a school principal

长辈 zhǎngbèi the elder generation

长进 zhǎngjìn to make progress: 这孩子大有长进。Zhè háizi dà yǒu zhǎngjìn. This child has made a lot of progress.

# 场  chǎng  cháng

chǎng ①the location or scene of an event or activity: 那场上还有别的队吗？Nà chǎng shang hái yǒu biéde duì ma? Are there any other teams on that playing-field? // 进场的时间到了。Jìn chǎng de shíjiān dào le. It's time to enter the arena (or any other site of a contest, performance etc.).

②a segment or scene (of a play): 第二幕第三场 dì èr mù dì sān **chǎng** Act 2, Scene 3

③(in physics) a field (of force etc.)

④[a measure word for performances of games, films, etc.]: 两场球赛 liǎng **chǎng** qiúsài two matches (football etc.)

操场 cāo**chǎng** a drill ground, sports ground

场合 **chǎng**hé a situation, occasion

磁场 cí**chǎng** a magnetic field

农场 nóng**chǎng** a farm

**cháng** ①a flat, open area, e.g. for threshing or drying grain: 二嫂正在场上晒谷子呢。Èr sǎo zhèng zài **cháng** shang shài gǔzi ne. Second sister-in-law is drying rice on the threshing ground.

②a country fair: 赶场 gǎn **cháng** to go to the fair

③[a measure word for events]: 一场大雨 yì **cháng** dà yǔ a downpour of rain

场院 **cháng**yuàn ⟨dial.⟩ a threshing ground

打谷场 dǎgǔ**cháng** a threshing ground

# 朝 **cháo → zhāo**

# 车 **chē　jū**

**chē** ①a wheeled vehicle: 开车 kāi **chē** to drive a car

②any wheel-like device

③to turn on a lathe: 把圆轴车光 bǎ yuán zhóu **chē**

guāng to smooth a round shaft on a lathe

④ to raise with a water-wheel：车水 chē shuǐ to raise water with a water-wheel

车床 chēchuáng a lathe

风车 fēngchē a windmill

火车 huǒchē a train

汽车 qìchē a car, automobile

jū　the counterpart of the rook in Chinese chess：车马炮 jū mǎ pào rook, knight, and cannon（in Chinese chess）

# 尺　chě → chǐ

# 称　chèn chēng → chèng

# 澄　chéng　dèng

chéng　①pure, limpid, still

②to clarify, make clear

澄彻 chéngchè clear, limpid：池水澄彻。Chíshuǐ chéngchè. The water in the pool is clear.

dèng　to clarify（a liquid）by allowing silt to settle：把水澄一澄 bǎ shuǐ dèng yi dèng to clarify water by allowing the silt to settle

*Polyphonic compound*：

澄清 chéngqīng ①clear, limpid：池水澄清，能见到底。Chíshuǐ chéngqīng, néng jiàndào dǐ. The water in the pool is clear; you can see to the bottom. ②to clarify（a situation, issue）：澄清事实 chéngqīng shìshí to clarify the facts

　　dèngqīng to clarify ( a liquid ) by allowing silt to set-
　　tle: 把水澄清 bǎ shuǐ dèngqīng to clarify water by
　　allowing the silt to settle

**盛**　chéng → shèng

**称**　chèng　chēng　chèn

chèng ( = 秤 ) a scales, balance, steelyard: 一杆称 yì gǎn
　　chèng a scales // 这称不准确。Zhè chèng bù
　　zhǔnquè. These scales are not accurate.

磅称 bàngchèng a platform scales

称锤 chèngchuí standard weights used with a steelyard

chēng ①to weigh: 这些菜称过了吗? Zhèxiē cài chēngguòle
　　ma? Have these vegetables been weighed?

　　② to call, give a name to: 人们都称他二老板。
　　Rénmen dōu chēng tā èr lǎobǎn. People call him
　　the number two boss.

　　③a name, title

　　④to say, declare, state: 连声称好 lián shēng chēng
　　hǎo to praise repeatedly

称呼 chēnghu to call, address; a form of address: 我该
　　怎么称呼你呢? Wǒ gāi zěnme chēnghu nǐ ne? How
　　should I address you? 我用什么称呼比较好? Wǒ
　　yòng shénme chēnghu bǐjiào hǎo? What form of ad-
　　dress would be better for me to use?

称赞 chēngzàn to praise; praise, acclaim: 大家都称赞
　　他的手艺。Dàjiā dōu chēngzàn tā de shǒuyì. Ev-

eryone praises his craftsmanship.

名称 míngchēng a name, term

宣称 xuānchēng to claim, assert：那个组织一贯宣称他们赞成民主政治。Nàge zǔzhī yíguàn xuānchēng tāmen zànchéng mínzhǔ zhèngzhì. That organisation has always asserted that it is in favour of democratic politics.

chèn fitting, suitable

称身 chènshēn to fit perfectly (of clothes)：裤子称身吗? Kùzi chènshēn ma? Do the trousers fit?

称心 chènxīn agreeable, satisfactory, to one's liking：这样的安排你称心吗? Zhèyàng de ānpái nǐ chènxīn ma? Is this arrangement satisfactory to you?

# 匙　chí　shi

chí a spoon

匙子 chízi a spoon

汤匙 tāngchí a soup-spoon

shi 钥匙 yàoshi a key

# 尺　chǐ　chě

chǐ ①a Chinese unit of length

②a rule, ruler

尺子 chǐzi a rule, ruler

公尺 gōngchǐ the metre (unit of length)

chě name of a note in certain traditional Chinese musical scales

工尺谱 gōngchěpǔ a type of traditional Chinese musical

notation

冲

chōng

**chōng    chòng**

chōng ① to charge toward：汽车失控，沿着坡道直冲下去。Qìchē shīkòng, yánzhe pōdào zhí **chōng** xiàqù. The car got out of control, and hurtled straight down the slope.

② to rinse, flush：把碗具用沸水冲一下。Bǎ wǎnjù yòng fèishuǐ **chōng** yíxià. Rinse the crockery with boiling water.

③ to pour boiling water on：冲茶 **chōng** chá to brew tea

④ a thoroughfare, strategic place

⑤ a flat area among hills

冲锋 **chōng**fēng a charge (e.g. through enemy ranks)：敌军发起的第一次冲锋被打退了。Díjūn fāqǐ de dì yī cì **chōng**fēng bèi dǎ tuì le. The first charge by the enemy forces was beaten back.

冲突 **chōng**tū a conflict

冲洗 **chōng**xǐ to rinse, wash; to develop (photographs)：冲洗地板 **chōng**xǐ dìbǎn to mop the floor // 冲洗相片 **chōng**xǐ xiàngpiàn to develop photographs

冲撞 **chōng**zhuàng to collide with, ram：两车在路中间冲撞，死伤多人。Liǎng chē zài lù zhōngjiān **chōng**zhuàng, sǐshāng duō rén. Two cars collided in the middle of the road, killing and injuring many people.

山冲 shān**chōng** a flat mountain valley

要冲 yàochōng a strategic thoroughfare

chòng ①facing toward: 冲东走 chòng dōng zǒu proceeding toward the east // 他这些话其实是冲着我来的。Tā zhèxiē huà qíshí shì chòngzhe wǒ lái de. His words were, in fact, directed at me.

②vigorous, forceful: 他干活真冲。Tā gànhuó zhēn chòng. He works really energetically.

③strong (of taste or smell): 这酒太冲。Zhè jiǔ tài chòng. This wine is very strong.

④punching (in metal-working)

冲劲儿 chòngjìnr strength and vigour; a strong smell or taste

冲压机 chòngyājī a punch (machine)

**重**　chóng → zhòng

**臭**　chòu　xiù

chòu foul-smelling; undesirable, unwelcome: 这厕所很臭。Zhè cèsuǒ hěn chòu. This toilet smells foul. // 名声很臭 míngshēng hěn chòu having a bad reputation

臭骂 chòumà to scold severely; a severe scolding: 把他臭骂一顿 bǎ tā chòumà yí dùn to give him a good scolding // 他挨了一顿臭骂。Tā ái le yí dùn chòumà. He received a severe scolding.

xiù an odour

无臭 wúxiù odourless

**处**　chǔ　chù

chǔ ①to get on (with other people): 处不来 chǔ bu lái unable to get on (with other people)

②situated

③to stay, live

④to manage

处罚 chǔfá to punish; punishment: 这种坏人真该处罚。 Zhè zhǒng huàirén zhēn gāi chǔfá. This kind of rascal really ought to be punished.

处境 chǔjìng unfavourable situation, plight

处理 chǔlǐ to manage, deal with: 把这事交给我处理吧。 Bǎ zhè shì jiāo gěi wǒ chǔlǐ ba. Give this matter to me to handle.

处女 chǔnǚ a virgin; maiden, first (voyage etc.)

处于 chǔyú to be in (a certain condition): 处于恶劣环境中 chǔ yú èliè huánjìng zhōng situated in a terrible environment

处置 chǔzhì to deal with, handle: 这批货物真难处置。 Zhè pī huòwù zhēn nán chǔzhì. It's really hard to know what to do with this lot of goods.

独处 dúchǔ to live alone: 长期独处对生理健康有影响。 Chángqī dúchǔ duì shēnglǐ jiànkāng yǒu yǐngxiǎng. Living alone for a long time has an effect on one's physical health.

相处 xiāngchǔ to get along together: 这街道上的邻里们相处得很好。 Zhè jiēdào shàng de línlǐmen xiāngchǔ de hěn hǎo. The people on this street get along together quite well.

**chù** ①a place

②an office or department

处所 chùsuǒ a place, locality

办事处 bànshìchù an office, bureau

到处 dàochù everywhere

好处 hǎochù a good point, advantage

人事处 rénshìchù a personnel office

住处 zhùchù a residence, lodgings

## 畜　chù　xù

**chù** domestic animals

畜生 chùshēng animals; a beast, inhuman swine

家畜 jiāchù domestic animals

**xù** to raise (livestock)

畜产品 xùchǎnpǐn livestock products

畜牧 xùmù to pasture sheep, cattle, etc.; animal husbandry

畜养 xùyǎng to raise (livestock): 今年我们畜养了一百只羊。Jīnnián wǒmen xùyǎngle yì bǎi zhī yáng. This year we have raised a hundred head of sheep.

## 揣　chuǎi　chuāi

**chuǎi** to estimate, measure

揣测 chuǎicè to conjecture, fathom: 他的意图难以揣测。Tā de yìtú nányǐ chuǎicè. It's hard to fathom what he's after.

揣摩 chuǎimó to think through in order to reach a conclu-
sion：我揣摩了半天，也想不出他的动机究竟是什
么。Wǒ chuǎimóle bàntiān, yě xiǎng bu chū tā de
dòngjī jiūjìng shì shénme. I speculated for a long
time, but couldn't think what his motive actually was.

chuāi 〈coll.〉 to conceal or carry in one's clothing：他把书揣在
怀里。Tā bǎ shū chuāi zài huái lǐ. He concealed the
book in his bosom.

# 传 chuán zhuàn

chuán ①to transmit, bequeath, infect, propagate：他把武艺传
给他们。Tā bǎ wǔyì chuán gěi tāmen. He passed on
his fighting skills to them.

②to summon：传他来。Chuán tā lái. Summon him to
come.

传道 chuándào to preach, do missionary work：到边远
地区传道 dào biānyuǎn dìqū chuándào to do missionary work in remote areas

传染 chuánrǎn to infect：苍蝇传染疾病。Cāngying
chuánrǎn jíbìng. Flies spread disease.

传统 chuántǒng tradition

宣传 xuānchuán to publicise; propaganda：宣传党的政
策 xuānchuán dǎng de zhèngcè to publicise the
party's policy

zhuàn a record, chronicle, biography

树碑立传 shù bēi lì zhuàn 〈often derogatory〉 to erect a
monument and write a biography = to build up

someone's public image

传记 zhuànjì a biography

自传 zìzhuàn an autobiography

**幢** chuáng → zhuàng

**创** chuàng chuāng

chuàng to begin, found, create

创始 chuàngshǐ originating, initiating, founding：创始会
员 chuàngshǐ huìyuán a founding member // 处于创始
阶段 chǔyú chuàngshǐ jiēduàn to be in the initial phase

创造 chuàngzào to create, produce：创造奇迹 chuàng
zào qíjì to produce miracles

chuāng a wound

创痕 chuānghén a scar

创伤 chuāngshāng wounds; trauma, distress, hurt

**差** cī → chā

**伺** cì → sì

**攒** cuán → zǎn

**撮** cuō zuǒ

cuō ①to pinch, bring together with the fingers：撮盐 cuō yán
to take a pinch of salt // 撮药 cuō yào to prepare medicine according to a prescription

②a pinch, a tiny amount：一撮盐 yì cuō yán a pinch of
salt // 一小撮坏人 yì xiǎo cuō huàirén a handful of
scoundrels

撮合 cuōhé to unite, bring together: 他俩的婚姻是由老李撮合的。Tā liǎ de hūnyīn shì yóu Lǎo Lǐ cuōhé de. Their marriage was arranged by Lao Li.

撮口呼 cuōkǒuhū (in traditional Chinese phonology) syllable-finals containing the sound [ü]

撮要 cuōyào to summarise; a synopsis: 撮要介绍一下 cuōyào jièshào yíxià to give a brief summary by way of introduction

zuǒ a tuft (of hair): 一撮黑毛 yì zuǒ hēi máo a tuft of black hair

# D

# 答 dá dā

dá ①an answer, reply, response

②to answer, reciprocate: 这个问题她答得不好。Zhège wèntí tā dá de bù hǎo. She did not answer this question well.

答非所问 dá fēi suǒ wèn to make an irrelevant reply

答谢 dáxiè to express thanks; an expression of thanks: 我答谢了她。Wǒ dáxiè le tā. I thanked her. // 我送她一篮苹果作为答谢。Wǒ sòng tā yì lán píngguǒ zuòwéi dáxiè. I sent her a basket of apples as an expression of gratitude.

回答 huídá to answer; an answer: 那家公司回答你没有? Nà jiā gōngsī huídá nǐ méiyǒu? Did the company give you an answer? // 我没听到他的回答。Wǒ méi tīng dào tā de huídá. I didn't hear his answer.

问答 wèndá question and answer

dā to answer [only in certain words, including the following]

答理 dālǐ to respond, acknowledge (a greeting etc.) [usually used with a negative]: 这地方的居民好像不爱答理陌生人。Zhè dìfāng de jūmín hǎoxiàng bú ài dālǐ mòshēng rén. The inhabitants of this place seem not to like greeting strangers.

答应 dāying to assent, promise: 他们答应下星期一动身。Tāmen dāying xià Xīngqīyī dòngshēn. They agreed to set out next Monday.

# 打　dǎ　dá

dǎ ①to hit, knock, strike: 打门 dǎ mén to knock on a door // 打球 dǎ qiú to play ball // 打钟 dǎ zhōng to strike a bell // 打扬琴 dǎ yángqín to play the dulcimer // 打铁 dǎ tiě to forge iron

②to fight, attack: 打架 dǎ jià to fight, come to blows // 打仗 dǎ zhàng to make war // 打他一顿 dǎ tā yí dùn to give him a beating

③[in many verbal expressions, and in many compound verbs, denotes the relevant activity]: 打电话 dǎ diànhuà to make a phone call // 打毛衣 dǎ máoyī to knit a pullover // 打伞 dǎ sǎn to hold (or put) up an

umbrella // 打行李 dǎ xíngli to pack one's luggage //
打枪 dǎ qiāng to fire a gun // 打水 dǎ shuǐ to draw
water // 打鱼 dǎ yú to catch fish // 打油 dǎ yóu to
buy oil // 打折扣 dǎ zhékòu to give a discount

④from; since：你打哪儿来? Nǐ dǎ nǎr lái? Where do
you come from? // 打那天起 dǎ nà tiān qǐ since that
day

打扮 dǎban to dress up, put on makeup：她总是打扮得
很漂亮。Tā zǒngshi dǎban de hěn piàoliàng. She
always makes up very beautifully.

打倒 dǎdǎo to overthrow; Down with ...：打倒专制政
权! Dǎdǎo zhuānzhì zhèngquán! Down with dictator-
ship!

打点 dǎdian to tidy up, pack：打点行装 dǎdian
xíngzhuāng to pack one's luggage

打发 dǎfa to send; to dismiss：打发孩子去买油 dǎfa
háizi qù mǎi yóu to send a child to buy oil

打扫 dǎsǎo to sweep, clean up 打扫教室 dǎsǎo jiàoshì
to clean up the classroom

打算 dǎsuàn to plan：她打算去上海度假。Tā dǎsuàn
qù Shànghǎi dùjià. She plans to go to Shanghai for the
holidays.

打消 dǎxiāo to give up, abandon：打消上大学的念头
dǎxiāo shàng dàxué de niàntou to give up the idea of
going to university

dá [used in transcribing foreign words]：一打 yì dá one dozen

苏打 sūdá soda

## 大　dà　dài

dà

① big, large in size or quantity：这房子真大。Zhè fángzi zhēn dà. This house is really big. // 音量太大了。Yīnliàng tài dà le. The sound is too loud. // 大山 dà shān a big mountain

② great, important：文化大革命 Wénhuà Dà Gémìng the "Great Cultural Revolution"

③ elder, eldest：大儿子 dà érzi eldest son // 她比我大。Tā bǐ wǒ dà. She is older than me.

④〔an indicator of respect for the other party's things or activities〕

⑤〔used before certain terms referring to days or years〕

⑥〔used to give force to a following time word〕：大白天 dà báitiān broad daylight // 大清早 dà qīngzǎo really early in the morning

大白 dàbái to come out, become known：真相大白。Zhēnxiàng dàbái. The whole truth has come out.

大伯 dàbó father's elder brother; uncle（polite form of address to an elder male）

大红 dàhóng bright red

大后天 dàhòutiān three days hence

大名 dàmíng（your）famous name

大前年 dàqiánnián three years ago

大事 dàshì an important matter, major event; in a big

way, enormously

大雨 dàyǔ heavy rain

大作 dàzuò (your) great **work**

dài　大夫 dàifu a physician, **medical doctor**

大黄 dàihuáng the Chinese rhubarb

# 逮　dǎi　dài

dǎi　to catch：猫逮老鼠。Māo dǎi lǎoshǔ. Cats catch mice.

// 逮住一个贼 dǎi zhù yí ge zéi to catch and hold a thief

dài　逮捕 dàibǔ to arrest：地方当局逮捕了四名嫌疑分子。

Dìfāng dāngjú dàibǔle sì míng xiányí fènzi. The local

authorities arrested four suspects.

# 大　dài → dà

# 待　dài　dāi

dài　①to wait：请稍待，我马上就来。Qǐng shāo dài，wǒ

mǎshàng jiù lái. Please wait a little. I'll come right

away.

②to treat, act towards：他们待我不错。Tāmen dài wǒ

bú cuò. They treated me well.

③about to：我待要拦住他，却又怕过于冒失。Wǒ dài

yào lánzhù tā，què yòu pà guòyú màoshi. I was

about to stop him, but then I was afraid that might be

too rash.

待命 dàimìng waiting for orders： 就地待命　jiùdì

dàimìng "on call"

待遇 dàiyù treatment；pay and conditions

招待 zhāodài to entertain guests：请好好招待这两位客
人。Qǐng hǎohāo zhāodài zhè liǎng wèi kèrén.
Please take good care of these two guests.

**dāi** to stay, hang around：待不住 dāi bu zhù unable to stay //
她待了很久。Tā dāile hěn jiǔ. She stayed a long while.

# 担　dān　dàn

**dān** ①to carry a burden：担水 dān shuǐ to carry water // 担
柴 dān chái to carry firewood

②to bear responsibility：身担重任 shēn dān zhòngrèn
to bear a heavy responsibility

担待 dāndài to take（blame or responsibility for）：万一
出了差错，我可担待不起呀！Wànyī chūle chācuò,
wǒ kě dāndài bu qǐ ya! If by any chance something
goes wrong, I can't be held responsible!

担任 dānrèn to fill a position, take responsibility：担任
要职 dānrèn yàozhí to fill an important position

担心 dānxīn to worry：别担心，有我呢！Bié dānxīn,
yǒu wǒ ne! Don't worry; I'm here!

担忧 dānyōu to worry：别为我担忧。Bié wèi wǒ
dānyōu. Don't worry about me.

**dàn** ①a burden, load（carried at the two ends of a shoulder-
pole）

②a unit of weight（ = 100 斤 jīn）

③〔a measure word for loads carried at the two ends of a
shoulder-pole〕：一担水 yí dàn shuǐ a pole-load of
water（i.e. two bucketfuls）// 两担肥料 liǎng dàn

féiliào two pole-loads of fertiliser

担子 dànzi a load carried on a shoulder-pole

货郎担 huòlángdàn a street vendor's load (carried on a shoulder-pole)

重担 zhòngdàn a heavy load; a heavy responsibility

**单** dān shàn chán

dān
①single, one: 单扇门 dān shàn mén a single door

②odd (of numbers)

③only, just: 不能单看表面现象。Bù néng dān kàn biǎomiàn xiànxiàng. One can't just take account of superficial appearances.

④simple, plain

⑤thin, weak

⑥a list

⑦a sheet

床单 chuángdān a bedsheet

单薄 dānbó thin, frail, flimsy: 衣服单薄 yīfu dānbó lightly dressed

单调 dāndiào monotonous: 颜色单调。Yánsè dāndiào. The colour is monotonous.

单独 dāndú alone, by oneself: 单独居住 dāndú jūzhù to live alone

单号 dānhào odd numbers

单衣 dānyī clothes without lining (e.g. for summer wear)

简单 jiǎndān simple, easy: 这房里的布置很简单。Zhè fáng li de bùzhì hěn jiǎndān. The decoration in this room is very simple.

名单 míngdān a roll, list of names

shàn ①〔a surname〕

②〔name of〕 a county in Shandong Province

chán 单于 chányú 〔the title of a Hun (匈奴) chief in ancient times〕

# 掸 dǎn shàn

dǎn ①to brush lightly, dust: 掸去尘土 dǎnqu chéntǔ to brush away dust

②a duster

掸子 dǎnzi a (feather) duster

shàn 〔name of〕 a minority people in Burma: 掸族 Shànzú the Shan people

# 石 dàn → shí

# 弹 dàn tán

dàn a pellet

飞弹 fēidàn a rocket, ballistic missile

原子弹 yuánzǐdàn a nuclear bomb

子弹 zǐdàn a bullet

tán ①to rebound: 那球弹得很高。Nà qiú tán de hěn gāo. The ball bounced high.

②to pluck; to play using the fingers: 弹琴 tán qín to play the harp, piano, etc.

弹劾 tánhé to impeach: 议会弹劾总统。Yìhuì tánhé zǒngtǒng. Parliament impeached the president.

弹簧 tánhuáng a spring

# 当 dāng dàng

dāng ①to act as, serve as: 他是个当兵的。Tā shì ge dāng bīng de. He is in the army. // 小李当了组长。Xiǎo Lǐ dāngle zǔzhǎng. Young Li has become a section chief.

②ought to: 当做的事就不该拖延。Dāng zuò de shì jiù bù gāi tuōyán. Things that ought to be done should not be deferred.

③equivalent to

④just when: 当我冲进门时，那小偷已经跳出窗外了。Dāng wǒ chōngjìn mén shí, nà xiǎotōu yǐjīng tiàochū chuāng wài le. Just as I rushed in the door, the thief jumped out of the window.

⑤to face, come face to face with: 当着他的面，把事情说清楚 dāngzhe tā de miàn, bǎ shìqing shuō qīngchu to explain the matter to him face to face

⑥to direct, manage: 你们这个家可不好当。Nǐmen zhège jiā kě bù hǎo dāng. This family of yours is not easy to manage.

⑦[onomatopoeia for the ringing of large bells]

当权 dāngquán to be in power: 当权派 dāngquánpài the party in power

当然 dāngrán of course, naturally: 骂人当然不对。Mà rén dāngrán bú duì. Cursing people is, of course, not right.

当时 dāngshí at that time

相当 xiāngdāng equivalent to, matching; rather, fairly: 两人地位相当。Liǎng rén dìwèi xiāngdāng. The two people's positions are equivalent. // 相当好 xiāngdāng hǎo rather good

应当 yīngdāng ought to; fitting, proper: 你应当留下。Nǐ yīngdāng liúxià. You ought to stay on. // 不应当这样做 bù yīngdāng zhèyàng zuò should not do it like this

dàng ①to consider, think, believe, regard as, treat as: 我当他不知道。Wǒ dàng tā bù zhīdào. I believe (or act as if) he doesn't know.

②to pawn: 他把冬天的衣服全当了。Tā bǎ dōngtiān de yīfu quán dàng le. He pawned all his winter clothes.

③suitable, appropriate: 用人不当 yòng rén bú dàng to have chosen unsuitable people (for a job etc.)

④to match; equal to: 他一人能当两人用。Tā yì rén néng dàng liǎng rén yòng. He has an ability equal to two men.

⑤the same (day, etc.)

当铺 dàngpù a pawn-shop

当天 dàngtiān the same day

当真 dàngzhēn to take seriously, regard as true: 别当真，那是闹着玩儿的。Bié dàngzhēn, nà shì nàozhe wánr de. Don't take it seriously; it's just a joke.

当做 dàngzuò to treat as, regard as, see as: 天黑看不
清，我把他当做老李了。Tiān hēi kàn bu qīng, wǒ
bǎ tā dàngzuò Lǎo Lǐ le. It was dark and hard to see,
and I mistook him for Lao Li.

上当 shàngdàng to be taken in, fall for a trick

## 叨　dāo　dáo　tāo

dāo　garrulous, talkative

叨叨 dāodao to talk incessantly

唠叨 láodao to talk incessantly: 那老太太整天唠叨。
Nà lǎo tàitai zhěng tiān láodao. That old lady talks
all day long.

dáo　叨咕 dáogu to mutter, grumble

tāo　to be favoured with

叨教 tāojiào to have the benefit of (your) advice; many
thanks for your advice

叨扰 tāorǎo to be favoured with (your) effort; thank you
for your trouble

## 倒　dǎo　dào

dǎo　①to fall over, collapse: 树倒了。Shù dǎo le. The tree
fell over.

②to take turns, work in shifts: 厂里的生产三班倒，人
歇机器不停。Chǎng lǐ de shēngchǎn sān bān dǎo,
rén xiē jīqì bù tíng. The factory works three shifts; the
people take rests but the machines work non-stop.

③to change, exchange: 把座位倒一下 bǎ zuòwèi dǎo yíxià to change seats // 去中关村得在哪儿倒车? Qù Zhōngguān Cūn děi zài nǎr dǎo chē? To get to Zhongguan Village, where do I change buses?

④to become hoarse: 他嗓子倒了。Tā sǎngzi dǎo le. He lost his voice.

⑤(of appetite) to be spoiled: 倒胃口 dǎo wèikǒu to spoil one's appetite

打倒 dǎdǎo to overthrow; Down with . . . !: 打倒独裁者! Dǎdǎo dúcáizhě! Down with the dictator!

倒闭 dǎobì to go bankrupt: 工厂倒闭了。Gōngchǎng dǎobì le. The factory went into liquidation.

倒卖 dǎomài to buy and sell at a profit: 做倒卖生意 zuò dǎomài shēngyi to do business buying and selling at a profit

倒霉 dǎoméi unfortunate, down on one's luck: 真倒霉，钱包丢了。Zhēn dǎoméi, qiánbāo diū le. What a misfortune! I've lost my wallet.

跌倒 diēdǎo to stumble and fall

dào ①to invert, reverse: 倒车 dào chē to reverse a car (cf. dǎo chē to change cars; see above)

②inverted, inverse: 你把画挂倒了。Nǐ bǎ huà guà dào le. You have hung the picture upside-down.

③to pour out: 倒茶 dào chá to pour tea // 水倒出来了。Shuǐ dào chulai le. The water poured out.

④but; on the contrary: 那倒不要紧。Nà dào bú

yàojǐn. But that's not important.

倒流 dàoliú to flow backward: 这真像是时光倒流了十几年。 Zhè zhēn xiàng shi shíguāng dàoliúle shí jǐ nián. It is just as if time had flowed backward a decade or more.

倒影 dàoyǐng a mirror image

倒转 dàozhuàn to turn in the reverse direction: 历史的车轮不能倒转。 Lìshǐ de chēlún bù néng dàozhuàn. The wheel of history cannot be turned back.

*Polyphonic compound*:

倾倒 qīngdǎo to topple over and fall; "head over heals" about: 那座古塔在强烈冲击下倾倒了。 Nà zuò gǔ tǎ zài qiángliè chōngjī xià qīngdǎo le. Under the strong impact the ancient tower toppled and fell. // 为她的美貌倾倒 wèi tā de měimào qīngdǎo overwhelmed by her beauty

qīngdào to toss out (e.g. rubbish): 倾倒工业废料 qīngdào gōngyè fèiliào to toss out industrial rubbish

# 得 dé de děi

dé ① to get: 今年的考试，她得了全优。 Jīnnián de kǎoshì, tā déle quán yōu. In this year's examinations she got top marks throughout.

② to result in (of calculations): 二三得六。 Èr sān dé liù. Twice three is six.

③fitting, proper

④complacent

⑤may, can: 未经批准不得外出。Wèi jīng pīzhǔn bù dé wàichū. Without permission one may not go outside.

⑥〈coll.〉finished, ready: 饭得了，来吃吧。Fàn dé le, lái chī ba. The meal is ready, so come and eat.

不得了 bùdéliǎo awfully, very; terrible, disastrous

得到 dédào to succeed in getting: 吴朋得到了耶鲁大学的奖学金。Wú Péng dédàole Yēlǔ Dàxué de jiǎngxuéjīn. Wu Peng got a scholarship to Yale University.

得体 détǐ befitting the occasion or one's position, appropriate: 在正式场合穿拖鞋，很不得体。Zài zhèngshì chǎnghé chuān tuōxié, hěn bù détǐ. It is quite inappropriate to wear slippers at a formal occasion.

得意 déyì proud, satisfied

自得 zìdé self-satisfied

de ①〔a verbal particle signifying ability or possibility〕: 看得见 kàn de jiàn able to see // 做得到 zuò de dào able to do // 拿得动 ná de dòng able to move (something)

②〔a particle introducing an adverbial phrase signifying manner or degree〕: 走得快 zǒu de kuài to walk quickly // 坏得很 huài de hěn very bad // 贵得没有人买 guì de méiyǒu rén mǎi so expensive that no one buys it

děi ①ought to, must: 我得去. Wǒ děi qù. I must go.

②sure to, bound to〔in the speaker's estimation〕: 你要是

不快走，就得迟到了。Nǐ yàoshi bú kuài zǒu, jiù **děi** chídào le. If you don't hurry, you're sure to be late.

必得 bì**děi** must

地 de → dì

的 de → dì

得 de děi → dé

澄 dèng → chéng

提 dī → tí

地 dì　de

dì　① earth, ground, territory, field：书掉在地上了。Shū diào zài **dì** shàng le. The book fell on to the floor. // 那块地是谁家的? Nà kuài **dì** shì shéi jiā de? Which family owns that piece of land? // 到地里干活去 dào **dì** li gàn huó qù to go to work in the fields

② a situation

③ a place, locality：两地分居 liǎng **dì** fēnjū to live separately in two places (of husband and wife or family members)

④ 〔used after 里 or 站〕distance：那村子离这儿只有两里地。Nà cūnzi lí zhèr zhǐ yǒu liǎng lǐ **dì**. The village is only two *li* from here.

地步 **dì**bù a situation

地图 **dì**tú a map

地位 **dì**wèi status

境地 jìngdì a situation

土地 tǔdì land

de 〔an adverbial particle comparable to English -ly〕: 偷偷地
tōutōu de stealthily

# 的   dì   dí   de

dì   a target, goal

鹄的 gǔdì ⟨lit.⟩ a shooting target

目的 mùdì an objective

无的放矢 wúdì-fàngshǐ to shoot without a target, to
shoot at random

dí   ①accurate, true

②proper

的当 dídàng ⟨lit.⟩ appropriate, proper

的确 díquè certainly, really

de   〔a genitive, adjectival, or subordinating particle〕: 我的
wǒ de my, mine // 好的 hǎo de good, fine, all right; a
good one // 他说的 tā shuō de what he says

# 鸟   diǎo → niǎo

# 调   diào   tiáo

diào   ①to interchange, transfer, shift: 上级把我调到他们局
里。Shàngjí bǎ wǒ diào dào tāmen jú li. The authorities moved me to their department.

②a tune: 她们唱的是一个调。Tāmen chàng de shì
yíge diào. What they sang was to the same tune.

③a musical mode or key: 这个调太高了。Zhège diào

tài gāo le. This is in too high a key.

④a tone (in linguistics)

调查 diàochá to investigate：调查飞机失事原因 diàochá fēijī shīshì yuányīn to investigate the cause of a plane crash

调动 diàodòng to transfer; a transfer：调动工作 diàodòng gōngzuò to transfer (someone) to a different posting

调换 diàohuàn to interchange：调换坐位 diàohuàn zuòwèi to exchange seats

调式 diàoshì a musical mode

调子 diàozi a tune

格调 gédiào (of a person, artwork, etc.) style, moral quality：此人格调低劣。Cǐ rén gédiào dīliè. This person is of low moral calibre.

声调 shēngdiào tone (in linguistics)

tiáo ①to adjust：把琴弦调好 bǎ qínxián tiáo hǎo to tune a stringed instrument

②to harmonise

③to mix：在牛奶里调点儿蜜 zài niúnǎi li tiáo diǎnr mì to mix a little honey with milk

④to make fun of

调羹 tiáogēng a spoon

调和 tiáohé to harmonise：调和两家关系 tiáohé liǎng jiā guānxi to harmonise relations between two families

调笑 tiáoxiào to tease, make fun of (flirtingly)：他喜欢

跟女人调笑。Tā xǐhuān gēn nǚrén tiáoxiào. He likes making fun of girls (flirtingly).

调整 tiáozhěng to adjust：调整座位 tiáozhěng zuòwèi to rearrange seating // 调整工资 tiáozhěng gōngzī to adjust salaries (usually upwards)

# 钉    dīng    dìng

dīng ①a nail, spike, rivet：一枚长钉 yì méi cháng dīng a long nail

②( = 盯 ) to follow persistently

钉梢 ( = 盯梢 ) dīngshāo to shadow or tail someone

钉鞋 dīngxié spiked shoes

钉子 dīngzi a nail

铁钉 tiědīng an iron nail

dìng ①to nail：钉书 dìng shū to staple or bind books // 钉钉子 dìng dīngzi to drive in a nail

②to sew on：钉扣子 dìng kòuzi to sew on buttons

# 酊    dǐng    dīng

dǐng 酩酊 míngdǐng dead drunk

dīng a tincture

碘酊 diǎndīng tincture of iodine

# 都    dōu    dū

dōu ①all, altogether：他们都走了。Tāmen dōu zǒu le. They have all left. // 他都知道。Tā dōu zhīdao. He knows it all. // 都是你，我们才误了火车。Dōu shì nǐ, wǒmen cái wùle huǒchē. It's all because of you that we missed the train.

②even: 他待她比亲爹都好。Tā dài tā bǐ qīn diē dōu hǎo. He treats her even better than her own father.

③already: 都十点了,你还不走。Dōu shí diǎn le, nǐ hái bù zǒu. It's already ten o'clock and you still haven't left.

dū ①a capital city

②a large city

③〔a surname〕

都市 dūshì a metropolis

首都 shǒudū a national capital

**斗** dǒu   dòu

dǒu ①a dipper-like measure for grain etc.

②〔a unit of dry measure, = one decalitre〕: 三斗米 sān dǒu mǐ three *dou* of rice

③any dipper-shaped object

④the Big Dipper; a constellation; a general term for stars

北斗星 Běidǒuxīng the Big Dipper, the Plough

漏斗 lòudǒu a funnel

烟斗 yāndǒu a (tobacco) pipe

星斗 xīngdǒu stars

dòu ①a fight, struggle, contest: 一场恶斗 yì chǎng è dòu a bitter contest

②to struggle, contest: 他们俩谁也斗不过谁。Tāmen liǎ shéi yě dòu bu guò shéi. Neither of them can win the struggle.

③to dovetail together

斗鸡 dòujī cockfighting; a gamecock

斗争 dòuzhēng a struggle, fight, conflict; to strive for, fight for: 为完成任务而斗争 wèi wánchéng rènwù ér dòuzhēng struggling in order to fulfil one's duty

都　dū → dōu

读　dú　dòu

dú　①to read, study: 他们家小三正在读小学二年级。Tāmen jiū Xiǎo Sān zhèngzài dú xiǎoxué èr niánjí. Their third child is studying second year at primary school. // 你最近在读什么书呢? Nǐ zuìjìn zài dú shénme shū ne? What books have you been reading lately?

②to pronounce (in reading out loud): 这个字该怎么读? Zhège zì gāi zěnme dú? How should this character be pronounced?

读本 dúběn a reader (for language study, etc.)

读音 dúyīn the literary pronunciation of a character

dòu　( = 逗 ) pauses in a sentence

句读 jùdòu the full stop and the comma; sentences and phrases

肚　dù　dǔ

dù　the belly

肚肠 dùcháng the intestines

肚脐眼 dùqíyǎn the navel

dǔ  the stomach (of animals), tripe

牛肚 niúdǔ beef tripe

*Polyphonic compound*:

肚子 dùzi the belly

　　dǔzi tripe

# 度　dù　duó

dù　①degree

②a unit of measurement for angles, temperature, etc.: 今天气温是 30 摄氏度。Jīntiān qìwēn shì sānshí Shèshì dù. The temperature today was thirty degrees Celsius. // 这酒有 60 度。Zhè jiǔ yǒu liùshí dù. This drink is sixty per cent alcohol.

③a system

④a limit

⑤a time, occasion: 一年一度 yì nián yí dù once a year

⑥to pass, spend time: 欢度节日 huān dù jiérì to celebrate a festival joyously

⑦disposition, personal attributes

⑧consideration, thought

程度 chéngdù a standard of attainment

风度 fēngdù demeanour, bearing: 风度翩翩 fēngdù piānpiān having an elegant bearing (describing a young man)

高度 gāodù height, altitude

过度 guòdù over the limit

速度 sùdù speed

态度 tàidù attitude

限度 xiàndù a limit

硬度 yìngdù hardness (a physical measure)

再度 zàidù a second time, again

制度 zhìdù a system

置之度外 zhì zhī dù wài to give no thought to：把个人安危置之度外 bǎ gèrén ānwēi zhì zhī dù wài to give no thought to one's own safety

duó　to calculate, estimate, guess：以己度人 yǐ jǐ duó rén to judge others by one's own subjective standards

揣度 chuǎiduó to conjecture, speculate, imagine：他的动机难以揣度。Tā de dòngjī nányǐ chuǎiduó. His motives are hard to conjecture.

**囤**　dùn → tún

**度**　duó → dù

**垛**　duò　　duǒ

duò　①to heap up：垛起来 duò qilai to heap up // 把干草垛在空地上 bǎ gāncǎo duò zài kòngdì shang to heap up hay in open ground

②a heap：灰垛 huī duò a heap of ashes // 草垛 cǎo duò a haystack

duǒ　a projecting structure, battlement

城垛口 chéngduǒkǒu a battlement

门垛子 ménduǒzi a door buttress

**驮**　duò → tuó

# E

阿  ē → ā

恶  è  wù  ě

è    evil, bad, foul, malignant

恶劣 èliè of bad quality, inferior, disgusting: 作风恶劣 zuòfēng èliè a disgusting way of doing things

恶名 èmíng a bad reputation

善恶 shàn'è good and evil

wù    ①to hate

②hateful

好恶 hàowù likes and dislikes, taste

可恶 kěwù damnable, hateful

厌恶 yànwù to detest: 我厌恶那种人。Wǒ yànwù nà zhǒng rén. I detest that kind of person.

ě    to disgust, nauseate

恶心 ěxīn nauseous; to be disgusted (also è xīn bad thoughts)

# F

发　fā　fà

fā　①to send out, issue: 发通知　fā tōngzhī　to send out a memo // 发布告　fā bùgào to issue an announcement

②to utter, express: 发音　fā yīn to utter a sound; to pronounce (also fāyīn pronunciation; see below) // 嗓子痛，发不出声来。Sǎngzi tòng, fā bu chū shēng lai. My throat is sore; I can't make a sound. // 所有的人都发了言。Suǒyǒu de rén dōu fā le yán. Everyone gave a talk.

③to shoot out, emit: 发光　fā guāng to emit light, shine

④to rise (by fermentation): 面发了。Miàn fā le. The dough has risen.

⑤to generate

⑥to open, expose, discover

⑦to become: 发烧　fā shāo to have a fever

⑧to give vent to: 发怒　fā nù to get angry

⑨to start, set out

出发　chūfā to set out; to proceed from: 部队出发了。Bùduì chūfā le. The unit has set out. // 从你的观点出发，结论当然不同。Cóng nǐ de guāndiǎn chūfā, jiélùn dāngrán bùtóng. Proceeding from your point of view, the conclusion is naturally different.

发表 fābiǎo to publish, issue; to express, state: 发表文章 fābiǎo wénzhāng to publish an article // 发表意见 fābiǎo yìjiàn to express an opinion

发电厂 fādiànchǎng an electric power station

发酵 fājiào to ferment; fermented; fermentation: 让面糊发酵一小时。Ràng miànhú fājiào yì xiǎoshí. Allow the paste to ferment for one hour.

发明 fāmíng to invent; an invention: 他又发明了一种新工具。Tā yòu fāmíngle yì zhǒng xīn gōngjù. He has invented another new kind of tool. // 一项新发明 yí xiàng xīn fāmíng a new invention

发音 fāyīn pronunciation: 他的英语发音不好。Tā de Yīngyǔ fāyīn bù hǎo. His English pronunciation is not good. (also fā yīn to pronounce; see above)

发展 fāzhǎn to develop; development: 这地区发展得很快。Zhè dìqū fāzhǎn de hěn kuài. This region is developing very quickly.

开发 kāifā to develop, open up, exploit: 开发旅游资源 kāifā lǚyóu zīyuán to exploit tourism resources // 开发山区 kāifā shānqū to develop mountain areas

蒸发 zhēngfā to evaporate: 水份在阳光下很快蒸发了。Shuǐfèn zài yángguāng xià hěn kuài zhēngfā le. The water soon evaporated in the sunshine.

fà ①hair

②an ancient (very small) unit of length

不差毫发 bú chà háo fà not differing by even the slightest amount, extremely accurate：每一部分的尺寸都符合标准，不差毫发。Měi yí bùfen de chǐcùn dōu fúhé biāozhǔn, bú chà háo fà. The size of every component conforms to the standard, with not the slightest discrepancy.

假发 jiǎfà a wig

理发 lǐfà to have a haircut (also lǐfà to cut hair)

**番**    fān    pān

fān    ①[a measure word for turns, times; types, kinds]：她这一番话把大家说得心服口服。Tā zhè yì fān huà bǎ dàjiā shuō de xīn fú kǒu fú. This speech of hers thoroughly convinced everyone. // 另有一番天地 lìng yǒu yìfān tiāndì (there is) an altogether different world

②barbarian, foreign

番茄 fānqié the tomato

轮番 lúnfān to take turns：轮番进攻 lúnfān jìngōng to attack by turns

三番五次 sānfān -wǔcì many times：她三番五次地劝我不去。Tā sānfān -wǔcì de quàn wǒ bú qù. She urged me time and again not to go.

生番 shēngfān a barbarian

pān    番禺 Pānyú a county in Guangdong Province

**坊**    fāng    fáng

fāng ①a neighbourhood, ward (often in place-names): 白纸坊 Báizhǐfāng White Paper Lane (a lane in Beijing)

②an archway

牌坊 páifāng a memorial archway

fáng a workshop, small factory

油坊 yóufáng a small factory for pressing vegetable oil

菲 fěi fēi

fěi ⟨lit.⟩ trifling, meagre, sparing, mean

菲薄 fěibó poor, mean; to belittle, despise: 礼品菲薄。 Lǐpǐn fěibó. ⟨humble⟩ (My) gift is meagre. // 妄自菲薄 wàng zì fěibó to belittle oneself improperly

菲仪 fěiyí ⟨humble⟩ (my) poor gift

fēi ①⟨lit.⟩ fragrant

②phenanthrene

③[used in transcribing foreign words]

菲菲 fēifēi ⟨lit.⟩ fragrant; beautiful, variegated: 芳草菲菲 fāngcǎo fēifēi ⟨lit.⟩ grasses (sending out) a fragrant aroma

菲律宾 Fēilǜbīn the Philippines

分 fēn fèn

fēn ①to divide, share, separate: 把人员分为四组 bǎ rényuán fēn wéi sì zǔ to divide people into four groups // 两家分住一栋楼。Liǎng jiā fēn zhù yí dòng lóu. The two families share one building.

②to distribute, assign, allot: 分传单 fēn chuándān to

distribute leaflets // 把这任务分给我们吧。Bǎ zhè rènwù **fēn** gěi wǒmen ba. Why not assign this task to us? // 她家分到了一个单元房。Tā jiā **fēn**dàole yí ge dānyuánfáng. Her family was allotted a flat to live in.

③to distinguish: 天太黑, 分不清谁是谁。Tiān tài hēi, **fēn** bu qīng shéi shi shéi. It had grown so dark that one couldn't distinguish who was who.

④division, branch: 他们在纽约有一家分公司。Tāmen zài Niǔyuē yǒu yì jiā **fēn** gōngsī. They have a branch in New York.

⑤a fraction: 三分之一 sān **fēn** zhī yī one third // 百分之五 bǎi **fēn** zhī wǔ five per cent

⑥〈coll.〉one tenth: 七分成绩, 三分错误 qī **fēn** chéngjì, sān **fēn** cuòwù 70% right, 30% wrong // 有十分把握 yǒu shí **fēn** bǎwò one hundred per cent certain

⑦various standard units of length, time, currency, etc.: 一寸三分长 yí cùn sān **fēn** cháng one and three tenths Chinese inches in length // 一分五十秒 yì **fēn** wǔshí miǎo one minute and fifty seconds // 东经一百度三十分 dōng jīng yì bǎi dù sānshí **fēn** 100 degrees 30 minutes east longitude // 七角八分钱 qī jiǎo bā **fēn** qián 0.78 yuan

⑧a point, mark (in games): 主队领先两分。Zhǔduì lǐngxiān liǎng **fēn**. The home team won by two points. //

期末考试她得了一百分。Qīmò kǎoshì tā déle yì bǎi fēn. She got full marks in the end-of-semester exam.

⑨ten per cent: 年利三分 niánlì sān fēn 30% interest per annum // 一分利不算高。Yì fēn lì bú suàn gāo. Ten per cent interest doesn't rate as high.

分布 fēnbù to be distributed, located: 矿藏主要分布在西北山区。Kuàngcáng zhǔyào fēnbù zài xīběi shānqū. The mineral deposits are mainly distributed in the mountainous regions of the north-west.

分工 fēngōng to divide work; division of labour: 咱们怎么分工? Zánmen zěnme fēngōng? How shall we divide up the work? // 这样分工不合理。Zhèyàng fēngōng bù hélǐ. This division of labour is not reasonable.

分行 fēnháng a branch (of a bank): 中国银行上海分行 Zhōngguó Yínháng Shànghǎi fēnháng the Shanghai branch of the Bank of China

分解 fēnjiě to solve, resolve, analyse: 分解方程式 fēnjiě fāngchéngshì to solve an equation (in algebra) // 水可以分解为氢和氧。Shuǐ kěyi fēnjiě wéi qīng hé yǎng. Water can be analysed into hydrogen and oxygen.

分歧 fēnqí divergence, dissension, dispute: 执政党内部产生了分歧。Zhízhèng dǎng nèibù chǎnshēngle fēnqí. Dissension developed within the ranks of the governing party.

分摊 fēntān to divide up, share out: 买机器的款项由众

人分摊。Mǎi jīqì de kuǎnxiàng yóu zhòngrén fēntān. The cost of purchasing the machine was shared by everyone.

分享 fēnxiǎng to share a pleasure：与朋友分享美味 yǔ péngyou fēnxiǎng měiwèi sharing delicious food with friends

分钟 fēnzhōng a minute

公分 gōngfēn a centimetre

难舍难分 nánshě-nánfēn cannot bear to separate

fèn ①a component：这水盐分太大。Zhè shuǐ yánfèn tài dà. The salt content of this water is too high. // 暴雨刚过，空气中充满水分。Bàoyǔ gāng guò, kōngqì zhōng chōngmǎn shuǐfèn. Just after the thunderstorm had passed, the air was saturated with moisture.

②( = 份 ) a duty, role, status：保卫祖国人人有分。Bǎowèi zǔguó rén rén yǒu fèn. Protecting the motherland is everyone's duty.

分量 fènliàng weight, quantity

分内 fènnèi duty bound

分外 fènwài excessive; beyond the scope of one's responsibility：分外高兴 fènwài gāoxìng extremely happy // 对我来说，这是分外事。Duì wǒ lái shuō, zhè shi fènwài shì. As far as I am concerned, this is outside my responsibility.

过分 guòfèn excessive, beyond reasonable limits

情分 qíngfèn mutual affection

# 冯　féng　píng

**féng**　〔a surname〕：冯妇 Féng Fù a legendary soldier said to have killed tigers = a person willing to take risks

**píng**　〈lit.〉暴虎冯河 bàohǔ-pínghé to fight a tiger without weapons and cross a river without a boat = rash, foolishly intrepid

# 缝　féng　fèng

**féng**　to sew, mend：缝衣服 féng yīfu to mend clothes // 缝口袋 féng kǒudài to sew a pocket // 缝伤口 féng shāngkǒu to suture a wound

缝补 féngbǔ to patch：请把那件破外套缝补好。Qǐng bǎ nà jiàn pò wàitào féngbǔ hǎo. Please patch up that worn-out coat.

缝合 fénghé to stitch together：把两块布片缝合起来 bǎ liǎng kuài bùpiàn fénghé qǐlai to sew together two pieces of cloth

**fèng**　a seam; a crack

缝隙 fèngxì crack, crevice

裂缝 lièfèng a crack or split

衣缝 yīfèng seams in a garment

# 佛　fó　fú

**fó**　the Buddha, Buddhist：那庙里有一尊大佛。Nà miào li yǒu yì zūn dà Fó. In that temple there is a large Buddha image. // 他信佛吃斋。Tā xìn Fó chī zhāi. He is a Buddhist and a vegetarian.

佛教 Fójiào Buddhism

佛陀 Fótuó the Buddha

fú    仿佛 fǎngfú to appear like; resembling

# 否    fǒu    pǐ

fǒu    not; or not? 〔expressing interrogation〕

否定 fǒudìng to negate: 对他所做的工作不应该完全否定。Duì tā suǒ zuò de gōngzuò bù yīnggāi wánquán fǒudìng. One should not negate all the work he had done.

是否 shìfǒu is it ... or not?

pǐ    ①⟨lit.⟩ bad, wicked, evil

②to censure

否极泰来 pǐ jí tài lái Out of the depths of misfortune come peace and happiness.

否运 pǐyùn bad luck

臧否 zāngpǐ ⟨lit.⟩ to pass judgment (on people): 臧否人物 zāngpǐ rénwù to pass judgment on people

# 佛    fú → fó

# 服    fú    fù

fú    ①clothing, dress

②to take (medicine): 服药 fú yào to take medicine // 这药得连服三天。Zhè yào děi lián fú sān tiān. This medicine has to be taken for three days in a row.

③to serve

④to be convinced or admiring: 你服不服? Nǐ fú bu fú?
Are you convinced? // 我真服了他了! Wǒ zhēn fúle
tā le! I really admire him!

⑤to obey, submit

⑥accustomed

服从 fúcóng to obey

服气 fúqì convinced

服务 fúwù to serve; service: 为人民服务 wèi rénmín
fúwù to serve the people

服役 fúyì to serve as a soldier: 他在部队里服役。Tā
zài bùduì li fúyì. He is serving in the army.

服装 fúzhuāng clothing

佩服 pèifú to admire: 我佩服你的勇气。Wǒ pèifú nǐ
de yǒngqì. I admire your courage.

水土不服 shuǐtǔ bù fú not acclimatised

西服 xīfú Western style dress

fù   ( = 付 ) a dose: 一服药 yí fù yào a dose of medicine

**脯**   fǔ   pú

fǔ   preserved and dried meat or fruit: 牛脯 niú fǔ dried beef
// 桃脯 táo fǔ preserved peaches

pú   the chest; the flesh of the chest

胸脯 xiōngpú the chest

# G

咖　gā → kā

嘎　gā　gá　gǎ

gā　①〔onomatopoeia〕

②〔used in transcribing foreign words〕

③〈dial.〉 solidified

嘎巴 gābā〔onomatopoeia for cracking or splitting sounds〕

嘎巴 gāba〈dial.〉 congealed; a solidified substance

gá　any spindle-shaped object (see polyphonic compound, below)

gǎ　①〈dial.〉 naughty：嘎小子 gǎ xiǎozi a naughty boy

②〈dial.〉 odd, eccentric：这个人真嘎。Zhège rén zhēn gǎ. This fellow is really odd.

*Polyphonic compound*：

嘎嘎 gāgā〔onomatopoeia for the sound of laughter〕

gága〈dial.〉 an oval wooden toy ball

轧　gá → yà

干　gān　gàn

gān　①dry：衣服干了。Yīfu gān le. The clothes have dried.

②dried food：地瓜干 dìguā gān dried sweet potato // 葡萄干 pútáo gān raisins

③empty, meaningless

④adopted into nominal kinship: 干儿子 **gān érzi** a nominally adopted son // 干娘 **gān niáng** a nominally adopted mother // 干爹 **gān diē** a nominally adopted father

⑤to be involved, concerned: 干你什么事！**Gān nǐ shénme shì!** None of your business!

⑥the "heavenly stems": 天干地支 **tiāngān dìzhī** the (ten) heavenly stems and (twelve) earthly branches

⑦to no avail, in vain: 干着急 **gān zháojí** worrying to no avail // 干等了一个小时 **gān děngle yíge xiǎoshí** waited in vain for an hour

饼干 **bǐnggān** biscuits

干巴巴 **gānbābā** dry; wizened; dry and dull: 干巴巴的土地 **gānbābā de tǔdì** dry, desolate land // 干巴巴的文章 **gānbābā de wénzhāng** a dry, boring essay

干净 **gānjìng** clean: 衣服很干净。**Yīfu hěn gānjìng.** The clothes are quite clean. // 干净的院落 **gānjìng de yuànluò** a clean compound

干涉 **gānshè** to interfere: 干涉他国内政 **gānshè tāguó nèizhèng** to interfere in another nation's internal affairs

干笑 **gānxiào** a hollow laugh; to laugh hollowly: 他干笑了几声。**Tā gānxiào le jǐ shēng.** He gave a few hollow laughs.

外强中干 **wài qiáng zhōng gān** outwardly strong but inwardly weak

**gàn** ①the trunk or main part of something

②to do, attend to, manage: 干活 gàn huó to work on a job, do manual labour // 你干不干? Nǐ gàn bu gàn? Will you do the job? // 干革命 gàn gémìng to carry out a revolution

③able, capable

干部 gànbù a cadre

干将 gànjiàng a capable leader

骨干 gǔgàn the backbone, spine

能干 nénggàn capable, competent

树干 shùgàn a tree trunk

# 杆　　gān　gǎn

gān　a long staff, pole, etc.

杆子 gānzi a pole

旗杆 qígān a flagpole

gǎn　①the shaft or arm of an object: 秤杆 chèng gǎn the beam of a steelyard // 枪杆 qiāng gǎn a rifle barrel

②[a measure word for long staff-like objects]: 一杆枪 yì gǎn qiāng one rifle

# 钢　　gāng　gàng

gāng　steel

不锈钢 búxiùgāng stainless steel

钢笔 gāngbǐ a pen (with metal nib)

钢琴 gāngqín a piano

钢铁 gāngtiě steel and iron

gàng　①to whet, strop: 钢菜刀 gàng càidāo to sharpen a

kitchen knife // 钢刀布 **gàngdāobù** a razor strop

②to reinforce a blade by adding extra steel and re-tempering

# 岗　**gǎng　gāng**

**gǎng** ①a sentry post; a place of duty：站岗 zhàn **gǎng** to stand guard

②a hillock, mound：黄土岗儿 huángtǔ **gǎng**r a hillock of loess

岗亭 **gǎng**tíng a sentry box

岗位 **gǎng**wèi one's post, place of duty

岗子 **gǎng**zi a hillock

**gāng** （＝冈）a ridge

山岗（properly 山冈）shāngāng a mountain ridge

# 咯　**gē　kǎ　lo　luò**

**gē** 〔onomatopoeia〕

咯噔 **gē**dēng〔onomatopoeia for clicking or creaking〕

咯咯 **gē**gē〔onomatopoeia for clucking, cackling, or chuckling〕

**kǎ** to cough up：咯血 **kǎ** xiě to cough up blood

**lo** 〔a sentence-final particle（＝了）〕：好咯！Hǎo lo! Good！

**luò** 〔used in transcribing foreign words〕

吡咯 bǐluò pyrrole

# 搁　**gē　gé**

**gē** ①to put：把书搁在桌子上。Bǎ shū **gē** zài zhuōzi

shàng. Put the books on the table. // 在牛奶里搁点糖 zài niúnǎi li **gē** diǎn táng to put a little sugar in the milk

②to put aside, leave over, shelve: 那机构办事官僚，把我的申请整整搁了一年。Nà jīgòu bàn shì guānliáo, bǎ wǒ de shēnqǐng zhěngzhěng **gē** le yì nián. That organisation works so bureaucratically, they put my application aside for an entire year.

搁浅 **gē**qiǎn to run aground: 轮船搁浅了。Lúnchuán **gē** qiǎn le. The liner ran aground.

搁置 **gē**zhì to shelve, lay aside: 搁置计划 **gē**zhì jìhuà to shelve a plan

gé　to bear, endure, tolerate

搁不住气 **gé** bu zhù qì unable to conceal one's anger; unable to hold one's temper

# 葛　gé　gě

gé　the kudzu vine (*Pueraria* sp.)

葛布 **gé**bù linen

葛根 **gé**gēn the root of the kudzu vine, used in herbal medicine

gě　[a surname]; [component of a surname]

诸葛 Zhū**gě** [a surname]

# 蛤　gé　há

gé　bivalve molluscs

蛤蚌 **gé**bàng a clam

蛤蚧 géjiè the gecko, a red-spotted lizard

há　蛤蟆 háma toads, frogs

合　gě → hé

个　gè/ge　gě

gè/ge ①〔usually in neutral tone: the most generally used measure word〕：三个苹果 sān ge píngguǒ three apples // 五个星期 wǔ ge xīngqī five weeks // 洗个澡 xǐ ge zǎo to have a bath // 打个电话 dǎ ge diànhuà to make a phone call

②〔usually in neutral tone: a particle used for mild emphasis〕：说个不停 shuō ge bù tíng to talk incessantly // 今儿个天气好。Jīnr ge tiānqì hǎo. The weather is good today.

③〔always in tone 4〕single, individual

个人 gèrén individual, personal

个体 gètǐ individual

个体户 gètǐhù a private (not state-owned) business

个性 gèxìng individual character：那人个性很强 。Nà rén gèxìng hěn qiáng. That person has a strong character.

个子 gèzi stature, build：他的个子大。Tā de gèzi dà. He has a big build.

那个 nàge that：那个东西 nàge dōngxi that thing

整个 zhěnggè the whole lot

gě　自个儿 zìgěr 〈coll.〉oneself

# 给　gěi　jǐ

**gěi**　①to give：给他钱。Gěi tā qián. Give him money.

②for：给他办事。Gěi tā bàn shì. Manage the affair for him.

③by〔in passive constructions〕：他给汽车撞伤了。Tā gěi qìchē zhuàng shāng le. He was knocked down and injured by a car.

④to let, allow：给她看看。Gěi tā kànkan. Let her have a look. // 他拿来一把椅子给我坐。Tā nálái yì bǎ yǐzi gěi wǒ zuò. He brought a chair for me to sit down.

⑤〔used before a verb to add emphasis〕：弟弟把书给撕了。Dìdi bǎ shū gěi sī le. Little brother has torn the book. // 我把钱包给丢了。Wǒ bǎ qiánbāo gěi diū le. I have lost my wallet.

**jǐ**　to supply, provide, give

供给 gōngjǐ to supply; a supply：供给生活用品 gōngjǐ shēnghuó yòngpǐn to supply the necessities of life // 你们部队里供给好吗？Nǐmen bùduì li gōngjǐ hǎo ma? Is your army unit being well supplied?

给与 jǐyǔ to give：对困难户应该给与补助。Duì kùnnan hù yīnggāi jǐyǔ bǔzhù. Assistance should be given to households in difficulty.

# 艮　gěn　gèn

**gěn**　〈dial.〉tough, plain, straightforward, obstinate：艮萝卜

gěn luóbo tough turnips // 这个人真艮。Zhège rén zhēn gěn. This fellow's really blunt.

gèn　one of the eight trigrams (connoting limitation)

# 更　gēng　gèng

gēng ①to change, revise

②the five watches of the night：三更 sān gēng the third watch of the night (about midnight)

③⟨lit.⟩ to experience

更迭 gēngdié to make a change：这地方终年温暖，四季更迭不明显。Zhè dìfang zhōng nián wēnnuǎn, sìjì gēngdié bù míngxiǎn. This place is warm all year round, and the change of seasons is not obvious.

更衣室 gēngyīshì a changing-room

更正 gēngzhèng to correct：更正错误 gēngzhèng cuòwù to correct mistakes

少不更事 shào bù gēng shì young and inexperienced

gèng even more, one more, further：更好 gèng hǎo even better // 更上一层楼 gèng shàng yì céng lóu to go up one more floor = to attain a still higher goal

更加 gèngjiā even more

# 红　gōng → hóng

# 供　gōng　gòng

gōng ①to supply

②for (the use or convenience of)：仅供参考 jǐn gōng cānkǎo just for reference // 大厅可供一千人候机。

Dàtīng kě **gōng** yì qiān rén hòu jī. The main hall can accommodate a thousand people waiting for planes.

供求 **gōng**qiú supply and demand：调查市场供求趋势 diàochá shìchǎng **gōng**qiú qūshì to investigate market trends in supply and demand

供应 **gōng**yìng to supply; a supply：这果园每月向城里 供应十来吨鲜果。Zhè guǒyuán měi yuè xiàng chéng lǐ **gōng**yìng shí lái dūn xiān guǒ. This orchard supplies the city with more than ten tonnes of fresh fruit each month.

提供 tí**gōng** to supply, provide：新闻稿由法新社提供。 Xīnwén gǎo yóu Fǎ Xīn Shè tí**gōng**. The news report was supplied by AFP.

**gòng** ① to offer in worship：供佛 **gòng** Fó to make offerings to the Buddha

② to testify, confess：犯人供出了五个同伙。Fànrén **gòng**chūle wǔ ge tónghuǒ. The convict named five accomplices.

③ a confession

供认 **gòng**rèn to confess on trial：那人供认了全部犯罪 经过。Nà rén **gòng**rènle quánbù fànzuì jīngguò. That person confessed to the crime in its entirety.

供桌 **gòng**zhuō a sacrificial altar

口供 kǒu**gòng** a verbal confession

*Polyphonic compound*：

供养 **gōng**yǎng to provide for：供养双亲 **gōng**yǎng

shuāngqīn to provide for one's parents

gòngyǎng offerings; to make offerings：庙里的供
养从不缺乏。Miào li de gòngyǎng cóng bù quēfá.
There's never a shortage of offerings in the temple.

**勾** gōu　gòu

gōu ①a tick mark indicating agreement or cancellation：请在
这一格上打一个勾。Qǐng zài zhè yì gé shang dǎ yí
ge gōu. Please put a tick in this space.

②to make a tick mark：请在这一格上勾一下。Qǐng zài
zhè yì gé shang gōu yíxià. Please tick in this space.

③to delineate, draw：勾一幅草图 gōu yì fú cǎotú to
draw a rough sketch

④to fill the joints in brickwork：勾墙缝 gōu qiáng fèng
to fill in cracks in a wall

⑤to entice：那娘儿们喜欢勾男人。Nà niángrmen
xǐhuān gōu nánrén. That woman likes enticing men.

⑥to collude with, conspire with：两人勾在一块儿商量
鬼点子。Liǎng rén gōu zài yíkuàir shāngliang
guǐdiǎnzi. The two of them conspired together, discussing their evil plot.

⑦the shortest side of a right-angled triangle

勾搭 gōuda to gang up with; to seduce：那俩人勾搭得
很紧。Nà liǎ rén gōuda de hěn jǐn. Those two are
closely ganged up together.

勾画 gōuhuà to draw the outline of, sketch：勾画居室
轮廓 gōuhuà jūshì lúnkuò to sketch the outline of a

living-room

勾结 gōujié to collude, gang up with：两个黑帮互相勾结。Liǎng ge hēibāng hùxiāng gōujié. Two criminal gangs colluded.

勾股定理 gōugǔ dìnglǐ Pythagorean theorem

勾销 gōuxiāo to strike out, write off：勾销旧帐 gōuxiāo jiù zhàng to write off old debts

勾引 gōuyǐn to seduce, tempt：勾引女人 gōuyǐn nǚrén to seduce women

gòu　勾当 gòudàng an underhand job

# 枸　gǒu　gōu　jǔ

gǒu　[a generic component of terms for various kinds of trees]

枸骨 gǒugǔ the holly, *Osmanthus aquifolium*

枸杞 gǒuqǐ the wolfberry, *Lycium chinense*

gōu　[a generic term for various kinds of trees]

枸橘 gōujú trifoliate orange; the shrub *Aegle sepiaria*

jǔ　[a generic term for various kinds of tree]

枸橼 jǔyuán the medicinal orange or citron, *Citrus medica*

# 估　gū　gù

gū　to estimate, appraise, reckon：你能估出这包东西的重量吗？Nǐ néng gū chū zhè bāo dōngxi de zhòngliàng ma? Can you estimate the weight of this bundle of things? // 给这衣服估个价。Gěi zhè yīfu gū ge jià. Appraise a price for this garment.

估计 gūjì to estimate, appraise：估计产量 gūjì

chǎnliàng to estimate production //估计各种可能性 gū jì gè zhǒng kěnéngxìng to appraise every possibility

估量 gūliàng to assess, appraise: 损失无法估量。 Sǔnshī wúfǎ gūliàng. The damage is impossible to assess.

gù 估衣 gùyī second-hand clothing or new clothes badly tailored and of poor material

# 骨　gǔ　gū

gǔ ①a bone: 头骨 tóu gǔ the skull // 腿骨 tuǐ gǔ the bones of the leg

②a framework

③one's character, spirit

骨骼 gǔgé a skeleton

骨气 gǔqì backbone, courage, moral integrity

骨肉 gǔròu flesh and blood; kinsfolk

骨头 gǔtou a bone

骨子 gǔzi a framework: 伞骨子 sǎn gǔzi the frame of an umbrella

gū 骨朵儿 gūduor an unopened bud

骨碌 gūlu rolling, spinning

# 鹘　gǔ → hú

# 贾　gǔ　jiǎ

gǔ ①⟨lit.⟩ a trader

②⟨lit.⟩ to invite, bring upon oneself

商贾 shānggǔ merchants

贾祸 gǔhuò 〈lit.〉 to invite disaster

jiǎ　〔a surname〕

# 观　guān　guàn

guān ①to look, view, observe

②appearance

③a viewpoint, attitude

观察 guānchá to observe, inspect：观察病情 guānchá bìngqíng to observe symptoms

观念 guānniàn a concept

观世音 Guānshìyīn the Bodhisattva Avalokitesvara

乐观 lèguān optimistic

奇观 qíguān a wonder, marvellous spectacle

壮观　zhuàngguān a marvellous sight：景象壮观 jǐngxiàng zhuàngguān marvellous scenery

guàn ①a Daoist temple

②a lookout tower

道观 Dàoguàn a Daoist temple

楼观 lóuguàn 〈lit.〉 storied buildings

# 冠　guān　guàn

guān ①a cap

②a bird's crest or comb

③a crown-like object

冠带 guāndài cap and sash = the literati

鸡冠 jīguān a cock's comb

树冠 shùguān the crown of a tree

guàn ①first place（in a contest）, the best

②to add an extra name or title: 小王写得一手好字，被同事们冠以"书法家"称号。Xiǎo Wáng xiě de yìshǒu hǎo zì, bèi tóngshìmen guàn yǐ "shūfǎjiā" chēnghào. Young Wang writes characters so well that his colleagues have given him the nickname Calligraphy Master.

③to put a cap on

冠词 guàncí an article（in grammar; e. g. English a, the）

冠军 guànjūn the champion

冠礼 guànlǐ an ancient capping ceremony marking a male's attainment of adulthood

# 莞　guān　guǎn　wǎn

guān ①a species of reed

②a mat made of such reeds

莞草 guāncǎo a species of reed

guǎn 东莞 Dōngguǎn a town in Guangdong Province

wǎn 莞尔 wǎn'ěr 〈lit.〉gently smiling

# 桄　guàng　guāng

guàng ①a skein, spool, or strand of thread: 一桄线 yí guàng xiàn a skein of thread

②a horizontal wooden bar or rung

③to wind on a spool: 把线桄上 bǎ xiàn guàng shang to wind thread on a spool

船桄 chuánguàng a wooden cross-piece in a boat

梯桄 tīguàng the rungs of a ladder

线桄 xiànguàng a reel or spool

guāng 桄榔 guāngláng the coir palm, *Arenga saccharifera*

# 龟

guī　jūn　qiū

guī　tortoises and turtles

龟甲 guījiǎ tortoise-shell

龟龄 guīlíng longevity

海龟 hǎiguī the green turtle

乌龟 wūguī a tortoise

jūn　龟裂 jūnliè (of earth, skin, etc.) cracked in a tortoise-shell pattern

qiū　龟兹 Qiūcí 〔name of an ancient state (in present Xinjiang Uygur Autonomous Region)〕

# 傀

guī → kuǐ

# 柜

guì　jǔ

guì　a cupboard, cabinet：衣柜 yīguì a wardrobe // 档案柜 dàng'àn guì a filing cabinet

柜台 guìtái a counter, desk (e.g. in a hotel lobby)

jǔ　trees of the willow family

柜柳 jǔliǔ a species of willow, *Pterocarya stenoptera*

# H

**哈**　hā　hǎ　hà

hā　①to expel air through the mouth (as if pronouncing [h]): 哈一口气 hā yì kǒu qì to blow a puff of air (with the mouth wide open)

②[onomatopoeia for the sound of laughter]: 哈哈大笑 hā hā dà xiào laughing Ha! Ha!

③[used in transcribing foreign words]

哈里发 hālǐfā a caliph

哈密瓜 hāmìguā the Hami melon

哈欠 hāqian a yawn

hǎ　①⟨dial.⟩ to reprimand: 哈他一顿 Hǎ tā yí dùn. Give him a reprimand.

②[used in transcribing foreign words]

哈巴狗 hǎbagǒu the Pekingese (breed of dog)

哈达 hǎdá a silk shawl used as a greeting gift by the Tibetans and Mongolians

hà　哈什蚂 hàshimǎ the Chinese forest frog (*Rana temporaria*)

**蛤**　há → gé

**咳**　hāi → ké

## 还　hái　huán

**hái** ①still, yet, in addition：还有 hái yǒu there are still...,
there is also ... // 她还没来。Tā hái méi lái. She
hasn't come yet. // 除了这两本书，我还带了一本词
典。Chúle zhè liǎng běn shū, wǒ hái dàile yì běn
cídiǎn. Besides these two books, I've also brought a
dictionary.

②rather, fairly：我的身体还好。Wǒ de shēntǐ hái
hǎo. My health is fairly good.

③even〔used for emphasis〕：这还不行吗？Zhè hái bù
xíng ma? Is even this not good enough? // 那还用说！
Nà hái yòng shuō! That goes without saying!

④〔used to signal the unexpected〕：他还真考了个第一
名。Tā hái zhēn kǎole ge dìyī míng. He really came
top in the exam.

**huán** ①to repay, return something borrowed：还钱 huán qián
to repay money

②to return：还乡 huán xiāng to return to one's home
town

## 汗　hàn　hán

**hàn** sweat：出汗 chū hàn to sweat // 他太紧张，汗都把衬
衫湿透了。Tā tài jǐnzhāng, hàn dōu bǎ chènshān
shītòu le. He was so tense that his shirt was soaked with
sweat.

汗马功劳 hànmǎ-gōngláo distinctions won in battle;

one's contributions in work

汗颜 hànyán 〈lit.〉 to feel deeply ashamed: 此事令我汗颜。Cǐ shì lìng wǒ hànyán. This matter makes me feel deeply ashamed.

血汗 xuèhàn blood and sweat ＝ hard toil

hán 〔used in transcribing foreign words〕

可汗 kèhán a khan

# 行　háng → xíng

# 吭　háng　kēng

háng 〈lit.〉 the throat

引吭高歌 yǐn háng gāo gē to sing lustily

kēng to utter a sound or word

吭哧 kēngchi 〔onomatopoeia for puffing and blowing (e.g. from exertion)〕

一声不吭 yì shēng bù kēng to keep silent, not utter a word

# 貉　háo　hé　mò

háo 貉绒 háoróng racoon dog fur

貉子 háozi racoon dog

hé 〈literary and figurative〉 the badger

一丘之貉 yì qiū zhī hé the badgers of one mound ＝ a gang of like-minded individuals

mò （＝ 貊）〔name of an ancient northern barbarian tribe〕

# 好　hǎo　hào

hǎo ①good, beautiful, fine, kind, well: 好朋友　hǎo

péngyou a good friend // 风景很好。Fēngjǐng hěn hǎo. The scenery is beautiful. // 庄稼长得好。Zhuāngjia zhǎng de hǎo. The crops are growing well. // 那人真好。Nà rén zhēn hǎo. That person is really kind. // 他待我好。Tā dài wǒ hǎo. He treats me well. // 你好! Nǐ hǎo! Hello! // 我病好了。Wǒ bìng hǎo le. I have recovered from my illness. // 我还好，别担心。Wǒ hái hǎo, bié dānxīn. I'm all right. Don't worry. // 真好吃 zhēn hǎo chī really delicious

②completed: 准备好 zhǔnbèi hǎo ready // 做好了 zuò hǎo le completed // 请坐好。Qǐng zuòhǎo. Please sit properly. or Please take a seat. // 饭好了，来吃吧。Fàn hǎole, lái chī ba. The food is ready, so come and eat.

③easy: 好懂 hǎo dǒng easy to understand // 这个问题好回答。Zhège wèntí hǎo huídá. This question is easy to answer. // 他这人好说话。Tā zhè rén hǎo shuō huà. He's easy to get on with. (also hào shuō huà; see below)

④very: 好难看 hǎo nánkàn very ugly // 好冷啊! Hǎo lěng a! So cold! // 好几年没回家 hǎo jǐ nián méi huí jiā not having returned home for many years

⑤all right: 好，就这么办吧。Hǎo, jiù zhème bàn ba. Right, so let's do it like this. // 好了，别说了。Hǎo le, bié shuō le. All right, don't say any more.

⑥may, can, able to: 不早了，你好走了。Bù zǎo le, nǐ hǎo zǒu le. It's late; you can go now. // 早些睡，明天好早起赶路。Zǎo xiē shuì, míngtiān hǎo zǎoqǐ gǎn lù. Go to bed early, so you can push on with your journey early tomorrow. // 吃饱了好干活。Chībǎole hǎo gàn huó. Eat well so you can work well.

好比 hǎobǐ to be just like, comparable to: 他俩好比一对鸳鸯。Tā liǎ hǎobǐ yí duì yuānyāng. Those two are just like a pair of love birds.

好歹 hǎodǎi good and bad; a mishap; in any case: 不知好歹 bù zhī hǎodǎi not knowing good from bad // 万一你们路上有个好歹，我可担不起这责任。Wànyī nǐmen lùshàng yǒu ge hǎodǎi, wǒ kě dān bu qǐ zhè zérèn. If you should have a mishap on the way, I can't take responsibility for that. // 你好歹吃点儿吧。Nǐ hǎodǎi chī diǎnr ba. In any case, eat a little.

好感 hǎogǎn a good opinion, a favourable impression

好汉 hǎohàn a true man, hero

好像 hǎoxiàng to seem, to be like

好转 hǎozhuǎn to take a turn for the better, improve: 情况好转。Qíngkuàng hǎozhuǎn. The situation is improving.

hào to like, be fond of, have a special liking for: 好说话 hào shuō huà fond of talking

好奇 hàoqí inquisitive, curious

嗜好 shìhào a fondness, weakness, hobby

# 号 hào háo

**hào** ① a trumpet

② 〔an ordinal indicator〕: 六号楼 liù hào lóu building No. 6 // 三号，请进。Sān hào, qǐng jìn. Number 3, please come in. // 九月十三号 jiǔ yuè shísān hào September 13th // 他穿中号衬衫。Tā chuān zhōng hào chènshān. His size in shirts is medium.

③ a mark, sign

④ an order, command

⑤ a title or name (additional to the original given name or 名 míng): 本人姓王，名颜，号梦柳。Běn rén xìng Wáng, míng Yán, hào Mèngliǔ. My surname is Wang, my given name is Yan, and my additional given name is Mengliu.

编号 biānhào a serial number (e.g. on a report); to number

别号 biéhào a person's extra name or style

符号 fúhào marks (e.g. for punctuation)

号令 hàolìng a verbal command, order

号码 hàomǎ a number, figure

号外 hàowài extra (of a newspaper)

军号 jūnhào a bugle

口号 kǒuhào a slogan

**háo** to howl, yell, wail

哀号 āiháo to wail in sorrow: 那母狼蹲在被打死的狼崽旁边哀号。Nà mǔláng dūn zài bèi dǎsǐ de lángzǎi pángbiān āiháo. The mother wolf sat wailing beside her pup, which had been beaten to death.

号哭 háokū to cry aloud, wail; a cry, wail: 那女人号哭不止。Nà nǚrén háokū bùzhǐ. The woman wailed incessantly.

怒号 nùháo to howl, roar: 狂风怒号 Kuángfēng nùháo. The gale howled.

**喝**　hē　hè

hè　①to drink: 喝酒 hē jiǔ to drink wine, take alcohol // 喝茶 hē chá to drink tea

②〔an interjection expressing surprise〕: 喝！这么贵！Hē! Zhème guì! Gosh! So expensive!

喝醉 hēzuì to get drunk

hè　to shout

喝彩 hècǎi to cheer, acclaim: 众人为她的表演喝彩。Zhòngrén wèi tā de biǎoyǎn hècǎi. The crowd applauded her performance.

喝令 hèlìng to shout an order: 门卫喝令来人止步。Ménwèi hèlìng láirén zhǐbù. The gatekeeper ordered the incoming people to halt.

**合**　hé　gě

hé　①to combine, mix, come together: 合在一起 hé zài yìqǐ to put (several items) together

②to suit, be in agreement: 合口味 hé kǒuwèi suiting one's taste

③to close：把盖子合上 bǎ gàizi hé shàng to close a lid

④whole, complete

⑤to be equal to, to add up to：一公顷合十五市亩。Yì gōngqǐng hé shíwǔ shìmǔ. One hectare equals 15 *mu*.

⑥name of a note in certain traditional Chinese musical scales

合并 hébìng to merge, amalgamate

合家欢 héjiāhuān the whole family happily together（esp. in a family photograph）

合适 héshì suitable

合眼 héyǎn to die; to sleep：她担心得一夜没合眼。Tā dānxīn de yí yè méi héyǎn. She was so worried that she did not sleep all night.

合作 hézuò to cooperate

**gě**　a traditional Chinese unit of dry measure for grain

**和** **hé**　hè　huó　huò　hú

**hé**

①with, and：我和你 wǒ hé nǐ you and I // 和她没关系。Hé tā méi guānxi. It has nothing to do with her.

②gentle（also -huo）

③harmony, peace：兄弟不和 xiōngdì bù hé brothers that don't get on together

④〈lit.〉together with：和衣而卧 hé yī ér wò to sleep in one's clothes

⑤to yield a tied result（in chess）：那盘棋和了。Nà pán qí hé le. The chess game was drawn.

⑥ the sum（result of adding numbers）两数之和 liǎng shù zhī hé the sum of the two numbers

⑦ Japan

⑧〔used in transcribing foreign words〕

和风细雨 hé fēng xì yǔ gentle wind and fine rain ＝ a gentle manner

和服 héfú Japanese-style clothing, *kimono*

和平 hépíng peace; peaceful; mild

和尚 héshàng a Buddhist monk

讲和 jiǎnghé to make peace, settle a dispute：双方讲和。Shuāngfāng jiǎnghé. The two parties are reconciled.

暖和 nuǎnhé（or -huo）pleasantly warm

hè  to match, keep in tune with：和韵 hè yùn to rhyme

附和 fùhè to echo; to chime in with：老李没主见，总是附和别人的发言。Lǎo Lǐ méi zhǔjiàn, zǒng shì fùhè biérén de fāyán. Lao Li doesn't have any opinions of his own; he always follows what others say.

huó  to knead：和面 huó miàn to knead dough // 和泥 huó ní to knead clay

huò  to mix in, stir in：和药 huò yào to grind and mix medicine // 和点儿糖 huò diǎnr táng to stir in a little sugar

和弄 huònòng to mix by stirring：面糊和弄好了吗？Miànhú huònòng hǎo le ma? Has the paste been stirred?

hú  a completed set in mahjong; to complete such a set：她和

了。Tā hú le. She's completed a set.

**荷** hé hè

hé ①the lotus

②the water-lily

③[used in transcribing foreign words]

荷包 hébāo a pouch or purse

荷花 héhuā lotus flowers

荷兰 Hélán Holland

荷叶 héyè lotus leaves

hè ①to carry, bear

②a burden

负荷 fùhè to bear a burden, bear responsibility; a load, burden

荷枪实弹 hè qiāng shí dàn armed with loaded guns

**貉** hé → háo

**吓** hè → xià

**横** héng hèng

héng ①horizontal, cross-wise

②to place horizontally：请把那根竹竿横过来。Qǐng bǎ nà gēn zhúgān héng guolai. Please place that bamboo pole horizontally across here.

③a horizontal stroke in calligraphy

④unrestrained; violent

横笛 héngdí the flute (played horizontally)

横断面 héngduànmiàn a cross-section

横扫 héngsǎo to sweep away, make a clean sweep of: 龙卷风横扫市区。Lóngjuǎnfēng héngsǎo shìqū. The tornado swept across the city area.

横竖 héngshù criss-cross; in any case

横行霸道 héngxíng bàdào to ride roughshod over; to tyrannise

hèng ①perverse, cruel

②unlucky, unexpected

③illegal

横暴 hèngbào cruel, tyrannical

横财 hèngcái ill-gotten gains

横祸 hènghuò unexpected disaster

横死 hèngsǐ a sudden and violent death; to die a sudden and violent death: 横死异乡 hèngsǐ yìxiāng to die a sudden and violent death in a foreign land

蛮横 mánhèng arbitrary, peremptory

强横 qiánghèng tyrannical, despotic

# 哄  hōng    hǒng

hōng ①(of a crowd) to make a loud noise; loud noise made by a crowd

②[onomatopoeia]

哄动 hōngdòng to create a sensation, cause a stir: 那条新闻曾在全国哄动一时。Nà tiáo xīnwén céng zài quán guó hōngdòng yìshí. That piece of news created a nation-wide sensation at the time.

哄堂大笑 hōngtáng dà xiào laughter that brings the

house down: 他的滑稽表演引得全场观众哄堂大笑。Tā de huáji biǎoyǎn yǐnde quán chǎng guānzhòng hōngtáng dà xiào. His comical performance brought the whole theatre down with laughter.

乱哄哄 luàn hōnghōng in noisy disorder, in an uproar

hǒng ①to cheat: 你别哄我了。Nǐ bié hǒng wǒ le. Don't you try to cheat me.

②to coax: 哄孩子 hǒng háizi to coax a child

哄骗 hǒngpiàn to swindle: 他可不容易哄骗。Tā kě bù róngyi hǒngpiàn. He's not easily deceived.

# 红　hóng　gōng

hóng ①red: 红色 hóng sè red colour // 红宝石 hóng bǎoshí the ruby

②a bonus

③successful and respected: 这个模特儿最近红得很。Zhège mótèr zuìjìn hóng de hěn. This model has recently been very popular.

分红 fēnhóng to share out profits: 年终分红 niánzhōng fēnhóng an end-of-year sharing out of profits

粉红 fěnhóng pink

红利 hónglì dividends, a bonus

红人 hóngrén a favourite with someone in power

红运 hóngyùn good luck

gōng（ = 工 ）work

女红 nǚgōng women's needlework

**和** hú → hé

**鹄** hú gǔ

hú　a species of crane

鸿鹄 hónghú the wild swan

鹄立 húlì to stand still and erect like a crane

gǔ　⟨lit.⟩ a target for archery：中鹄 zhòng gǔ to hit the mark

鹄的 gǔdì a target

**糊** hú hū hù

hú　①paste, glue：面糊 miàn hú paste made from flour

②to paste, glue（also hū）：把纸糊在墙上 bǎ zhǐ hú zài qiáng shàng to paste paper on a wall

③burnt, over-cooked：饭糊了。Fàn hú le. The rice has burned.

裱糊 biǎohú to paste up wall-paper; to mount scrolls：裱糊字画 biǎohú zìhuà to mount calligraphy scrolls

糊口 húkǒu to eke out a living, make ends meet

糊涂 hútu befuddled; slipshod; in a mess：奶奶年纪大了，有时难免糊涂。Nǎinai niánjì dà le, yǒushí nánmiǎn hútu. Granny is getting old, so she's bound to get confused sometimes. // 他粗心大意，办事糊涂。Tā cūxīn dàyì, bàn shì hútu. He is careless and does things in a slipshod manner. // 那几个孩子把屋子里弄得一塌糊涂。Nà jǐ ge háizi bǎ wūzi li nòng de yìtāhútú. Those children got the room into a real mess.

hū to seal or block up with any thick paste-like substance：把墙缝用灰浆糊上 bǎ qiángfèng yòng huījiāng **hū** shàng to block up cracks in a wall with mortar

hù ①a paste（food）：辣椒糊 làjiāo hù chilli paste

②a glutinous soup：麦糊 mài hù oatmeal porridge

糊弄 hùnong to do carelessly; to fool, deceive：你别糊弄人，我知道那是你编出来的故事。Nǐ bié hùnong rén, wǒ zhīdào nà shì nǐ biān chulai de gùshi. Don't try to fool people. I know you made up that story.

# 哗　huā　huá

huā 〔onomatopoeia for clanging, crashing, or gurgling sounds〕：哗的一声 huā de yì shēng with a clanging sound

哗啦 huālā 〔onomatopoeia for crashing sounds, or for the sound of rushing water〕

huá a hubbub, tumult

喧哗 xuānhuá an uproar, hubbub

# 华　huá　huà

huá ①China

②splendid, beautiful

③the best part, epitome

④〔an honorific prefix〕

⑤〔used in transcribing foreign words〕

华诞 huádàn 〈hon.〉 a birthday

华丽 huálì magnificent, gorgeous

华侨 huáqiáo overseas Chinese

华盛顿 Huáshèngdùn Washington

精华 jīnghuá the epitome, quintessence

中华 Zhōnghuá China

huà ①〔a surname〕

②〔a place-name〕：华山 Huà Shān Mount Huashan（in Shaanxi Province）

# 划 huá huà

huá ①to paddle, row：划船 huá chuán to row a boat // 把船划到江心 bǎ chuán huá dào jiāng xīn to row a boat to the middle of a river

②to cut the surface of：她在纸板中间划了一刀。Tā zài zhǐbǎn zhōngjiān huále yì dāo. She made a slice with the knife along the middle of the cardboard. // 我手被划破了。Wǒ shǒu bèi huápò le. My hand is cut.

③to scratch：划火柴 huá huǒchái to strike a match

④to pay, be to one's profit：干这个太划不来了。Gàn zhège tài huá bu lái le. This is not worth doing.

划拳 huáquán the game of guess-fingers（played at drinking parties）

划算 huásuàn to calculate, weigh up; to be to one's profit：这趟旅行总共该花多少钱，你得划算划算。Zhè tàng lǚxíng zǒnggòng gāi huā duōshao qián, nǐ děi huásuàn huásuàn. You have to weigh up what the total cost of this trip will be. // 这衣服这么贵，太不划算。Zhè yīfu zhème guì, tài bù huásuàn. This garment is so expensive; it's not worth it.

huà　①to demarcate：划清界限 huà qīng jièxiàn to make a clear demarcation

②to plan

③to cross out：划掉一行字 huà diào yì háng zì to cross out a line of characters

划分 huàfēn to divide; to differentiate; differentiation：划分区域 huàfēn qūyù to divide up territory // 作这种划分意义不大。Zuò zhè zhǒng huàfēn yìyì bú dà. Making this sort of distinction does not mean much.

划一 huàyī to unify (e.g. prices); uniform, standardised：那几排木桩安置得整齐划一，十分美观。Nà jǐ pái mùzhuāng ānzhì de zhěngqí huàyī, shífēn měiguān. Those lines of wooden posts are arranged so neatly and regularly; they really look good.

计划 jìhuà a plan; to plan：你们该把明年的工作好好计划一下了。Nǐmen gāi bǎ míngnián de gōngzuò hǎohāo jìhuà yíxià le. You ought to plan next year's work carefully.

豁　huá → huō

化　huà　huā

huà　①to change, transform：传说那美女化成了这座山峰。Chuán shuō nà měinǚ huàchéngle zhè zuò shānfēng. Legend has it that that beautiful girl was transformed into this mountain peak.

② to melt, dissolve, digest: 雪化了。Xuě huà le. The snow has melted. // 用水化开 yòng shuǐ huà kāi to dissolve in water

③ [a suffix equivalent to English -ise, -isation]

④ (of Buddhist monks and Daoist priests) to beg alms

⑤ to cremate

焚化 fénhuà to cremate: 焚化尸体 fénhuà shītǐ to cremate a body

化石 huàshí a fossil

化学 huàxué chemistry

化缘 huàyuán (of Buddhist monks and Daoist priests) to beg alms

化装 huàzhuāng to make up; to disguise; make-up: 我最讨厌化装。Wǒ zuì tǎoyàn huàzhuāng. I really detest making up. // 那便衣侦探化装得太蹩脚。Nà biànyī zhēntàn huàzhuāng de tài biéjiǎo. That plain-clothes detective is very poorly disguised. // 她的化装很适合她的脸型。Tā de huàzhuāng hěn shìhé tā de liǎnxíng. Her make-up suits her face very well.

食古不化 shí gǔ bú huà to swallow ancient learning without digesting it = to be pedantic

现代化 xiàndàihuà to modernise; modernisation

消化 xiāohuà digestion; to digest: 消化不良 xiāohuà bùliáng indigestion // 这食物不容易消化。Zhè shíwù bù róngyi xiāohuà. This food is not easy to digest.

huā （ ＝ 花 ）to use up, expend：化钱 huā qián to spend money // 化时间 huā shíjiān to use up time

叫化子 jiàohuāzi a beggar

## 还　huán → hái

## 晃　huǎng　huàng

huǎng　①dazzling

②to flash past： 他在窗外一晃就不见了。 Tā zài chuāng wài yì huǎng jiù bú jiàn le. He flashed past outside the window and disappeared.

白晃晃 báihuǎnghuǎng dazzlingly white

晃眼 huǎngyǎn dazzling; momentary：亮得晃眼 liàng de huǎngyǎn dazzlingly bright // 晃眼的工夫 huǎngyǎn de gōngfu "the twinkling of an eye", an instant

huàng　to sway, shake

晃荡 huàngdàng to sway, oscillate：那吊篮不停地晃荡。 Nà diàolán bùtíng de huàngdàng. The hanging basket swayed incessantly.

摇晃 yáohuàng to sway, rock：江心浪大，小船摇晃得很厉害。 Jiāng xīn làng dà, xiǎo chuán yáohuàng de hěn lìhài. In the middle of the river the waves were big, and the small boat rocked violently.

## 会　huì　kuài

huì ① to gather, come together: 全组准八点会齐，请勿迟到。Quán zǔ zhǔn bā diǎn huìqí, qǐng wù chídào. The whole group will be gathering at eight o'clock sharp, so please don't be late.

② to meet: 会一面 huì yí miàn to meet (once), come together (once) // 我想会会他。Wǒ xiǎng huì huì tā. I would like to meet him.

③ a meeting: 开一次会 kāi yí cì huì to hold a meeting // 全厂大会 quán chǎng dà huì a general meeting of the whole factory

④ a society, union, association: 青年会 qīngnián huì a youth association

⑤ able to: 她会英文。Tā huì Yīngwén. She can speak English.

⑥ an opportunity

⑦ a capital, chief city

⑧ certainly will, bound to: 我会还你钱的。Wǒ huì huán nǐ qián de. I will definitely return your money. // 他会遵守诺言的。Tā huì zūnshǒu nuòyán de. He is sure to keep his promise.

⑨ to pay a bill (e.g. in a restaurant): 饭钱我会过了。Fàn qián wǒ huìguo le. I've paid for the meal.

⑩ to understand

⑪ a moment: 一会儿 yí huìr a moment // 等会儿 děng huìr in a moment, shortly

报告会 bàogàohuì a meeting to give a report

都会 dūhuì a capital city

工会 gōnghuì a trade union

会客 huìkè to receive guests：会客室 huìkèshì a guest
reception room // 局长正在会客。Júzhǎng zhèngzài
huìkè. The bureau chief is receiving guests right now.

会师 huìshī to join forces：两军会师 liǎng jūn huìshī
two army units meeting and joining forces（on the battle-
field）

会心 huìxīn understanding, knowing：他俩会心地笑了。
Tā liǎ huìxīn de xiào le. The two of them gave a knowing smile.

会议 huìyì a meeting, conference

会账 huìzhàng to pay a bill：这顿饭由谁会账？Zhè
dùn fàn yóu shéi huìzhàng? Who is paying for this
meal?

会诊 huìzhěn a consultation of doctors：专家会诊
zhuānjiā huìzhěn a consultation of medical specialists

机会 jīhuì an opportunity

省会 shěnghuì a provincial capital

适逢其会 shì féng qí huì to chance upon an opportunity

误会 wùhuì to misunderstand：请别误会，我没那个意
思。Qǐng bié wùhuì, wǒ méi nàge yìsi. Please don't
get me wrong. That's not what I meant.

心领神会 xīnlǐng-shénhuì to understand intuitively：他
对老板的意图总是心领神会。Tā duì lǎobǎn de
yìtú zǒngshi xīnlǐng-shénhuì. He always intuitively

understands the boss's intention.

kuài 会计 kuàijì accounting, book-keeping; an accountant

# 混 hùn hún

hùn ①to mix without distinction: 你把两码子不同的事搞混
了。Nǐ bǎ liǎng mǎzi bù tóng de shì gǎo hùn le.
You have mixed up two quite different matters. // 混在
一起 hùn zài yìqǐ to confuse, mix up (two or more matters) // 跟他们混得很熟 gēn tāmen hùn de hěn
shú to mix and become familiar with them

②to pass for, pass oneself off as: 那关卡查得很严，不
容易混过去。Nà guānqiǎ chá de hěn yán, bù
róngyi hùn guoqu. That checkpoint is very strict. It's
not easy to slip through.

③to muddle along, drift along: 混日子 hùn rìzi to muddle along through life // 混饭吃 hùn fàn chī to get by
from one meal to the next

④disorderly, chaotic; thoughtlessly, indiscriminately

混合 hùnhé to mix, blend, mingle: 混合两种药品
hùnhé liǎng zhǒng yàopǐn to mix together two types of
medicine

混乱 hùnluàn confused, in disorder: 会场里混乱得很。
Huìchǎng li hùnluàn de hěn. The meeting room was in
great disorder.

混杂 hùnzá mixed: 那帮人成分混杂，有的来历不明。
Nà bāng rén chéngfèn hùnzá, yǒu de láilì bù míng.
They are a mixed lot of people, and it's not clear where

some of them are from.

混战 hùnzhàn a wild battle, a melee: 军阀混战 jūnfá hùnzhàn a wild battle between warlords

混浊 hùnzhuó fouled, turbid, muddy: 空气混浊。Kōngqì hùnzhuó. The air is foul.. // 混浊的河水 hùnzhuó de héshuǐ turbid river water

蒙混 ménghùn to get by: 蒙混过关 ménghùn guò guān to get through on false pretences

hún （ = 浑 ) turbid, dirty

混蛋 húndàn a scoundrel, a son-of-a-bitch

## 豁　huō　huò　huá

huō ①a crack

②to crack; cracked, split: 那墙豁开了一个口子。Nà qiáng huōkāile yí ge kǒuzi. A crack opened up in the wall.

③to sacrifice: 豁出命来干 huō chu mìng lái gàn to sacrifice one's whole life to achieve something // 豁出一年时间把中文学好 huō chu yìnián shíjiān bǎ Zhōngwén xué hǎo to sacrifice a year to master Chinese

豁子 huōzi a crack in a vessel; a breach in a wall; a person with a harelip

huò ①to exempt

②open, clear

豁达 huòdá open-minded, generous: 为人豁达 wéi rén huòdá open-minded toward people

豁亮 huòliàng open and well lit：这屋子又干净又豁亮。Zhè wūzi yòu gānjìng yòu huòliàng. This room is clean and also open and well lit.

豁免 huòmiǎn to exempt：请告诉我，哪几项物品的关税可以豁免。Qǐng gàosu wǒ, nǎ jǐ xiàng wùpǐn de guānshuì kěyǐ huòmiǎn. Could you please tell me which goods are exempt from customs duty?

huá 豁拳（＝划拳）huáquán the game of guess-fingers (played at drinking parties)

**和** huó huò → hé

# J

**奇** jī → qí

**缉** jī qī

jī ①to arrest, capture

②to spin, twist threads：缉麻 jī má to make hemp into rope

缉拿 jīná to arrest

缉私 jīsī to seize smugglers or smuggled goods：缉私船 jīsī chuán a boat used for seizing smugglers

通缉 tōngjī to order the arrest of a criminal at large：当局

下令在全国范围内通缉那个逃犯。Dāngjú xià lìng zài quánguó fànwéi nèi tōngjī nàge táofàn. The authorities ordered a nation-wide search to arrest the escaped prisoner.

qī　close stitching; to stitch closely: 缉鞋口 qī xiékǒu to apply close stitching around the opening of〈Chinese cloth〉shoes（for added strength）

稽　jī　qǐ

jī　①to investigate

②〈lit.〉to delay, hinder

③〈lit.〉to check, ascertain

④〈lit.〉to argue

反唇相稽 fǎnchún-xiāngjī〈lit.〉to make mutual recriminations: 他对我的指责反唇相稽。Tā duì wǒ de zhǐzé fǎnchún-xiāngjī. He responded to my accusation with mutual recriminations.

滑稽 huájī（formerly pronounced gǔjī）comical, clowning

稽查 jīchá to investigate; an official engaged in such work: 稽查处 jīcháchù investigation unit

稽留 jīliú to delay; to be detained: 因事稽留 yīn shì jīliú delayed by some business

无稽之谈 wú jī zhī tán a baseless, fantastic tale

qǐ　稽首 qǐshǒu to kowtow

几　jǐ　jī

jǐ　①how many?: 他上过几年学? Tā shàngguo jǐ nián

xué? How many years has he been studying at school? // 共有几个人? Gòng yǒu jǐ ge rén? How many people were there altogether?

②a few: 他上过几年学。Tā shàngguo jǐ nián xué. He has been studying at school for a few years. // 共有几个人。Gòng yǒu jǐ ge rén. There were several people altogether. // 二十几张纸 èrshí jǐ zhāng zhǐ twenty-odd sheets of paper // 几十年 jǐ shí nián a few decades

几何学 jǐhéxué geometry

jī ①a small table
②almost

茶几 chájī a tea table

几乎 jīhū almost

**给** jǐ → gěi

**系** jì → xì

**济** jì jǐ

jì ①to aid
②help, benefit
③〈lit.〉to cross over (a river)

济贫 jìpín to help the poor

经济 jīngjì economy; financial situation; economic; economical: 社会经济 shèhuì jīngjì social economy // 家庭经济宽裕 jiātíng jīngjì kuānyù well-off as regards the family's financial situation // 经济植物 jīngjì zhíwù commercial plants // 经济小吃 jīngjì xiǎochī economical (cheap) snacks

救济 jiùjì to aid, relieve distress: 红十字会救济难民。Hóngshízìhuì jiùjì nànmín. The Red Cross aids refugees.

同舟共济 tóngzhōu-gòngjì "in the same boat" = pulling together in time of misfortune

无济于事 wú jì yú shì of no help

jǐ ①numerous (of people)

②〔a place-name〕

济济 jǐjǐ plentiful, numerous (of people): 科学院里人才济济。Kēxuéyuàn li réncái jǐjǐ. There are plenty of talented people in the academy of science.

济南 Jǐnán the city of Jinan (capital of Shandong Province)

## 荠  jì  qí

jì  gorse and other plants

荠菜 jìcài the shepherd's purse (*Capsella bursa-pastoris*)

qí  荸荠 bíqí the water-chestnut

## 夹  jiā  jiá

jiā ①an instrument for squeezing; a clip, clamp, folder, etc.

②to press from both sides, to place in between: 用两片木板把断肢夹住 yòng liǎng piàn mùbǎn bǎ duàn zhī jiā zhù to splint a broken limb using two boards // 用小镊子把邮票夹起来 yòng xiǎo nièzi bǎ yóupiào jiā qǐlai to pick up a postage stamp with tweezers // 鞋太小, 夹脚。Xié tài xiǎo, jiā jiǎo. The shoes are too small. They pinch the feet. // 把相片夹在书里 bǎ xiàngpiàn jiā zài shū li to put photos between the pages of a book // 夹在中间 jiā zài zhōngjiān to squeeze in between

③ to mix, mingle: 狂风夹着暴雨 kuángfēng jiāzhe bàoyǔ a wild wind combined with heavy rain

夹带 jiādài to carry secretly; something carried secretly (e.g. contraband): 旅客入境时不许夹带危险品。Lǚkè rùjìng shí bù xǔ jiādài wēixiǎnpǐn. Travellers are not permitted to conceal dangerous goods on their persons when entering the country.

夹道 jiādào a narrow lane; to line both sides of the street: 夹道欢迎贵宾 jiādào huānyíng guìbīn lining both sides of the street to welcome an important guest

夹攻 jiāgōng to attack from both sides in a pincer movement; a pincer attack: 敌军经不住两面夹攻, 终于败退。Díjūn jīng bu zhù liǎng miàn jiāgōng, zhōngyú bàituì. The enemy forces could not resist the pincer attack, and finally fell back defeated.

夹生饭 jiāshēngfàn incompletely cooked rice

夹杂 jiāzá to mix or blend in: 那小偷夹杂在一大群游客中走开, 很快失去踪影。Nà xiǎotōu jiāzá zài yí dà qún yóukè zhōng zǒukāi, hěn kuài shīqù zōngyǐng. The thief blended into a large crowd of tourists, and was soon lost to view.

夹子 jiāzi pincers

讲义夹 jiǎngyìjiā a clip binder

jiá　　double-layered

夹袄 jiá'ǎo a lined jacket

**茄**　jiā → qié

**贾**　jiǎ → gǔ

**假**　jiǎ　jià

jiǎ　①false, artificial, an imitation: 那朵花是假的。Nà duǒ huā shì jiǎ de. That flower is artificial.

②if, supposing

③〈lit.〉to borrow

假冒 jiǎmào to pass off as; to palm off (a false imitation): 假冒名牌产品 jiǎmào míngpái chǎnpǐn imitations of brand-name goods // 谨防假冒。Jǐnfáng jiǎmào. Beware of imitations.

假面具 jiǎmiànjù a mask

假如 jiǎrú if, supposing: 假如他来了，我们就包饺子。Jiǎrú tā lái le, wǒmen jiù bāo jiǎozi. If he comes, we will make dumplings.

假设 jiǎshè if, supposing: 假设你是检查官，你会怎么处理这事? Jiǎshè nǐ shì jiǎncháguān, nǐ huì zěnme chǔlǐ zhè shì? If you were the inspection officer, how would you handle this matter? // 这个假设不合逻辑。Zhège jiǎshè bù hé luóji. This postulate is not logical.

假手于人 jiǎ shǒu yú rén 〈lit.〉to get someone else to do one's dirty work

假说 jiǎshuō a hypothesis

jià　leave of absence：放假 fàng **jià** to have a holiday

假期 jiàqī a holiday period

## 价　jià　jie

jià　a price

价格 jiàgé a price

价值 jiàzhí value

jie　〈dial.〉〔an adverb-forming suffix equivalent to 地 de〕：成天价闹 chéng tiān jie nào making a noise all the time // 锣鼓敲得震天价响，谁也听不清他讲了什么。Luógǔ qiāo de zhèn tiān jie xiǎng, shéi yě tīng bu qīng tā jiǎng le shénme. The gongs and drums were so loud that no one could hear what he said.

## 间　jiān　jiàn

jiān　①between, among：天地之间 tiān dì zhī jiān between heaven and earth // 同学之间 tóngxué zhī jiān among schoolmates

②within a certain time or space

③a room; a space

④〔a measure word for rooms〕：这间屋子 zhè jiān wūzi this room // 两间卧室 liǎng jiān wòshì two bedrooms // 一间门面 yì jiān ménmiàn a single-bay shop-front

房间 fángjiān a room

人世间 rénshìjiān (in) the human world

时间 shíjiān time

田间 tiánjiān (in) the fields

外间 wàijiān an outer room; ⟨lit.⟩ outside circles

夜间 yèjiān (at) night

衣帽间 yīmàojiān a cloakroom

中间 zhōngjiān the middle

jiàn ①a crevice or intervening space

②to divide, separate, discontinue: 晴间多云 qíng jiàn duō yún alternately clear and overcast

③to sow discord

④alternately, in turn

间断 jiànduàn to interrupt, break off: 几年来他从未间断过锻炼。Jǐ nián lái tā cóng wèi jiànduànguo duànliàn. For the past few years he has never broken off exercising.

间隔 jiàngé an interval, a space between: 这两行字间隔太大。Zhè liǎng háng zì jiàngé tài dà. The space between these two lines of characters is too large. // 音乐会上下场间隔十分钟。Yīnyuèhuì shàng xià chǎng jiàngé shí fēnzhōng. The interval between the first and second sessions of the concert is ten minutes.

间接 jiànjiē indirectly: 我间接打听他的情况。Wǒ jiànjiē dǎtīng tā de qíngkuàng. I have indirectly enquired about his situation.

间隙 jiànxì a cleft, intervening space; a misunderstanding

间作 jiànzuò to rotate (crops): 农作物间作很有好处。Nóngzuòwù jiànzuò hěn yǒu hǎochù. Rotating crops is very beneficial.

离间 líjiàn to sow seeds of discord, create division: 你们双方应该互相谅解，不要被坏人离间了。Nǐmen shuāngfāng yīnggāi hùxiāng liàngjiě, bú yào bèi huàirén líjiàn le. You two ought to seek mutual understanding and not let evil people divide you.

相间 xiāngjiàn to alternate with: 黑白相间 hēi bái xiāngjiàn alternating black and white, in a black and white checker pattern

监 jiān jiàn

jiān ①to supervise

②a prison: 送进监里 sòngjìn jiān li to put in prison // 男监 nán jiān a male prison

监督 jiāndū to supervise, inspect; a supervisor: 这些学生不够自觉，需要严加监督。Zhè xiē xuéshēng bú gòu zìjué, xūyào yán jiā jiāndū. These students are not responsible enough, so they must be strictly supervised.

监护 jiānhù to protect, supervise and guard; a guardian (e.g. for a minor): 法庭将那少年交由街道委员会监护。Fǎtíng jiāng nà shàonián jiāo yóu jiēdào wěiyuánhuì jiānhù. The court put that juvenile under the supervision and protection of the community association.

监狱 jiānyù a prison

jiàn ①an official government establishment

②a eunuch

国子监 guózǐjiàn the Imperial Academy

太监 tàijiàn a eunuch

# 见　jiàn　xiàn

jiàn ①to see, be seen: 那种服装现在已经见不到了。Nà zhǒng fúzhuāng xiànzài yǐjīng jiàn bu dào le. That kind of clothing is now no longer seen.

②to come in contact with, encounter, meet: 他今天很高兴，见人就笑。Tā jīntiān hěn gāoxìng, jiàn rén jiù xiào. He is very happy today, and smiles at anyone. // 别让它见阳光。Bié ràng tā jiàn yángguāng. Don't let it be exposed to sunlight.

③to appear, look: 日久见人心 rì jiǔ jiàn rénxīn time reveals a person's heart = it takes time to know a person

④See … [used in directing attention to a note or location in written material]: 见下文。Jiàn xiàwén. See below. // 请见注释。Qǐng jiàn zhùshì. Please see explanatory note.

⑤to visit, call on: 你去见他了吗? Nǐ qù jiàn tā le ma? Have you been to see him?

⑥a view, opinion

⑦〈lit.〉[an adverb indicating passive voice or expressing the speaker's perspective]

⑧〔a surname〕

会见 huìjiàn to meet formally: 总理会见美国大使。
Zǒnglǐ huìjiàn Měiguó dàshǐ. The premier met the US
ambassador.

见好 jiànhǎo (of a patient's condition) to get better: 吃
了那药病见好了。Chīle nà yào, bìng jiànhǎo le.
After taking that medicine, the illness got better.

见笑 jiànxiào to belittle, laugh at, joke at: 请别见笑。
Qǐng bié jiànxiào. Please don't laugh at me.

见效 jiànxiào efficacious: 这药一点儿也不见效。Zhè
yào yìdiǎnr yě bú jiànxiào. This medicine is not at all
efficacious.

见证 jiànzhèng witness; testimony

看见 kànjiàn to see: 看见一只狼 kànjiàn yì zhī láng to
see a wolf

意见 yìjiàn opinion, view: 他们意见不统一。Tāmen yì
jiàn bù tǒngyī. Their views are not united.

xiàn 〈lit.〉 ( = 现 ) to become visible: 图穷匕首见。Tú
qióng bǐshǒu xiàn. When the picture-scroll is unrolled,
the dagger is revealed. = The hidden intention is revealed
in the end.

# 槛    jiàn    kǎn

jiàn    a cage for animals; prison cell; railings, bars

井槛 jǐngjiàn a railing around a well

囚槛 qiújiàn a prison

兽槛 shòujiàn an animal cage

kǎn  a threshold, door-sill

门槛 ménkǎn a door-sill

# 将    jiāng   jiàng

jiāng ① to take, use; by means of: 将公款挪为私用 jiāng gōngkuǎn nuó wéi sī yòng to misappropriate public funds for one's private use

② 〔a preposition equivalent to 把 bǎ〕: 将门关上 jiāng mén guān shàng to shut the door

③ about to, going to; will: 他们将在这儿建一座工厂。 Tāmen jiāng zài zhèr jiàn yí zuò gōngchǎng. They will build a factory here.

④ 〔a particle indicating commencement of an action〕: 打将起来 dǎ jiāng qilai to start fighting

⑤ to check (in chess): 将军! Jiāng jūn! Check!

⑥ to put on the spot: 这几个问题把他将住了, 他什么话也说不出来。 Zhè jǐ ge wèntí bǎ tā jiāngzhù le, tā shénme huà yě shuō bu chūlái. These few questions stumped him, and he couldn't say a word.

⑦ both . . . and . . . : 将信将疑 jiāngxìn-jiāngyí half believing, half doubting

⑧ to look after (one's health)

将功折罪 jiānggōng-zhézuì to expiate one's crimes with good deeds

将计就计 jiāngjì-jiùjì to turn someone's trick against him, to beat someone at his own game

将军 jiāngjūn a general

将来 jiānglái in the future

将息 jiāngxī to rest and recuperate：休闲在家，将息一段时日 xiūxián zài jiā, jiāngxī yí duàn shírì to rest at home and recuperate for a period

将养 jiāngyǎng to nourish; to recuperate：好生将养，早日康复 hǎo shēng jiāngyǎng, zǎo rì kāngfù to take a good rest and recover soon

将要 jiāngyào about to; will：她将要去美国留学。Tā jiāngyào qù Měiguó liúxué. She is about to go to the US to study.

**jiàng** ①military ranks at the level of general

②the principal piece in Chinese chess

将领 jiànglǐng a high-ranking military officer

将校 jiàngxiào generals and field officers

## 浆　jiāng　jiàng

**jiāng** ①any thick liquid

②to starch：浆衣服 jiāng yīfu to starch clothes

豆浆 dòujiāng soybean milk

浆果 jiāngguǒ any type of berry

**jiàng** ( = 糨 ) starch; starchy, thick (of rice porridge etc.)

浆糊 jiànghu starch paste

浆子 jiàngzi starch paste

## 降　jiàng　xiáng

**jiàng** ①to descend, fall：那气球降得很低，都快碰到地面了。Nà qìqiú jiàng de hěn dī, dōu kuài pèng dào dìmiàn le. The balloon has descended very low, and it's about to hit the ground.

②to lower: 降旗 jiàng qí to lower the flag (e.g. at sunset)

③to decrease, decline, be reduced: 蔬菜价格近来降了不少。Shūcài jiàgé jìnlái jiàngle bù shǎo. The price of vegetables has dropped a lot recently.

降价 jiàngjià to lower prices; to fall in price: 目前多种商品降价，是购物的好时机。Mùqián duō zhǒng shāngpǐn jiàngjià, shì gòu wù de hǎo shíjī. Right now the prices of many goods have been reduced, so it's a good time to buy.

降落 jiàngluò to land (an aeroplane): 飞机安全降落。Fēijī ānquán jiàngluò. The plane landed safely.

降生 jiàngshēng to be born (e.g. the founder of a religion): 又一个孩子降生了。Yòu yí ge háizi jiàngshēng le. One more child is born.

xiáng ①to surrender, submit

②to subdue

投降 tóuxiáng to surrender: 敌军无条件投降。Díjūn wú tiáojiàn tóuxiáng. The enemy army surrendered unconditionally.

降伏 xiángfú to subdue, tame, vanquish: 驯兽师轻易地降伏了那只老虎。Xùnshòushī qīngyì de xiángfú le nà zhī lǎohǔ. The animal tamer easily subdued the tiger.

**强**  jiàng → qiáng

**教**  jiāo  jiào

jiāo  to teach [used as an independent verb]: 他教我。Tā jiāo wǒ. He teaches me. // 教书 jiāo shū to teach (book-learning)

jiào  ①to teach [as a component of compound verbs]

②a teaching, religion, directive

教会 jiàohuì a church

教室 jiàoshì a classroom

教育 jiàoyù education

教员 jiàoyuán a teacher

宗教 zōngjiào religion

*Polyphonic compound*:

教学 jiāoxué to teach (usually academically): 他教学二十年，学生众多。Tā jiāoxué èrshí nián, xuéshēng zhòngduō. He has been teaching for twenty years, and has had many students.

教学 jiàoxué teaching and learning (of any kind); the process of teaching: 教学相长。Jiàoxué-xiāngzhǎng. Teaching and being taught are mutually beneficial. // 教学改革 jiàoxué gǎigé educational reform

**嚼**  jiáo  jué  jiào

jiáo  ①〈coll.〉to chew

②glib, talkative

嚼舌 jiáoshé glib, gossiping; to gossip

嚼子 jiáozi a horse's bit

细嚼慢咽 xì jiáo màn yàn to chew carefully and swallow slowly

味同嚼蜡 wèitóngjiáolà like chewing wax = tasteless, uninteresting

jué ⟨lit., fig.⟩ to chew

咀嚼 jùjué to chew (carefully); to "chew over", ponder: 陈教授的这篇讲演，我得细细咀嚼。Chén Jiàoshòu de zhè piān jiǎngyǎn, wǒ děi xìxì jǔjué. I'll have to ponder carefully on this lecture by Professor Chen.

jiào 倒嚼 dàojiào to chew the cud

# 角　jiǎo　jué

jiǎo ①a horn: 牛角 niú jiǎo an ox horn // 鹿角 lù jiǎo deer's antlers

②any horn-shaped object

③an angle or corner: 正方形有几个角？Zhèngfāngxíng yǒu jǐ ge jiǎo？How many angles does a square have? // 墙角 qiáng jiǎo the corner of a wall // 东北角 dōngběi jiǎo the northeast corner (of a region)

④a coin equal to one-tenth of a yuan: 三元五角 sān yuán wǔ jiǎo three yuan fifty fen

⑤an ancient kind of military wind instrument

号角 hàojiǎo a bugle, horn

角落 jiǎoluò a corner; a remote place

三角形 sānjiǎoxíng a triangle

直角 zhíjiǎo a right angle

jué　（also written 脚）a role, personage in a play; an actor

角色 juésè a role

主角 zhǔjué the leading role

# 脚　jiǎo　jué

jiǎo　①the foot（part of body）

②the leg or base of an object

赤脚 chìjiǎo barefoot

脚本 jiǎoběn the script of a play

脚踏车 jiǎotàchē a bicycle

山脚 shānjiǎo the foot of a mountain

jué　（more often written 角）a role, personage in a play; an actor

脚色 juésè a role

# 觉　jiào → jué

# 校　jiào → xiào

# 结　jié　jiē

jié　①to tie：在绳子上结一个疙瘩 zài shéngzi shàng jié yíge gēda to tie the rope with a knot

②a knot：把这条带子打一个结 bǎ zhè tiáo dàizi dǎ yí ge jié to tie a knot in this tape

③to unite

④to solidify：天太冷，池面上结了冰。Tiān tài lěng, chí miàn shàng jiéle bīng. The weather is really cold. The pond has frozen over.

⑤to end, conclude: 结账 jié zhàng to settle accounts

⑥〈arch.〉an undertaking, written guarantee: 具结 jù jié 〈arch.〉to provide a written guarantee

活结 huójié a running knot

结构 jiégòu a structure

结果 jiéguǒ a result, outcome (cf. jiē guǒ to produce fruit; see below)

结合 jiéhé to combine, unite, integrate; the act of uniting: 共同的苦难使他们结合在一起了。Gòngtóng de kǔnàn shǐ tāmen jiéhé zài yìqǐ le. Shared hardships brought them together.

结婚 jiéhūn to marry: 他俩昨天结婚了。Tā liǎ zuótiān jiéhūn le. They got married yesterday.

结束 jiéshù to conclude, wind up; the end: 结束了学生生活 jiéshùle xuéshēng shēnghuó having finsihed student life

结子 jiézi a knot (cf. jiē zǐ to produce seeds; see below)

jiē　to fruit: 树上结了不少果子。Shù shàng jiēle bùshǎo guǒzi. A lot of fruit developed on the tree.// 桑树结实了。Sāng shù jiē shí le. The mulberry tree has been bearing fruit. // 结果 jiē guǒ to produce fruit (cf. jiéguǒ a result, outcome; see above) // 结子 jiē zǐ to produce seeds (cf. jiézi a knot; see above)

结巴 jiēba to stammer; a stammerer; stammering

结实 jiēshi solid, sturdy (also jiē shí; see above)

桔　jié　jú

jié　桔槔 jiégāo a well-sweep

桔梗 jiégěng the root of the balloon-flower ( *Platycodon grandiflorus* )

jú　( = 橘 ) the mandarin ( fruit )

**解**　jiě　jiè　xiè

jiě　①to loosen, untie, free: 解鞋带 jiě xiédài to untie shoe-laces // 把绳子解了 bǎ shéngzi jiě le to untie a rope

②to dispel, allay: 喝点茶解油腻。Hē diǎn chá jiě yóunì. Drink a little tea to get rid of the oily taste.

③to divide, separate

④to explain

⑤to understand

⑥to excrete

⑦to solve: 解方程式 jiě fāngchéngshì to solve an equation ( in algebra )

⑧a solution ( in mathematics ): 这道题无解。Zhè dào tí wú jiě. This ( mathematical ) problem has no solution.

解除 jiěchú to remove, relieve: 解除禁令 jiěchú jìnlìng to lift a ban

解放 jiěfàng to liberate: 盟军解放了这座城市。Méngjūn jiěfàngle zhè zuò chéngshì. The allied army liberated this city.

解决 jiějué to solve, resolve: 解决一项纠纷 jiějué yí xiàng jiūfēn to resolve a dispute

解渴 jiěkě to quench thirst: 吃西瓜解渴 chī xīguā jiěkě to quench one's thirst by eating watermelon

解释 jiěshì to explain; an explanation: 他们无法解释这一现象。Tāmen wú fǎ jiěshì zhè yí xiànxiàng. They have no way of explaining this phenomenon.

了解 liǎojiě to understand: 我不了解这件事的内幕。Wǒ bù liǎojiě zhè jiàn shì de nèimù. I don't know what lies behind this matter.

求解 qiújiě to find a solution: 求解方程式 qiújiě fāngchéngshì to solve an equation (in algebra)

瓦解 wǎjiě to disintegrate: 通过政治宣传来瓦解敌军 tōngguò zhèngzhì xuānchuán lái wǎjiě díjūn to disintegrate enemy forces using political propaganda

小解 xiǎojiě ⟨polite⟩ to urinate; urine

jiè　to send under guard

解送 jièsòng to send (a prisoner) under guard: 犯人被解送到沈阳。Fànrén bèi jièsòng dào Shěnyáng. The criminal was sent under guard to Shenyang.

解元 jièyuán the top candidate in provincial imperial examinations in the Ming and Qing dynasties

xiè　①[a surname]

②⟨arch.⟩ acrobatic skills

解数 xièshù martial arts skills

# 价

jiè → jià

# 禁

jīn → jìn

# 尽

jìn　jǐn

jìn　①finished, exhausted: 废气已排尽了。Fèiqì yǐ pái jìn

le. The waste air has been completely expelled. // 我已用尽了气力，不能再坚持了。Wǒ yǐ yòngjìnle qìlì, bù néng zài jiānchí le. I have already used up all my energy, and I can't carry on any further.

②to exhaust, use up (energy, resources, etc.), to do all that should or can be done: 尽人事 jìn rénshì to do one's best; to do whatever can be done // 尽责任 jìn zérèn to do one's duty; to have done one's duty

③to the utmost, to the limit

④all, the totality

尽力 jìnlì to do one's best: 他们尽力把陷入泥坑的大车拉出。Tāmen jìnlì bǎ xiànrù níkēng de dà chē lā chū. They did their best to pull the cart out of the mudhole.

尽善尽美 jìnshàn-jìnměi the acme of perfection

尽收眼底 jìnshōu-yǎndǐ having a panoramic view

无穷无尽 wúqióng-wújìn boundless, endless, inexhaustible

一言难尽 yìyán-nánjìn hard to explain in a few words, (it's) a long story

jǐn    ①as ... as possible

②to let, allow, give free rein to: 尽您吩咐 jǐn nín fēnfù give whatever instructions you like

③always, constantly: 这几天尽下雨。Zhè jǐ tiān jǐn xià yǔ. These few days it's been raining constantly.

④within the limits of: 尽着两天把工作完成 jǐnzhe

liǎng tiān bǎ gōngzuò wánchéng to get the job
finished within two days

⑤to give priority to: 饭不多，尽着孩子们先吃。Fàn
bù duō, jǐnzhe háizimen xiān chī. There's not much
food, so let the children eat first.

尽管 jǐnguǎn feel free to; even though: 饭菜多着呢，尽
管吃吧！Fàn cài duō zhe ne, jǐnguǎn chī ba!
There's plenty of food, so eat as much as you like! // 尽
管下大雨，她还是来了。Jǐnguǎn xià dà yǔ, tā
háishi lái le. Although it was raining hard, she still
came.

尽快 jǐnkuài as soon as possible

尽早 jǐnzǎo as early as possible

# 劲    jìn → jìng

# 禁    jìn    jīn

jìn    ①to prohibit: 禁烟 jìn yān to prohibit smoking

②to imprison

③a ban; what is forbidden by law or custom: 解禁 jiě jìn
to lift a ban

④not open to the public (e.g. a royal residence)

监禁 jiānjìn to imprison: 那个难民曾被无理监禁过三
年。Nàge nànmín céng bèi wúlǐ jiānjìn guò sān
nián. That refugee was jailed for three years without
justification.

禁忌 jìnjì a taboo; to taboo: 老李向来禁忌烟酒。Lǎo Lǐ

xiànglái jìnjì yān jiǔ. Lao Li never touches tobacco or alcohol.

禁止 jìnzhǐ to prohibit: 此处禁止吸烟。Cǐ chù jìnzhǐ xī yān. Smoking is prohibited here.

紫禁城 Zǐjìnchéng the Forbidden City (in Beijing)

jīn　①to withstand, endure, bear: 这鞋太不禁穿了。Zhè xié tài bù jīn chuān le. These shoes are not at all durable.

②to restrain oneself: 听到那消息，他不禁笑出声来。Tīngdào nà xiāoxi, tā bù jīn xiào chū shēng lái. On hearing the news, he could not restrain himself from laughing.

弱不禁风 ruòbùjīnfēng very feeble

# 劲　jìng　jìn

jìng　strong, violent

劲敌 jìngdí a powerful enemy

劲风 jìngfēng a gale

劲旅 jìnglǚ crack troops

jìn　①strength, stamina, energy: 使劲打 shǐ jìn dǎ to beat with force // 用劲拉 yòng jìn lā to pull strongly // 她有使不完的劲儿。Tā yǒu shǐ bù wán de jìnr. She has inexhaustible energy.

②spirit, manner, (active or exciting) air: 她真有那股劲儿。Tā zhēn yǒu nà gǔ jìnr. She really has that kind of spirit. // 瞧你那骄傲劲儿! Qiáo nǐ nà jiāo'ào jìnr! Look at your arrogant manner!

③interest：真没劲 zhēn méi jìn really uninteresting

干劲 gànjìn vigour，enthusiasm

劲儿 jìnr〈coll.〉strength；fondness；bearing，manner

劲头 jìntóu strength，stamina，drive

起劲 qǐjìn enthusiastic；vigorously，energetically，enthusi-
astically：他打扑克很起劲。Tā dǎ pūkè hěn qǐjìn．
He is very enthusiastic in playing poker．

**车**    jū → chē

**桔**    jú → jié

**锔**    jú    jū

  jú    the element curium（Cm）

  jū    ①a kind of metal staple used for mending broken crockery

    ②to employ such staples：锔碗 jū wǎn to mend broken
crockery using metal staples

  锔子 jūzi a metal staple for mending broken crockery

**枸**    jǔ → gǒu

**柜**    jǔ → guì

**据**    jù    jū

  jù    ①on the basis of，according to：据新华社提供的消息 jù
Xīnhuáshè tígōng de xiāoxi according to a report from
Xinhua News Agency

    ②evidence：有根有据 yǒu gēn yǒu jù based on good
grounds or evidence

    ③to occupy，take，seize，take possession of：据为己有

jù wéi jǐ yǒu to appropriate, take for one's own use

④ to rely on, depend on: 据险顽抗 jù xiǎn wánkàng ⟨derogatory⟩ to resist stubbornly, taking advantage of a natural barrier

根据 gēnjù on the basis of, according to; basis, grounds: 根据他们的调查报告, 这地区的霍乱仍未根除。Gēnjù tāmen de diàochá bàogào, zhè dìqū de huòluàn réng wèi gēnchú. According to the report from their investigation, cholera has not yet been eradicated from this region.

据说 jùshuō according to what they say, allegedly: 据说那事儿是真的。Jùshuō nà shìr shì zhēn de. According to what they say, it's true.

收据 shōujù a receipt

jū　拮据 jiéjū short of money, in financial difficulty: 他们家只靠老王一人的工资生活, 一向十分拮据。Tāmen jiā zhǐ kào Lǎo Wáng yì rén de gōngzī shēnghuó, yíxiàng shífēn jiéjū. Their family depends entirely on Lao Wang's salary to survive, so they're always in financial difficulty.

圈　juān juàn → quān

卷　juǎn　juàn

juǎn　① a roll: 铺盖卷儿 pūgai juǎnr a bedding roll

② to roll up or roll along: 卷铺盖 juǎn pūgai to roll up one's bedding; ⟨fig.⟩ to be forced to leave, be sacked

③rolled, wavy or curly: 她的头发是卷的。Tā de tóufa shì juǎn de. Her hair is curly.

④〔a measure word for rolled objects〕: 一卷手纸 yì juǎn shǒuzhǐ a roll of toilet paper

卷发 juǎnfà curly hair

卷入 juǎnrù rolled up in; drawn into; involved in: 他被卷入旋涡。Tā bèi juǎnrù xuánwō. He was sucked into the vortex. // 卷入一场官司 juǎnrù yì chǎng guānsi involved in a court case

juàn ①a book, document, scroll, examination paper

②〔a measure word for volumes of a book〕: 第五卷 dì wǔ juàn volume five

画卷 huàjuàn a painting scroll

手不释卷 shǒubúshìjuàn never without a book in one's hand = engrossed in studies

文卷 wénjuàn documents

*Polyphonic compound*:

卷子 juǎnzi a small rolled object; a steamed roll
        juànzi an examination paper

# 角 jué → jiǎo

# 觉 jué jiào

jué ①to feel, be conscious of

②to waken

觉得 juéde to feel: 你吃药后觉得好些了吗? Nǐ chī yào hòu juéde hǎo xiē le ma? Do you feel a bit better since taking the medicine?

觉悟 juéwù to realize, become aware; consciousness, awareness: 他终于觉悟了，不再跟那帮人鬼混。Tā zhōngyú juéwù le, bú zài gēn nà bāng rén guǐhùn. He has finally woken up to himself, and won't be fooling around with that crowd any more. // 他在这方面觉悟很低。Tā zài zhè fāngmiàn juéwù hěn dī. His awareness in this regard is very low.

觉醒 juéxǐng to awaken; an awakening: 人民觉醒了。Rénmín juéxǐng le. The people have awakened. // 被压迫者的觉醒 bèi yāpò zhě de juéxǐng an awakening of the oppressed

听觉 tīngjué the sense of hearing

jiào ①to sleep

②a sleep, nap

睡觉 shuìjiào to (go to) sleep: 妈妈正在睡觉，别吵醒她。Māma zhèngzài shuìjiào, bié chǎoxǐng tā. Mother's asleep, so don't make a noise and wake her.

午觉 wǔjiào a siesta

# 倔 jué juè

jué tough, obstinate, surly

倔强 juéjiàng stubborn, unbending

juè tough, obstinate, surly: 脾气很倔 píqi hěn juè of surly disposition

倔巴棍子 juèba gùnzi 〈dial.〉 a surly, roughly-spoken fellow

**脚**   jué → jiǎo

**蹶**   jué   juě

jué   to suffer a setback

一蹶不振 yìjué -búzhèn to collapse after one setback and never recover

juě   to kick back

尥蹶子 liào juězi ( of a horse etc. ) to give a backward kick

**嚼**   jué → jiáo

**龟**   jūn → guī

# K

**咖**   kā   gā

kā   〔used in transcribing foreign words〕

咖啡 kāfēi coffee

gā   〔used in transcribing foreign words〕

咖哩 gālí curry

**卡**   kǎ   qiǎ

kǎ   〔used in transcribing foreign words〕：圣诞卡 shèngdàn kǎ a Christmas card // 资料卡 zīliào kǎ a reference card

// 十轮大卡 shí lún dà kǎ a ten-wheeled truck

卡车 kǎchē a truck

卡片 kǎpiàn a card

qiǎ ①to become wedged in, stuck: 鱼刺卡了嗓子。Yúcì qiǎ le sǎngzi. A fishbone became stuck in (his) throat.

②a clip or fastener

③a checkpoint

④to block: 卡住敌人的退路 qiǎ zhù dírén de tuìlù to block the enemy's line of retreat

发卡 fàqiǎ a hairpin

关卡 guānqiǎ a checkpoint

卡子 qiǎzi a pair of pincers; 〈coll.〉 a customs office, checkpoint

**喀** kǎ → gē

**槛** kǎn → jiān

**看** kàn  kān

kàn ①to look at, watch, see: 请看那座山。Qǐng kàn nà zuò shān. Look at that mountain. // 看电视 kàn diànshì to watch television // 看不见 kàn bu jiàn can't see // 看球赛 kàn qiúsài to watch a ball-game

②to read: 看书 kàn shū to read (books) // 看报 kàn bào to read the newspaper

③to observe, think, consider: 看问题 kàn wèntí to consider a problem // 你看他人品如何? Nǐ kàn tā rénpǐn rúhé? What do you think of him as a person?

④〈coll.〉to visit: 去看朋友 qù kàn péngyou to visit
　　friends // 看大夫 kàn dàifu to see a doctor

⑤to look after, mind, take care of: 别跑，看摔着。Bié
　　pǎo, kàn shuāizhe! Don't run or you'll fall!

⑥ to try and see how something turns out: 尝尝看
　　chángcháng kàn to taste and see // 做做看 zuòzuò
　　kàn to give it a try // 等等看 děngděng kàn to wait
　　and see

⑦to depend on: 看情况 kàn qíngkuàng depending on
　　the situation

观看 guānkàn to watch, view: 观看演出 guānkàn
　　yǎnchū to watch a show

看穿 kànchuān to see through, perceive accurately: 看
　　穿他的心思 kànchuān tā de xīnsi to see his point of
　　view // 看穿敌人的阴谋 kànchuān dírén de yīnmóu
　　to see through the enemy's schemes

看待 kàndài to look on, regard: 这两种情况不能等同
　　看待。Zhè liǎng zhǒng qíngkuàng bù néng
　　děngtóng kàndài. These two situations cannot be re-
　　garded as the same.

看顾 kàngù to look after: 看顾孩子 kàngù háizi to look
　　after a child

看望 kànwàng to visit, go and see: 看望病人 kàn
　　wàng bìngrén to visit the sick

小看 xiǎokàn to look down on, belittle, underestimate:
　　小看人 xiǎokàn rén to look down on people // 对这个

问题不可小看。Duì zhège wèntí bù kě xiǎokàn.
Don't underestimate this problem.

**kān** to take care of, guard, keep watch over: 看家 kān jiā to mind a house // 看着孩子 kānzhe háizi to look after a child

看守 kānshǒu to watch over; to detain

看押 kānyā to take into custody

## 咳 ké hāi

**ké** to cough, spit: 咳血 ké xiě to cough up blood // 她咳得厉害。Tā ké de lìhài. She's coughing badly.

咳嗽 késou to cough; a cough: 连声咳嗽 liánshēng késou coughing continuously // 你的咳嗽好点了吗? Nǐ de késou hǎodiǎn le ma? Is your cough a little better?

**hāi** [an interjection expressing regret, or calling attention]: 咳，可惜! Hāi, kěxī! Ah, what a pity!

## 可 kě kè

**kě** ①can, able to: 这种草可作中药用。Zhè zhǒng cǎo kě zuò Zhōngyào yòng. This herb can be used in Chinese medicine. // 没什么可说的了。Méi shénme kě shuō de le. Nothing more can be said.

②but: 我想去，可他不愿意。Wǒ xiǎng qù, kě tā bú yuànyì. I would like to go, but he is not willing to.

③[used to add feeling to a statement or question]: 你可来了! Nǐ kě lái le! So you've come! // 可不是吗? Kě bú shì ma? How could it be otherwise? // 他可是听见

了的! Tā kě shì tīngjiàn le de! He did indeed hear it!

④〔used to indicate doubt or questioning〕: 你可知道? Nǐ kě zhīdao? You know, perhaps? *or* Do you know?

可爱 kě'ài lovable

可靠 kěkào reliable

可口 kěkǒu tasty

可能 kěnéng possible

可是 kěshì but

可以 kěyǐ can, able to

kè    〔used in transcribing foreign words〕

可汗 kèhán a khan

吭    kēng → háng

空    kōng    kòng

kōng ①empty, hollow: 空箱子 kōng xiāngzi an empty box // 大厅里空空的。Dàtīng li kōngkōng de. The hall is quite empty. // 空手 kōng shǒu empty-handed

②space, sky, emptiness

③for nothing, in vain: 空忙 kōng máng to make fruitless efforts // 他没来, 让我空等。Tā méi lái, ràng wǒ kōng děng. He didn't come. I waited for nothing. // 空跑一趟 kōng pǎo yí tàng to make a trip for nothing, go on a wild goose chase

航空 hángkōng aviation, air transport

空气 kōngqì the atmosphere, air

空虚 kōngxū hollow, empty, vacuous

kòng ①leisure, free time：你有空吗？Nǐ yǒu kòng ma? Are you free? // 我最近空得很。Wǒ zuìjìn kòng de hěn. I've had a lot of leisure time recently.

②to make or leave vacant：把座位空出来 bǎ zuòwèi kòng chulai to leave a seat vacant

③ unoccupied, vacant：车厢里空得很。Chēxiāng li kòng de hěn. There's a lot of room in the boot.

④a vacancy, empty space, blank：每行之间多留点儿空。Měi háng zhī jiān duō liú diǎnr kòng. Leave a little more space between the lines.

空白 kòngbái blank：空白纸 kòngbái zhǐ blank paper

空额 kòng'é vacancies（for enrolment etc.）

空隙 kòngxì a space, gap, interval

空闲 kòngxián idle, free：没有空闲时间 méiyǒu kòng xián shíjiān to have no free time

会　kuài → huì

傀　kuǐ　guī

kuǐ　傀儡 kuǐlěi a puppet

guī　①〈lit.〉great, large

②〈lit.〉strange

傀奇 guīqí〈lit.〉strange, odd

傀然独立 guī rán dúlì〈lit.〉like a standing giant

# L

## 拉 lā lá lǎ

lā ①to pull, draw, seize: 拉绳子 lā shéngzi to pull a rope // 拉车 lā chē to pull a cart, rickshaw, etc. // 一把拉住他 yì bǎ lāzhù tā grabbed and held him

②to move the bowels: 拉屎 lā shǐ to have a bowel movement // 拉肚子 lā dùzi to have diarrhoea // 一天拉了好几次。Yì tiān lāle hǎo jǐ cì. He had many bowel movements in a single day.

③〔used in transcribing foreign words〕

拉链 lāliàn a zip fastener

拉客 lākè to solicit customers

拉稀 lāxī 〈coll.〉to have diarrhoea

拉丁 Lādīng Latin

lá 〈dial.〉to cut, slash: 手上拉了个口子 shǒu shàng lále ge kǒuzi received a cut to the hand

lǎ 半拉 bànlǎ 〈dial.〉a half

## 喇 lǎ lá lā

lǎ ①a horn

②〔used in transcription〕

喇叭 lǎba a trumpet

喇嘛 lǎma a lama

lá 哈喇子 hālázi 〈dial.〉saliva dripping from the mouth

lā 　哗喇 huālā〔onomatopoeia for thumping sounds〕

落　là → luò

蜡　là　zhà

là　wax: 蜂蜡 fēng là beeswax // 地板蜡 dìbǎn là floor wax
// 给地板打蜡 gěi dìbǎn dǎ là to wax the floor

蜡染 làrǎn to make batik; batik

蜡烛 làzhú a (wax) candle

zhà　蜡祭 zhàjì an ancient year-end sacrifice

莨　làng　liáng

làng　莨菪 làngdàng the henbane

liáng　薯莨 shǔliáng a tuberous plant whose juice is used for
　　　　preserving fishing nets

姥　lǎo　mǔ

lǎo　姥姥 lǎolɑo a maternal grandmother; an old woman

mǔ　( = 姆，母 ) a governess, matron

天姥山 Tiānmǔ Shān Tianmu Mountain ( in Zhejiang
Province)

络　lào → luò

烙　lào　luò

lào　to burn, brand; to bake in a pan: 在皮上烙一个印记
zài pí shang lào yí ge yìnjì to brand a mark on the skin //
烙饼 lào bǐng to bake cakes ( also làobǐng; see below)

烙饼 làobǐng baked wheat cakes ( also lào bǐng; see
above)

烙铁 làotie iron; soldering iron

烙印 làoyìn a brand or mark burnt into something

**luò**　炮烙 páoluò an ancient form of punishment using heated metal pillars

**落**　lào → luò

**乐**　lè → yuè

**勒**　lè  lēi

**lè**　①to compel

②to rein in: 勒住马 lè zhù mǎ to rein in a horse // 勒住缰绳 lè zhù jiāngshéng to pull on the reins

③a bridle

勒令 lèlìng to compel (by law etc.): 勒令案犯交出赃款 lèlìng ànfàn jiāochū zāngkuǎn to compel a convicted person to surrender illicitly acquired money

勒索 lèsuǒ to extort, blackmail; extortion, blackmail: 赃官勒索百姓。Zāngguān lèsuǒ bǎixìng. The corrupt officials practised extortion on the people.

马勒 mǎlè a bridle

**lēi**　to tighten (a rope etc.): 她把皮带勒了一下。Tā bǎ pídài lēi le yíxià. She tightened the strap.// 他是被人勒死的。Tā shì bèi rén lēisǐ de. He was strangled.

勒紧 lēijǐn to pull tight: 勒紧腰带 lēijǐn yāodài to tighten one's belt

**了**　le → liǎo

# 勒

lēi → le

# 擂

léi　lèi

léi　①to pound, pulverise：擂碎 léi suì to pulverise

②to hit, punch：擂了一拳 léi le yì quán gave（someone）a punch

擂钵 léibō mortar（a vessel）

lèi　to strike, beat：擂鼓 lèi gǔ to beat a drum

擂台 lèitái a stage for martial arts contests

# 累

lèi　lěi　léi

lèi　①tired：很累 hěn lèi very tired// 累死了 lèi sǐ le dead tired

②tiring：累活 lèi huó tiring work

③to make tired：这么重的活，会把人给累坏的。
Zhème zhòng de huó, huì bǎ rén gěi lèihuài de.
Such heavy work can exhaust a person.

④to work hard：为完成这个项目，她累了整整一年。
Wèi wánchéng zhège xiàngmù, tā lèile zhěngzhěng yì nián. In order to complete this project, she worked hard all year.

劳累 láolèi tired from hard work

lěi　①to accumulate

②repeatedly

③to implicate

积累 jīlěi to accumulate：张教授积累了大量的数据资料。Zhāng Jiàoshòu jīlěile dàliàng de shùjù zīliào.

Professor Zhang accumulated a large amount of data.

经年累月 jīng nián lěi yuè year after year, month after month

累犯 lěifàn a frequent offender

累计 lěijì to add up; cumulative: 累计数据 lěijì shùjù cumulative data // 全年累计，产量已达九万公斤。Quán nián lěijì, chǎnliàng yǐ dá jiǔ wàn gōngjīn. Production for the entire year totalled ninety thousand kilos.

连累 liánlěi to implicate, get someone else into trouble: 你不该连累别人。Nǐ bù gāi liánlěi biérén. You shouldn't get other people involved in trouble.

léi 累累 léiléi abundant: 果实累累 guǒshí léiléi fruit hanging in clusters

累赘 léizhui a nuisance, tiresome

# 哩 lī li lǐ

lī 哩哩啰啰 līliluōluō 〈coll.〉 mumbling, rambling in speech

li [a sentence-final particle]: 他没来哩。Tā méi lái li. He hasn't come.

lǐ 〈old written form〉 the English mile: 一哩 yì lǐ one English mile

# 蠡 lí lǐ

lí a calabash, dipper; seashell

蠡测 lícè 〈lit.〉 using a calabash to measure the ocean = having a shallow understanding lǐ [a component of certain place-names]: 蠡园 Lǐ Yuán a well-known garden in Wuxi City // 蠡县 Lǐ Xiàn Li County in central Hubei Province

# 丽 lì lí

lì beautiful, elegant

风和日丽 fēnghé-rìlì glorious weather

美丽 měilì beautiful

壮丽 zhuànglì majestic, glorious

lí 高丽 Gāolí Korea

# 俩 liǎ liǎng

liǎ [a fusion of 两个 liǎng ge] two; a few: 俩人 liǎ rén two people // 咱俩 zán liǎ we two // 俩钱儿 liǎ qiánr 〈dial.〉 a few coins

liǎng 伎俩 jìliǎng a sly trick, cunning manoeuvre

# 凉 liáng liàng

liáng ①cool, cold: 开水凉了。 Kāi shuǐ liáng le. The boiled water has cooled. // 凉水 liáng shuǐ cool water

②to feel disheartened: 心里凉了 xīn li liáng le became disheartened

③[name of a dynasty]: 北凉 Běi Liáng the Northern Liang Dynasty (A.D. 397 – 439)

凉快 liángkuài comfortably cool

liàng to make cool: 凉一凉再喝。 Liàng yi liàng zài hē. Let it cool off before drinking it.

# 莨 liáng → làng

# 量　liáng　liàng

liáng　to measure, evaluate: 量体温 liáng tǐwēn to take someone's temperature // 把绳子量一下 bǎ shéngzi liáng yíxià to measure a rope

测量 cèliáng to survey, measure; a survey: 测量山地海拔高度 cèliáng shāndì hǎibá gāodù to measure a mountain's height above sea level

量规 liángguī a gauge

商量 shāngliáng to discuss: 你们自己商量着办吧，不用再来问我了。Nǐmen zìjǐ shāngliángzhe bàn ba, bú yòng zài lái wèn wǒ le. Do it by discussing among yourselves. There's no need to come back and ask me.

liàng　①capacity: 饭量 fànliàng eating capacity // 他酒量很大。Tā jiǔ liàng hěn dà. He has a big capacity for alcohol.

②quantity: 给的量太少了。Gěi de liàng tài shǎo le. The amount they give is too small. // 保质保量 bǎo zhì bǎo liàng to guarantee both quality and quantity

③to estimate

④⟨arch.⟩ a general name of measures of capacity: 度量衡 dù liàng héng weights and measures

量变 liàngbiàn a quantitative change

量词 liàngcí a measure word (e.g. 个，支)

量力而行 liànglì-érxíng to act within one's abilities

量入为出 liàngrù-wéichū to estimate income in planning expenditure = to live within one's means

量子 liàngzǐ a quantum (in physics)

容量 róngliàng capacity (of a container)

**俩** liǎng → liǎ

**跟** liàng  liáng

liàng 跟跄 liàngqiàng to limp, walk unsteadily

liáng 跳跟 tiàoliáng ⟨lit.⟩ to jump about, hop around

**撩** liāo  liáo

liāo ①to lift: 撩起来 liāo qilai to raise (a curtain etc.)

②to sprinkle with the hand: 撩水 liāo shuǐ to sprinkle water with the hand

liáo to attract, lure, entice, provoke, challenge, waken: 春色撩人。Chūnsè liáo rén. The spring scenery attracts people. // 那姑娘把他撩得心神不定。Nà gūniang bǎ tā liáo de xīnshén-búdìng. That girl attracts him so much that he is all in a flutter.

撩动 liáodòng to arouse: 撩动肝火 liáodòng gānhuǒ to arouse one's spleen

撩乱 liáoluàn chaotic, confused: 眼花撩乱 yǎnhuā liáoluàn dazzled

**燎** liáo  liǎo

liáo to burn

燎泡 liáopào a blister caused by burning

星火燎原 Xīnghuǒ-liáoyuán. A spark can start a prairie fire.

liǎo to singe: 燎了他的眉毛 liǎole tā de méimao singed his

eyebrows

了　　**liǎo　le**

liǎo　①to complete: 没完没了 méi wán méi liǎo endless, never-ending // 把那事儿给了了 bǎ nà shìr gěi liǎo le finished the matter off // 就这么了啦。Jiù zhème liǎo la. Let's leave it at that.

②( = 瞭) to understand

③〔a verbal complement signifying possibility〕: 办不了这件事 bàn bu liǎo zhè jiàn shì can't handle this affair // 他来得了吗? Tā lái de liǎo ma? Is he able to come? // 受不了 shòu bu liǎo can't tolerate; can't endure // 不得了 bù déliǎo desperately serious; extremely

了断 liǎoduàn to decide, settle: 他们两家的官司至今无法了断。Tāmen liǎng jiā de guānsi zhì jīn wúfǎ liǎoduàn. The court case between their two families has still not been settled.

了结 liǎojié to finish, settle, bring to a conclusion: 这事应该了结了吧? Zhè shì yīnggāi liǎojié le ba? This matter should have been finished, shouldn't it?

了解 liǎojiě to understand, have insight into: 我对那案情不了解。Wǒ duì nà ànqíng bù liǎojiě. I know nothing about that case.

了如指掌 liǎorúzhǐzhǎng to know like the back of one's hand: 老王对当地情况了如指掌。Lǎo Wáng duì dāngdì qíngkuàng liǎorúzhǐzhǎng. Lao Wang knows the situation there like the back of his hand.

了无牵挂 liǎowú qiānguà absolutely free of concerns: 他是个单身汉，了无牵挂。Tā shì ge dānshēnhàn, liǎowú qiānguà. He's a single man, completely free of concerns.

le [a particle signifying completion or transition]: 完了 wán le finished // 他走了。Tā zǒu le. He has left. // 算了！Suàn le! Enough! That will do! Forget it!

## 钌 liǎo liào

liǎo the element ruthenium (Ru)

liào 〈dial.〉钌吊儿 liàodiàor an old-style window latch

## 咧 liē liě lie

liē 大大咧咧 dàdaliēliē〈dial.〉careless, casual
骂骂咧咧 màmaliēliē〈dial.〉foul-mouthed, incessantly cursing

liě to stretch or open the lips sideways
咧开嘴 liěkāi zuǐ to open the mouth sideways

lie [a sentence-final particle]: 她没来咧。Tā méi lái lie. She hasn't come yet.

## 淋 lín lìn

lín ①to sprinkle, pour liquid on: 淋湿 lín shī wet through by rain // 给面条淋点麻油 gěi miàntiáo lín diǎn máyóu to sprinkle a little sesame oil on the noodles
②[used in transcribing foreign words]
淋巴 línbā lymph
淋浴 línyù a shower bath

lìn    to filter: 过淋 guòlìn to pass through a filter

　　淋病 lìnbìng gonorrhoea

令    lìng    lǐng

lìng    ①to cause, command: 令部队转移 lìng bùduì zhuǎnyí
　　　　to order the troops to move

　　②a command, law

　　③a season

　　④⟨lit., hon.⟩ good, your: 令名 lìng míng your good
　　　　name // 令郎 lìng láng your son

　　⑤〔an ancient official title〕

　　⑥a form of poem

　　发号施令 fāhào-shīlìng to issue orders; to order people
　　　　about

　　酒令 jiǔlìng a drinkers' betting game

　　命令 mìnglìng to command; a command: 命令部队停止
　　　　前进 mìnglìng bùduì tíngzhǐ qiánjìn to order an army
　　　　to stop advancing // 服从命令 fúcóng mìnglìng to
　　　　obey orders

　　时令 shílìng a season

　　夏令 xiàlìng summer

　　县令 xiànlìng an ancient grade of county official

　　小令 xiǎolìng a form of poem

lǐng    〔transcription of English "ream"〕: 一令纸 yì lǐng zhǐ a
　　ream of paper

溜    liū    liù

liū ①to slip, slip away: 书从手中溜下去。Shū cóng shǒu zhōng liū xiàqu. The book slipped from his/her hand. // 悄悄溜出会场 qiāoqiāo liūchū huìchǎng to quietly slip away from a meeting // 她溜走了。Tā liūzǒu le. She slipped away. // 不到半小时，听众全溜光了。Bú dào bàn xiǎoshí, tīngzhòng quán liūguāng le. Within half an hour the entire audience had slipped away.

②to glance at: 溜了一眼 liūle yì yǎn cast a glance at

③very slippery, smooth

④a method of cooking: 溜虾仁 liū xiārén prawns stir-fried with starchy sauce

溜冰 liūbīng to ice-skate

溜达 liūda to take a short stroll: 出去溜达溜达，散散心 chūqu liūda liūda, sàn sàn xīn to go out for a short stroll and relax

溜光 liūguāng very smooth: 大理石桌面溜光滑亮。Dàlǐshí zhuōmiàn liūguāng huáliàng. The marble tabletop was smooth and shiny. (cf. liù guāng, see above)

liù ①rapids

②a row: 一溜儿房子 yí liùr fángzi a row of houses

③an eaves gutter

④〈dial.〉quick; fluent: 他英语说得溜极了。Tā Yīngyǔ shuō de liù jíle. He speaks English extremely fluently.

顺溜 shùnliù orderly; going smoothly

檐溜 yánliù an eaves gutter

## 陆 liù → lù

## 咯 lo → gē

## 笼 lóng　lǒng

lóng ①a cage, basket, or trunk made of strips of bamboo, wood, or iron: 把鸡鸭关在笼里 bǎ jī yā guān zài lóng li to pen chickens and ducks in cages

②a basket-like utensil for steaming food: 那笼里蒸着馒头。Nà lóng li zhēngzhe mántou. In that steamer there are buns being steamed.

③〈dial.〉to put one's hands inside one's sleeves: 笼着手 lóngzhe shǒu with one's hands in one's sleeves

鸡笼 jīlóng a chicken coop

蒸笼 zhēnglóng a bamboo vessel for steaming food

lǒng ①a large box or chest

②to envelop, cover

笼络 lǒngluò to win over, "rope in": 那老板常用些小恩小惠来笼络员工。Nà lǎobǎn cháng yòng xiē xiǎo ēn xiǎo huì lái lǒngluò yuángōng. That boss often uses small incentives and rewards to win over his staff.

笼统 lǒngtǒng general, sweeping, not specific, not clear enough: 这报告过于笼统，必须重新写过。Zhè bàogào guòyú lǒngtǒng, bìxū chóngxīn xiě guò.

This report is too sweeping and vague, and will have to be rewritten.

笼罩 lǒngzhào to envelop, shroud: 会场被一种紧张气氛笼罩着。Huìchǎng bèi yì zhǒng jǐnzhāng qìfēn lǒngzhàozhe. The meeting place was enveloped in a kind of tense atmosphere.

箱笼 xiānglǒng all kinds of luggage containers

## 弄 lòng → nòng

## 喽 lóu lou

lóu ( = 偻 ) a lackey

喽罗 lóuluo bandits' lackeys

lou [an attention-drawing particle indicating completion]: 好喽! Hǎo lou! Good! Done!

## 搂 lǒu lōu

lǒu ①to embrace: 母亲把孩子搂得紧紧的。Mǔqīn bǎ háizi lǒu de jǐnjǐn de. The mother embraced the child very tightly. // 搂住他不放 lǒu zhù tā bú fàng embraced him and did not let go

②a measure of girth (e.g. of a tree) equal to that encompassed by a person's embracing arms: 一搂干柴 yì lǒu gān chái an armful of dry firewood

搂抱 lǒubào to embrace: 互相搂抱 hùxiāng lǒubào to embrace each other

lōu ①to gather up, rake together: 搂柴火 lōu cháihuo to rake up twigs etc. for fuel // 搂钱 lōu qián to rake in money by any means

② to tuck up: 捋起袖子 lōu qǐ xiùzi to tuck up one's sleeves

③ ⟨dial.⟩ to check, audit

捋算 lōusuàn ⟨dial.⟩ to check an account, to audit: 你捋算一下吧，这批货该值多少？ Nǐ lōusuàn yíxià ba, zhè pī huò gāi zhí duōshao? You check it over. How much should these goods be worth?

**露** lòu → lù

**陆** lù liù

lù ① dry land, the shore

② [a surname]

大陆 dàlù the mainland

陆军 lùjūn the army, ground forces

陆路 lùlù by land, a land route

陆续 lùxù continuous

水陆两栖 shuǐlù liǎngqī amphibious

liù six [used in writing cheques etc.]

陆拾陆元 liùshíliù yuán sixty-six yuan

**露** lù lòu

lù ① dew

② a syrup or beverage distilled from leaves, flowers, or fruit: 果子露 guǒzi lù a fruit drink // 柠檬露 níngméng lù lemon juice

③ to become exposed, appear in view

暴露 bàolù to reveal, expose, lay bare: 阴谋暴露了。
Yīnmóu bàolù le. The plot has been exposed.

表露 biǎolù to show, reveal: 他在那封信里表露了心
迹。Tā zài nà fēng xìn lǐ biǎolù le xīnjì. In that letter
he revealed his true feelings.

露水 lùshuǐ dew

露天 lùtiān open to the sky, out of doors

露营 lùyíng an open-air camp

透露 tòulù to reveal, divulge, disclose: 透露内情 tòulù
nèiqíng to divulge inside information

lòu 〈coll.〉 to emerge, appear, show, reveal: 他在众人面前
露了一手。Tā zài zhòngrén miànqián lòule yì shǒu.
He showed off in front of everyone.

露马脚 lòu mǎjiǎo "let the cat out of the bag", give the
show away

露面 lòumiàn to show one's face, appear: 他向来不爱
在公共场合露面。Tā xiànglái bú ài zài gōnggòng
chǎnghé lòumiàn. He has never liked appearing on
public occasions.

# 捋    lǚ    luō

lǚ    to stroke and smooth out with the fingers: 捋胡子 lǚ húzi
to stroke one's beard // 把皮毛捋平 bǎ pímáo lǚ píng to
stroke and smooth out fur

luō    to rub a long object lengthwise: 捋奶 luō nǎi to milk (a
cow) // 捋虎须 luō hǔ xū to stroke the tiger's whiskers =
to offend the powerful

# 绿　lǜ　lù

**lǜ**　green：绿色 lǜ sè green colour // 绿地 lǜ dì parkland, green areas // 叶子很绿。Yèzi hěn lǜ. The leaves are very green.

**lù**　green〔used only in a few special terms〕

绿林豪杰 lùlín háojié "heroes of the greenwood" of the Robin Hood type

鸭绿江 Yālù Jiāng the Yalu River（on the China-Korea border）

# 率　lǜ　shuài

**lǜ**　a rate

百分率 bǎifēnlǜ a percentage

兑换率 duìhuànlǜ an exchange rate

**shuài**　①to lead：率军出征 shuài jūn chū zhēng to lead an army out to battle

②handsome（more usually 帅）：长得很率 zhǎng de hěn shuài grown very handsome

③careless, rash, hasty

④frank

草率 cǎoshuài careless, perfunctory：工作草率 gōngzuò cǎoshuài to work carelessly

轻率 qīngshuài rash, hasty, indiscreet：为人轻率 wéirén qīngshuài having a reckless and frivolous personality

率领 shuàilǐng to lead：率领军队 shuàilǐng jūnduì to

lead troops

直率 zhíshuài forthright, direct：性格直率 xìnggé zhíshuài forthright by nature

# 论 lùn lún

lùn ①to discuss, analyse

②according to：鸡蛋论斤卖。Jīdàn lùn jīn mài. Eggs are sold by the *jin* (half kilo).

③a theory

④an analytical or explanatory essay

⑤a view, opinion

⑥to say, mention：论业务，她比谁都强。Lùn yèwù, tā bǐ shéi dōu qiáng. Professionally, she is better than anyone else.

⑦to decide on, determine

不论 búlùn no matter whether; regardless of：不论你去不去 búlùn nǐ qù bu qù regardless of whether you go or not // 不论年龄 búlùn niánlíng regardless of age

高论 gāolùn enlightening remarks, brilliant views

结论 jiélùn a conclusion, verdict

理论 lǐlùn theory, principle; a theory

论功行赏 lùngōng-xíngshǎng to reward according to merit

论罪 lùnzuì to decide on the nature of the guilt：法官宣布对被告按过失杀人论罪，判决十年监禁。Fǎguān xuānbù duì bèigào àn guòshī shā rén lùnzuì, pànjué shí nián jiānjìn. The magistrate announced that the accused was guilty of manslaughter, and sentenced him to ten years imprisonment.

讨论 tǎolùn to discuss: 讨论问题 tǎolùn wèntí to discuss a problem or issue

文论 wénlùn a piece of scholarly writing

相对论 xiāngduìlùn the theory of relativity

相提并论 xiāngtí-bìnglùn to mention in the same breath, place at the same level or in the same category: 这两件事不能相提并论。Zhè liǎng jiàn shì bù néng xiāngtí-bìnglùn. These two matters cannot be discussed together (as if they were in the same category).

舆论 yúlùn public opinion

争论 zhēnglùn a controversy, debate; to debate, dispute: 争论是非 zhēnglùn shìfēi to argue about right and wrong

lún　论语 Lúnyǔ the *Analects of Confucius*

**捋**　luō → lǚ

**络**　luò　lào

luò　①to wrap, connect, enmesh

②to fasten with a net: 络着发网 luòzhe fàwǎng wearing a hairnet

③something shaped like a net, network

④a halter

联络 liánluò to get in touch, be in contact, allied; a linkage, contact, liaison: 他们联络了不少组织，共同发

起抗议。Tāmen liánluò le bù shǎo zǔzhī, gòngtóng fāqǐ kàngyì. They contacted quite a few organisations to start a protest together. // 请保持联络。Qǐng bǎochí liánluò. Please keep in touch.

笼络 lǒngluò to win over, "rope in": 笼络人心 lǒngluò rénxīn to win over people's hearts

马络头 mǎluòtou a horse's halter

网络 wǎngluò a network

lào　络子 làozi a carrying net, string bag

**咯** luò → gē

**烙** luò → lào

**落** luò　lào　là

luò　①to fall, drop, go down: 树叶落了。Shùyè luò le. The leaves have fallen. 太阳落山。Tàiyáng luò shān. The sun set.

②to decline, wane: 落到这步田地 luò dào zhè bù tiándì to have declined to this state

③to settle, remain

④a settlement

⑤to lag behind, fall behind

⑥to get, receive (as a result): 我干得这么辛苦, 反而落个埋怨。Wǒ gàn de zhème xīnkǔ, fǎn'ér luò ge mányuàn. I work so hard, and then I get the blame.

⑦to leave behind (a trace etc.): 不落痕迹 bú luò hénjì to leave no trace

⑧to fall to, rest with: 权力落在他们手中。Quánlì luò zài tāmen shǒu zhōng. Authority passed into their hands. // 重任落在我们肩上。Zhòng rèn luò zài wǒmen jiān shàng. A heavy responsibility rests on our shoulders.

部落 bùluò a tribe

降落 jiàngluò to descend, land: 跳伞员安全降落地面。Tiàosǎnyuán ānquán jiàngluò dìmiàn. The parachutist landed safely on the ground.

落后 luòhòu to fall behind; backward: 最后一场比赛红队落后两分。Zuìhòu yì chǎng bǐsài hóng duì luòhòu liǎng fēn. In the last match the red team fell behind by two points. // 这地区的工业很落后。Zhè dìqū de gōngyè hěn luòhòu. Industry in this region is very backward.

落户 luòhù to settle, set up house: 在农村落户 zài nóngcūn luòhù to settle in a farming village

落空 luòkōng to come to nothing, fail: 希望落空 xīwàng luòkōng hopes come to nothing

落选 luòxuǎn to lose an election: 张先生今年落选，未当上区议员。Zhāng xiānsheng jīnnián luòxuǎn, wèi dāng shàng qū yìyuán. Mr. Zhang lost this year's election, so he didn't become the district's member of parliament.

落叶 luòyè fallen leaves

没落 mòluò to decline, die out, become forgotten: 家道

没落。Jiādào mòluò. The family fortunes declined.

lào ①〈dial.〉 to fall, decline

②〈dial.〉 to get: 落好儿 lào hǎor to receive favourable comment

落价 làojià to fall in price: 西瓜落价了。Xīguā làojià le. Watermelons have dropped in price.

落色 làoshǎi to fade: 布料落色了。Bùliào làoshǎi le. The cloth has faded.

là ①〈coll.〉 to omit, forgetfully leave behind: 这里落了两个字。Zhèlǐ là le liǎng ge zì. Two characters have been left out here. // 我把书落在家里了。Wǒ bǎ shū là zài jiā li le. I (forgetfully) left my books at home.

②〈coll.〉 to fall behind: 落在大家后头 là zài dàjiā hòutou to fall behind the others

*Polyphonic compound*:

落下 luòxià to fall down: 升降机缓缓落下。Shēngjiàngjī huǎnhuǎn luòxia. The lift slowly descended.

　　làoxià 〈dial.〉 to get, end up with: 他在矿坑里干了二十年，落下一身风湿病。Tā zài kuàngkēng lǐ gànle èrshí nián, làoxià yì shēn fēngshī bìng. He worked in the mines for twenty years, and ended up with rheumatism all over.

　　làxia 〈coll.〉 to omit, forgetfully leave behind: 你走得慢些，别把那孩子落下。Nǐ zǒu de màn xiē, bié bǎ nà háizi làxia. Walk slower so you don't leave the child behind.

# M

**抹**　mā → mǒ

**蚂**　mǎ　mà　mā

mǎ　蚂蟥 mǎhuáng leech

　　蚂蚁 mǎyǐ ants

mà　蚂蚱 màzha〈dial.〉a kind of locust

mā　蚂螂 mālang〈dial.〉dragonflies

**埋**　mái　mán

mái　to bury, conceal: 把管子埋在地下 bǎ guǎnzi mái zài dì xià to bury pipes in the ground

埋伏 máifú an ambush; to lie in ambush: 中了埋伏 zhòngle máifú caught in an ambush // 埋伏在树林中 máifú zài shùlín zhōng lying in ambush in the forest

埋没 máimò to bury, cover up; to neglect, stifle: 泥石流把整个村庄埋没了。Níshíliú bǎ zhěnggè cūnzhuāng máimò le. The mud slide buried the entire village. // 天才被埋没了。Tiāncái bèi máimò le. The genius was overlooked.

埋葬 máizàng to bury (the dead); to get rid of: 埋葬尸

体 máizàng shītǐ to bury a body // 埋葬专制王朝 mái zàng zhuānzhì wángcháo to get rid of the autocratic monarchy

mán 埋怨 mányuàn to blame, complain, grumble; a grumbling complaint: 别埋怨我, 是你自己不小心。Bié mányuàn wǒ, shì nǐ zìjǐ bù xiǎoxīn. Don't hold it against me. It was your own carelessness. // 我受不了那种埋怨。Wǒ shòu bu liǎo nà zhǒng mányuàn. I can't endure that kind of grumbling.

# 脉 mài mò

mài ①arteries and veins
②pulse
③vein (of a leaf): 叶脉 yè mài leaf vein
④something in the shape of a network of blood vessels
脉搏 màibó pulse
脉络 màiluò a network of blood vessels; thread of thought
山脉 shānmài a mountain chain

mò 脉脉 mòmò affectionate, lovingly: 脉脉含情 mòmò hánqíng with loving eyes, full of tender affection

# 蔓 màn wàn mán

màn ①creeping plants
②to grow and spread (like creeping plants)
蔓草 màncǎo creeping grasses
蔓延 mànyán to grow and spread; widespread: 野火蔓延到了湖边。Yěhuǒ mànyán dàole hú biān. The

blaze spread to the edge of the lake.

**wàn** 〈dial.〉a creeping tendril vine

蔓儿 guāwànr a melon vine

**mán** 蔓菁 mánjing the rape-turnip

没 **méi　mò**

**méi** not; to have not; there is not: 没事 méi shì not busy; nothing important // 没法子。Méi fǎzi. There's no solution, no hope. // 他没去。Tā méi qù. He didn't go.

没趣 méiqù snubbed, put out: 觉得没趣 juéde méiqù to feel snubbed // 自讨没趣 zì tǎo méiqù to leave oneself open to a snub

没有 méiyǒu to have not; there is not

**mò** ①to sink, submerge: 没入水中 mò rù shuǐ zhōng to sink into water

②to overflow, rise beyond: 水深没顶。Shuǐ shēn mò dǐng. The water is deep enough to go over a person's head. // 洪水没过堤岸。Hóngshuǐ mòguò dī'àn. The flood waters rose beyond the embankment.

③to disappear, vanish

④to confiscate

沉没 chénmò to sink, drown: 那巨轮在离岸二十里处沉没。Nà jùlún zài lí àn èrshí lǐ chù chénmò. The supertanker sank at a spot twenty *li* from the shore.

泯没 mǐnmò to vanish: 那古迹早已泯没，无法寻到踪影了。Nà gǔjì zǎo yǐ mǐnmò, wúfǎ xúndào zōngyǐng le. That historic site vanished a long time ago, and there is no way of discovering any trace of it.

没收 mòshōu to confiscate：没收走私品 mòshōu zǒusīpǐn to confiscate contraband goods

**麇** méi → mí

**闷**　mèn　mēn

mèn ①depressed, bored：我闷得很，得出去散散心。Wǒ mèn de hěn, děi chūqu sàn sàn xīn. I'm awfully bored. I must go outside for a break.

②tightly closed, sealed

烦闷 fánmèn unhappy, worried, and taciturn

闷罐车 mènguànchē a sealed boxcar

闷葫芦 mènhúlu a complete mystery

闷闷不乐 mèn mèn bú lè unhappy, sullen

mēn ①stuffy：窗没开，屋里闷得很。Chuāng méi kāi, wū li mēn de hěn. The window has not been opened so the room is very stuffy.

②silent; dull-sounding：闷声不响 mēnshēng-bùxiǎng to remain silent // 闷声闷气 mēnshēng-mēnqì muffled, dull (of a sound or voice)

③to keep shut so air cannot circulate：刚沏的茶，闷一会儿再喝。Gāng qī de chá, mēn yíhuìr zài hē. The tea has just been made. Let it draw a while before drinking it.

④to shut inside：别老闷在屋里。Bié lǎo mēn zài wū li. Don't always shut yourself indoors.

闷热 mēnrè hot and sultry

# 蒙　　méng　měng　mēng

méng ①to cover: 蒙住眼睛 méng zhù yǎnjīng blindfolded // 蒙上一层灰 méng shàng yì céng huī covered with a layer of ash; to cover with a layer of ash

②to deceive, cover up, hide: 蒙在鼓里 méng zài gǔ lǐ to be kept inside a drum = to be "kept in the dark"

③to receive (help, kindness, etc.): 蒙您指引, 十分感谢。Méng nín zhǐyǐn, shífēn gǎnxiè. I am really grateful to have received your guidance.

④to suffer (injury, loss, etc.)

⑤ignorant, illiterate

⑥one of the 64 hexagrams, signifying youthful inexperience

⑦[a surname]

承蒙 chéngméng to be obliged (for a kindness); to be granted a favour: 承蒙张教授夸奖, 令我很受鼓舞。Chéngméng Zhāng jiàoshòu kuājiǎng, lìng wǒ hěn shòu gǔwǔ. I'm obliged to Professor Zhang for his praise; it gave me a lot of encouragement.

蒙蔽 méngbì to deceive, hide the truth from: 蒙蔽大家 méngbì dàjiā to hide the truth from everybody // 被人蒙蔽 bèi rén méngbì deceived by people

蒙难 méngnàn to meet with disaster(esp. violent death): 先父是二十年前蒙难的。Xiānfù shì èrshí nián qián méngnàn de. It was twenty years ago that my father was killed.

蒙受 méngshòu to suffer, sustain (injury, loss): 蒙受
不白之冤 méngshòu bù bái zhī yuān to suffer false
accusation

启蒙 qǐméng to enlighten, initiate, teach the ignorant:
启蒙教育 qǐméng jiàoyù enlightened education

**měng**　Mongolia

蒙古 Měnggǔ Mongolia

**mēng**　①to cheat, deceive: 他蒙人。Tā mēng rén. He cheated
people.

②unconscious: 他给打蒙了。Tā gěi dǎ mēng le. He
was knocked senseless.

③to make wild guesses: 你不懂行，就别瞎蒙了。Nǐ bù
dǒng háng, jiù bié xiā mēng le. If you don't understand the subject area, then don't make wild guesses.

蒙蒙亮 mēngmēngliàng the first glimmer of dawn

蒙骗 mēngpiàn to hoodwink, cheat

# 眯　mī　mí

**mī**　①to narrow one's eyes: 眯着眼 mīzhe yǎn narrowing the
eyes

②〈dial.〉to take a nap: 眯一会儿 mī yí huìr to take a
short nap

**mí**　to get something (e.g. dust) in one's eyes: 我眯了眼了。
Wǒ míle yǎn le. Something got in my eye.

# 糜　mí　méi

mí　①rice-gruel：糜粥 mí zhōu rice-gruel

②rotten

③extravagant

④〔a surname〕

糜费 mífèi to waste, spend extravagantly：糜费钱财 mífèi qiáncái to waste money

糜烂 mílàn rotten; dissolute：水果糜烂了。Shuǐguǒ mí làn le. The fruit is rotten. // 生活糜烂 shēnghuó mílàn to live dissolutely

méi　糜子 méizi a variety of panicled millet

# 靡　mǐ　mí

mǐ　①knocked over; blown away by the wind

②extravagant, elaborate

靡丽 mǐlì extravagantly magnificent, gorgeous

靡靡之音 mǐmǐ zhī yīn soft and sentimental music or songs

披靡 pīmǐ blown about by wind; routed (e.g. an army)

mí　①rotten

②( = 糜 ) extravagant

靡费 mífèi to waste, spend extravagantly

# 泌　mì　bì

mì　to excrete, secrete

分泌 fēnmì to secrete; secretions：树干上分泌出一种胶状液体。Shùgàn shang fēnmì chū yìzhǒng jiāozhuàng yètǐ. From the trunk of the tree a sticky liquid is secreted.

泌尿管 mìniàoguǎn the urinary passage

bì　泌水 Bìshuǐ a river in Henan Province

泌阳 Bìyáng a county in Henan Province

# 秘　mì　bì

mì　①secret

②to keep secret

密而不宣 mì ér bù xuān to keep secret

秘方 mìfāng a secret recipe

秘密 mìmì secret, clandestine

秘书 mìshū a secretary

bì　①( ＝ 闭 ) clogged, blocked

②［used in transcribing foreign words］

秘鲁 Bìlǔ Peru

便秘 biànbì constipation

# 无　mó → wú

# 模　mó　mú

mó　①a model, standard

②to copy, imitate

模仿 mófǎng to copy, imitate：那学生模仿老师的动作。Nà xuéshēng mófǎng lǎoshī de dòngzuò. The student imitated the teacher's movements.

模糊 móhu blurred, unclear

模棱两可 móléng liǎng kě vague and ambiguous

模型 móxíng a model (of a building etc.)

mú 〈mainly coll.〉mould, pattern

模样 múyàng appearance, shape, figure

模子 múzi a mould, form, die

# 磨　mó　mò

mó ①to grind, polish, rub: 磨刀 mó dāo to hone a knife //
磨光 mó guāng to polish, burnish

②to wear down, wear out: 这件大衣的袖口已经快磨
破了。Zhè jiàn dàyī de xiùkǒu yǐjīng kuài mópò le.
The cuffs of this overcoat are almost worn out.

③to trouble, pester: 磨嘴皮子 mó zuǐpízi〈coll.〉to
pester with incessant talk

④suffering

好事多磨。Hǎo shì duō mó. The path to happiness is
strewn with suffering/frustration.

磨灭 mómiè to wipe out, obliterate: 岁月无法磨灭他
铭刻心底的仇恨。Suìyuè wúfǎ mómiè tā míngkè
xīndǐ de chóuhèn. Time cannot obliterate the deep-
seated hatred in his heart.

磨难 mónàn hardships, sufferings

mò ①a mill: 一盘磨 yì pán mò one mill

②to grind: 磨豆腐 mò dòufu to grind soybeans

③〈dial.〉to turn: 这么重的东西，你一个人能把它磨
过来吗? Zhème zhòng de dōngxi, nǐ yí ge rén néng
bǎ tā mò guolai ma? Can you turn such a heavy thing
by yourself?

磨坊 mòfáng a mill（house）

磨盘 mòpán the lower millstone

**抹**　mǒ　mā　mò

mǒ　①to smear

　　②to eliminate: 抹脖子 mǒ bózi 〈coll.〉to slit one's throat

　　抹黑 mǒhēi to besmirch, blacken someone's name: 别老往我脸上抹黑! Bié lǎo wǎng wǒ liǎn shàng mǒhēi! Don't keep blackening my name!

　　抹杀 mǒshā to obliterate, deny, write off: 抹杀别人的功绩 mǒshā biérén de gōngjì to write off someone else's achievements

mā　to wipe: 抹桌子 mā zhuōzi to wipe the table // 你想抹抹脸吗? Nǐ xiǎng mā mā liǎn ma? Would you like to wipe your face? // 我实在是抹不下脸来。Wǒ shízài shì mā bu xià liǎn lái. I really can't put on a straight face.

　　抹布 mābù a cleaning rag

mò　①to plaster, smooth down: 抹墙 mò qiáng to plaster a wall

　　②to skirt, bypass

　　转弯抹角 zhuǎn wān mò jiǎo tortuous; to "beat about the bush"

**没**　mò → méi

**脉**　mò → mài

**貉**　mò → háo

**模**    mú → mó
**姥**    mǔ → lǎo

# N

**南**    nā → nán
**哪**    nǎ    na    né

nǎ    which?：哪所房子？Nǎ suǒ fángzi?（coll. also něi ...
        or nǎi ... ）which house?

        哪个 nǎge（coll. also něige or nǎige ）which?：哪个
        人？Nǎge rén? Which person?

        哪里？Nǎli? Where?

na    〔a sentence-final particle〕：好得很哪！Hǎo de hěn na !
        Really good!

né    〔used in transcribing foreign words〕

        哪吒 Nézhā Nata（a demon-king in Buddhism; a divine
        warrior in Chinese mythology）

**那**    nà    nā

nà    that, those：那种人 nà zhǒng rén（coll. also nèi ... or
        nè ... ）that sort of person

        那个 nàge（coll. also nèige or nège）that：那个人
        nàge rén that person

那里 nàlǐ there

nā ①〔a surname〕

②〔used in transcribing foreign words〕

那落迦 nāluòjiā hell（Sanskrit *naraka*）

## 娜 nà → nuó

## 南 nán　nā

nán ①south：从这儿往南走，十分钟就到。Cóng zhèr wǎng nán zǒu, shí fēnzhōng jiù dào. Go south from here and you'll be there in ten minutes.

②〔a surname〕

南方 nánfāng the south, the southern region

指南针 zhǐnánzhēn a magnetic compass

nā 〔used in transcribing Sanskrit words〕

南无 nāmó Hail!（Sanskrit *namo*）

## 难 nán　nàn

nán ①difficult, hard, troublesome：这工作难做。Zhè gōngzuò nán zuò. This work is hard to do. // 路难走。Lù nán zǒu. The road is bad. // 难听 nán tīng difficult to hear（also nántīng unpleasant sounding; see below）

②to put somebody into a difficult position：这事儿可把我难住了。Zhè shìr kě bǎ wǒ nán zhù le. This matter has put me in a difficult position.

③bad, unpleasant

难保 nánbǎo hard to say/know for sure：今天难保不下雨。Jīntiān nánbǎo bú xià yǔ. One can't be sure it won't rain today.

难道 nándào 〔used to introduce an emphatic rhetorical question〕：难道你忘了吗？ Nándào nǐ wàng le ma? Can you really have forgotten?

难过 nánguò sad; hard to bear

难受 nánshòu to feel unwell or unhappy：心里难受 xīn lǐ nánshòu feeling unhappy

难听 nántīng unpleasant sounding（also nán tīng difficult to hear; see above）

难为情 nánwéiqíng embarrassed, ashamed; embarrassing

难为 nánwei to cause difficulty for, to press; difficult to do：你太难为他了。 Nǐ tài nánwei tā le. You've been too much trouble to him.

nàn　①a disaster：这真是一个大难。 Zhè zhēn shi yí ge dà nàn. This really is a big disaster.

②to take to task, call to account

发难 fānàn to rebel; to launch an attack（usually verbal）：反对党抓住这次机会向执政党发难。 Fǎnduìdǎng zhuā zhù zhè cì jīhuì xiàng zhízhèngdǎng fānàn. The opposition seized this opportunity to launch an attack on the governing party.

难民 nànmín refugees

灾难 zāinàn a disaster

责难 zénàn to censure, blame：不要轻易责难别人。 Bú yào qīngyì zénàn bié rén. Don't lightly blame others.

# 哪

né → nǎ

# 呢

ní ne

ní ①a woollen fabric：呢大衣 ní dàyī a woollen overcoat

②〔onomatopoeia for chirping etc.〕

毛呢 máoní coarse woollens

呢喃 nínán〔onomatopoeia for chirping or murmuring, esp. of small birds〕

呢绒 níróng woollen materials

ne ①〔an interrogative sentence-final particle indicating ellipsis〕：你呢? Nǐ ne? And you?

②〔a sentence-final particle indicating incompleteness or continuation of an action〕：他还没来呢。Tā hái méi lái ne. He hasn't come yet. // 他们在吃饭呢。Tāmen zài chī fàn ne. They are eating.

③〔a particle signalling a pause within a sentence〕：我妈妈呢，她已经回去了。Wǒ māma ne, tā yǐjīng huíqù le. As for my mother, she's already gone back.

# 泥

ní nì

ní ①mud, clay：衣服沾上泥了。Yīfu zhān shang ní le. The clothes are splashed with mud. // 泥墙 ní qiáng a clay wall（also nì qiáng; see below）

②any paste-like substance

泥土 nítǔ mud and soil; muddy land

水泥 shuǐní cement

挖泥船 wāníchuán a dredge

印泥 yìnní a stamp pad for use with seals

nì ①to daub with mud or clay: 泥墙 nì qiáng to plaster over cracks in a wall (also ní qiáng; see above)

②stubborn, bigoted, obstinate

③to linger: 泥着不走 nìzhe bù zǒu hanging around persistently

拘泥 jūnì (also jūní) to adhere rigidly to (formalities etc.): 过分拘泥于形式 guòfèn jūnì yú xíngshì to adhere too rigidly to formalities

泥古 nìgǔ ultra-conservative

# 粘 nián zhān

nián ( = 黏 ) sticky, glutinous, viscous: 粘米 nián mǐ glutinous rice // 这胶水很粘。Zhè jiāoshuǐ hěn nián. This glue is really sticky.

粘土 niántǔ clay

粘性 niánxìng viscosity

粘液 niányè mucus

zhān to glue, stick, paste: 粘信封 zhān xìnfēng to seal up an envelope

粘连 zhānlián adhesions (after surgery)

# 鸟 niǎo diǎo

niǎo birds

鸟蛋 niǎodàn a bird's egg

鸟类 niǎolèi birds (of every type)

diǎo ⟨coll., often abusive⟩ the male genitals

# 尿　niào　suī

**niào**　①urine

②to urinate：尿床 niào chuáng to wet the bed

尿道 niàodào the urethra

尿素 niàosù urea

**suī**　〈coll.〉urine：小孩尿了一泡尿。Xiǎo hái niào le yì pāo suī. The child passed a bladderful of urine.

尿泡 suīpāo the bladder

# 拧　níng　nǐng　nìng

**níng**　to pinch, twist：拧他一把。Níng tā yì bǎ. Give him a pinch. // 拧毛巾 níng máojīn to wring out a towel // 拧眉瞪眼 níng méi dèng yǎn to twist the eyebrows and open the eyes wide ＝ to look at angrily

**nǐng**　①to twist, screw：拧开瓶盖 nǐng kāi píng gài to screw open a bottle // 拧水龙头 nǐng shuǐlóngtóu to turn a tap

②mistaken：我听拧了，把王林当成王力。Wǒ tīng nǐng le, bǎ Wáng Lín dàng chéng Wáng Lì. I heard wrongly, and took Wang Lin for Wang Li.

③at cross-purposes：他俩说拧了，谁也不服谁。Tā liǎ shuō nǐng le, shéi yě bù fú shéi. They were talking at cross-purposes, and neither would listen to the other.

**nìng**　〈dial.〉dogged, stubborn

拧性 nìngxìng stubbornness：他那拧性一辈子也改不了。Tā nà nìngxìng yíbèizi yě gǎi bu liǎo. His stubborn disposition can never be changed.

拧种 nìngzhǒng an incurably stubborn person: 那孩子是
个拧种，别理他! Nà háizi shì ge nìngzhǒng, bié lǐ
tā! That child is an incurably stubborn type. Take no
notice of him!

# 宁　nìng　níng

nìng ①rather, would rather, would better

②[a surname]

宁可 nìngkě would rather: 我宁可走着，也不坐他的
车。Wǒ nìngkě zǒuzhe, yě bú zuò tā de chē. I
would rather walk than go in his car.

宁缺毋滥 nìng quē wú làn rather go without than have
something shoddy = to put quality first

níng quiet, peaceful

安宁 ānníng at peace, composed: 孩子吵得大家都不
安宁。Háizi chǎo de dàjiā dōu bù ānníng. The children made so much noise that everyone was disturbed.

宁静 níngjìng peaceful and quiet: 宁静的夜晚 níngjìng
de yèwǎn a quiet evening

宁夏 Níngxià Ningxia (Hui Autonomous Region in north-
west China)

# 拗　niù → ǎo
# 弄　nòng　lòng

nòng to handle, perform, play with: 弄饭 nòng fàn to prepare
food // 小心点，别把仪器弄坏了。Xiǎoxīn diǎn, bié

bǎ yíqì nòng huài le. Be careful. Don't damage the apparatus.

玩弄 wánnòng to dally with, play with; to resort to: 玩弄女性 wánnòng nǚxìng to philander, dally with women // 玩弄词句 wánnòng cíjù to juggle with words // 玩弄鬼花招 wánnòng guǐ huāzhāo to resort to evil tricks

lòng ⟨dial.⟩ a small lane

里弄 lǐlòng lanes and alleys; a neighbourhood

弄堂 lòngtáng a small lane

# 疟　nüè　yào

nüè malaria

疟疾 nüèjì malaria

疟蚊 nüèwén the malaria-bearing mosquito

yào 疟子 yàozi ⟨coll.⟩ malaria

# 娜　nuó　nà

nuó tender, graceful

婀娜 ēnuó graceful (of a female figure)

nà 〔used in transcribing foreign words〕

安娜 Ānnà Anna

# 喏　nuò　rě

nuò 〔an attention-calling interjection〕: 喏，这不是你的书吗？Nuò, zhè bú shì nǐ de shū ma? Hey, isn't this your book?

rě ⟨arch.⟩〔a polite reply of assent〕

唱喏 chàngrě ⟨arch.⟩ to salute respectfully

# O

区　　ōu → qū

沤　　òu　ōu

òu　①to soak in water：沤麻 òu má to soak or ret hemp

②constantly damp

沤肥 òuféi to make（wet）compost

ōu　bubbles

浮沤 fú'ōu ⟨lit.⟩ froth, foam

# P

扒　　pá → bā

耙　　pá　bà

pá　①to rake：把地耙平 bǎ dì pá píng to rake the soil level

②a rake

耙子 pázi a rake

bà ①to harrow or plough: 耙地 bà dì to harrow the ground

②a harrow

圆盘耙 yuánpánbà a disc harrow

# 排 pái pǎi

pái ①a row, rank, volley: 一排树木 yì pái shùmù a row of trees

②to place in order, set out in rows: 把椅子排整齐 bǎ yǐzi pái zhěngqí to line up chairs neatly // 排队 pái duì to form a queue // 排字 pái zì to set type (in printing) // 排节目 pái jiémù to arrange a programme

③to push out, discharge, exclude: 排脓 pái nóng to discharge pus // 排水 pái shuǐ to drain off water

④a platoon

⑤to rehearse: 排戏 pái xì to rehearse a play

⑥a raft: 竹排 zhú pái a bamboo raft

安排 ānpái to arrange: 明天的活动都安排好了吗? Míngtiān de huódòng dōu ānpái hǎo le ma? Have tomorrow's activities all been arranged?

排斥 páichì to exclude: 排斥外人 páichì wàirén to exclude outsiders

排除 páichú to remove, get rid of: 排除异己 páichú yìjǐ to get rid of dissidents; to discriminate against those with views different from one's own

排骨 páigǔ ribs

排挤 páijǐ to push aside, elbow out: 互相排挤 hùxiāng páijǐ each trying to squeeze the other out

排演 páiyǎn to rehearse：排演一出戏 páiyǎn yì chū xì
　　to rehearse a play

**pǎi**　排子车 pǎizichē〈dial.〉a kind of hand-pulled cart for
　　transporting goods

迫　pǎi → pò

番　pān → fān

胖　pán → pàng

膀　pāng páng → bǎng

磅　páng → bàng

胖　pàng　pán

**pàng**　fat, stout（of people）

肥胖 féipàng fat

胖子 pàngzi a fat person

**pán**　〈lit.〉comfortable and contented, fit and happy

心广体胖 xīnguǎng-tǐpán When the heart is contented,
　　the body grows fat. = healthy in mind and body

刨　páo　bào

**páo**　①to dig up：刨土 páo tǔ to dig the ground

②to deduct, exclude：刨去 páo qù exclusive of, not
　　counting

刨根儿 páogēnr〈coll.〉to investigate thoroughly, get to
　　the bottom of（a matter）

**bào**　①to plane wood：刨木头 bào mùtou to plane wood

②a plane（for woodworking）

刨床 bàochuáng a planing machine

刨花 bàohuā wood shavings

刨子 bàozi a plane (for woodworking)

# 跑 pǎo pǎo

pǎo ①to run: 她跑得很快。Tā pǎo de hěn kuài. She ran quickly.

②to flee: 犯人跑了。Fànrén pǎo le. The criminal fled.

③to leak (e.g. a tyre): 车胎跑气了。Chē tāi pǎo qì le. The tyre leaked. // 轮胎气跑光了。Lúntāi qì pǎo guāng le. All the air has leaked out of the tyre.

④to run errands, go about doing business: 跑买卖 pǎo mǎimai to work as a travelling salesperson or a commercial traveller

跑步 pǎobù to go jogging: 在操场上跑步 zài cāochǎng shang pǎobù jogging on a sports ground

跑道 pǎodào a runway (for planes); a running track (for athletes)

跑电 pǎodiàn leakage of electricity

跑腿儿 pǎotuǐr to run errands

pǎo to paw the ground

虎跑泉 Hǔpǎo Quán a spring in Hangzhou (from a tale about a tiger pawing the ground there)

# 泡 pào pāo

pào ①a bubble, blister: 起泡儿 qǐ pàor to raise a blister

②to infuse, soak, pickle: 泡茶 pào chá to brew tea //

泡菜 pào cài to pickle vegetables (also pàocài; see below)

③to dawdle: 别瞎泡了! Bié xiā pào le! Stop dawdling!

泡菜 pàocài pickled vegetables (also pào cài; see above)

泡沫 pàomò foam, froth

泡泡糖 pàopaotáng bubble gum

pāo ①〈coll.〉 spongy, light, insubstantial: 面包很泡。 Miànbāo hěn pāo. The bread is very light.

②anything puffy and soft: 豆腐泡儿 dòufu pāor bean-curd puffs

③[a measure word for portions of liquid]: 一泡尿 yì pāo niào one passage of urine

# 炮　　pào　bāo　páo

pào a cannon

炮火 pàohuǒ artillery fire

炮手 pàoshǒu a gunner

炮仗 pàozhang firecrackers

bāo ①to quick-fry: 炮肉 bāo ròu quick-fried meat

②to heat: 炮干 bāo gān to dry by heating

páo ①to refine by heating

②to roast

炮炼 páoliàn to refine or decoct medicine by heating: 炮炼丹丸 páoliàn dān wán to make pills (e.g. Daoist immortality pills, by heat refining)

炮烙 páoluò an ancient form of punishment using heated

metal pillars

炮制 páozhì to refine medicine by heating; to concoct (a scheme)：炮制中药 páozhì Zhōngyào to make Chinese medicine using heat// 炮制出一套反革命的方案 páozhì chū yí tào fǎn gémìng de fāng'àn to concoct a counter-revolutionary scheme

## 喷　pēn　pèn

pēn　to spurt out：喷出来 pēn chūlai to come spraying or gushing out // 泉水喷得很高。Quánshuǐ pēn de hěn gāo. The water from the spring spurted very high.

喷射 pēnshè to spray, spurt：火花不断地从炉顶上喷射出来。Huǒhuā búduàn de cóng lú dǐng shàng pēnshè chūlai. Sparks continuously shoot out from the top of the furnace.

喷水池 pēnshuǐchí a fountain

喷嚏 pēntì a sneeze

pèn　①〈dial.〉strong (of odours)

②[a measure word for certain crops, harvests (e.g. cotton)]：头喷儿棉花 tóu pènr miánhuā the first crop of cotton

③the season (e.g. for a certain fruit)：西瓜正在喷儿上。Xīguā zhèngzài pènr shang. Watermelons are in season right now.

喷香 pènxiāng strongly fragrant, very delicious

## 澎　péng　pēng

péng 澎湖 Pénghú the Pescadores (Islands)

澎湃 péngpài roaring (of waves)

pēng 〈dial.〉 to splash; splashing：泥浆澎了我一身。Níjiāng pēngle wǒ yì shēn. The mud splashed all over me.

# 劈 pī pǐ

pī ①to chop, split, or cleave using an axe or heavy chopper：劈柴 pī chái to chop wood (also pǐchái; see below) // 劈山开路 pī shān kāi lù to cut away hillsides to build roads

②to strike with a sudden vertical movement：他让雷给劈了。Tā ràng léi gěi pī le. He was struck by lightning.

③right against (one's face etc.)

④[onomatopoeia]

⑤a wedge

劈刀 pīdāo a chopper for splitting wood etc.; sabre fighting

劈里啪啦 pīlipālā [onomatopoeia for cracking or banging sounds]

劈面 pīmiàn right in the face

劈头盖脸 pītóu-gàiliǎn right in the face

pǐ ①to divide, split, separate：他把绳劈成三股。Tā bǎ shéng pǐ chéng sān gǔ. He separated the rope into three strands.

②to spread the legs or fingers widely：劈开双腿 pǐ kāi shuāng tuǐ to spread one's legs wide

劈叉 pǐchà to do the splits; the act of doing the

splits

劈柴 pǐchái wood chips for kindling or fuel（also pī chái; see above）

## 否 pǐ → fǒu

## 辟 pì bì

pì

①to open up（new land，field of study）：在密林中辟出一条通道 zài mìlín zhōng pì chū yì tiáo tōngdào to open a road through dense forest

②to refute

③penetrating，incisive

④〈arch.〉law; a law，statute

大辟 dàpì〈arch.〉law concerning capital punishment

精辟 jīngpì incisive：精辟的分析 jīngpì de fēnxì an incisive analysis

开辟 kāipì to open up，develop（new land etc.）：开辟田地 kāipì tiándì to open up agricultural land // 开辟新的研究领域 kāipì xīn de yánjiū lǐngyù to open up new areas of research

辟谣 pìyáo to refute a rumour：张贴布告辟谣 zhāngtiē bùgào pìyáo to put up notices refuting a rumour

bì

①〈lit.〉monarch

②to fight off，escape，avoid

辟邪（also 避邪）bìxié to ward off evil spirits：大门口上边那面小镜子是用来辟邪的。Dà ménkǒu shàngbian nà miàn xiǎo jìngzi shì yònglái bìxié de.

That small mirror over the main door is to ward off evil spirits.

复辟 fùbì to restore the monarchy: 那王朝是在哪年复辟的? Nà wángcháo shì zài nǎ nián fùbì de? In which year was that dynasty restored?

# 便 pián → biàn

# 片 piàn piān

piàn ①a piece, slice: 肉片 ròu piàn slices of meat

②a small card

③to slice: 片肉 piàn ròu to slice meat

④[a measure word for flat portions]: 一片汪洋 yí piàn wāngyáng a vast expanse of water // 一片草原 yí piàn cǎoyuán a stretch of grassy plain

⑤uncompleted, partial, brief

⑥[a measure word, used with 一 yí, for scenes, situations, speech, feelings, etc.]: 一片繁忙景象 yí piàn fánmáng jǐngxiàng a vast scene of busy activity // 一片春光 yí piàn chūnguāng a vast spring scene // 一片欢呼声 yí piàn huānhūshēng a vast scene of loud rejoicing // 一片胡言乱语 yí piàn húyán luànyǔ a load of utter nonsense // 一片真情 yí piàn zhēnqíng total sincerity

⑦a small area within a larger region: 这工厂是他们那一片的, 不归我们管。Zhè gōngchǎng shì tāmen nà yí piàn de, bù guī wǒmen guǎn. This factory belongs to their region, so is not under our administration.

唱片 chàngpiàn a gramophone record

名片 míngpiàn a name-card

片面 piànmiàn one-sided, biased

相片 xiàngpiàn a photograph

piān ⟨coll.⟩ a piece, slice, etc.

相片儿 xiàngpiānr a photograph

*Polyphonic compound*:

片子 piànzi a sheet or slice: 铁片子 tiě piànzi a sheet of iron

piānzi ⟨coll.⟩ a cinema film; an X-ray photograph; a gramophone record

# 漂 piāo piǎo piào

piāo to drift, float: 许多树叶漂在湖面。Xǔduō shùyè piāo zài hú miàn. Quite a lot of leaves were floating on the lake.

漂浮 piāofú to drift: 那船马达坏了，只能顺流漂浮。Nà chuán mǎdá huài le, zhǐ néng shùn liú piāofú. The boat's motor broke down, so it could only drift with the current.

水漂儿 shuǐpiāor a float or buoy

piǎo ①to bleach

②to rinse out: 把衣服漂一漂。Bǎ yīfu piǎo yi piǎo. Rinse out the clothes.

漂白 piǎobái to bleach: 漂白布料 piǎobái bùliào to bleach cloth

**piào** ①〈dial.〉to come to nothing, fail：漂账 piào zhàng to fail to pay debts // 这事要漂了。Zhè shì yào piào le. This affair will be a failure.

②beautiful

漂亮 piàoliàng beautiful, pretty

**朴** piáo → pǔ

**撇** piē   piě

**piē** ①to throw away, desert, abandon：他把朋友全撇下不管了。Tā bǎ péngyou quán piēxià bù guǎn le. He abandoned his friends and gave no more thought to them. // 她忙于工作，把家务事全撇开了。Tā máng yú gōngzuò, bǎ jiāwù shì quán piēkāi le. She was so busy with her job that she completely neglected the housework.

②to skim：撇油 piē yóu to skim off oil

**piě** ①the stroke 丿 in calligraphy：一撇 yì piě a brush-stroke of the form 丿

②to curl (the lips) in contempt, disappointment, unhappiness, etc.：撇了撇嘴 piě le piě zuǐ curled the lips (as if about to cry)

③to throw horizontally：撇瓦片 piě wǎpiàn to throw (horizontally) pieces of tile // 把妈说的话撇到脑后 bǎ mā shuō de huà piě dào nǎo hòu to ignore Mother's words completely ("toss them to the back of one's mind")

④〔a measure word for objects having the shape 丿〕：两
撇胡子 liǎng piě húzi a pair of sweeping moustaches

**冯** píng → féng

**屏** píng　bǐng

píng ①a screen

②a set of scrolls

③to screen, shield

屏蔽 píngbì to screen; a screen, barrier：屏蔽在山后的
小村 píngbì zài shān hòu de xiǎo cūn a village
screened behind the hills

屏风 píngfēng a movable door-screen

屏条 píngtiáo a set of hanging scrolls

屏障 píngzhàng a barrier

bǐng ①to reject

②to stop：屏着气不敢出声 bǐngzhe qì bù gǎn chū
shēng holding one's breath, not daring to make a sound

屏弃 bǐngqì to discard：屏弃不良习惯 bǐngqì bùliáng
xíguàn to discard bad customs

屏息 bǐngxī to hold one's breath：屏息静听 bǐngxī jìng
tīng to hold one's breath and listen quietly

**朴** pō pò → pǔ

**泊** pō → bó

**迫** pò　pǎi

**pò**　①to compel, force, press

②urgent, pressing

③to press toward

被迫 bèipò forced (into some course of action)：被迫卖淫 bèipò màiyín forced into prostitution

紧迫 jǐnpò pressing, urgent：时间紧迫 shíjiān jǐnpò pressed for time

迫不及待 pòbùjídài critically urgent, requiring immediate action; too impatient to wait

迫害 pòhài to persecute; persecution：迫害无辜儿童 pòhài wúgū értóng to persecute innocent children

迫近 pòjìn to press on toward (a goal, destination); to draw near：敌军迫近城市。Díjūn pòjìn chéngshì. The enemy forces pressed on toward the city.

**pǎi**　迫击炮 pǎijīpào a mortar (artillery)

# 铺　pū　pù

**pū**　to set out in order, lay out：铺铁轨 pū tiěguǐ to lay railway tracks // 铺砖 pū zhuān to lay bricks // 铺床 pū chuáng to make the bed

铺垫 pūdiàn bedding; foreshadowing：为故事高潮作铺垫 wèi gùshi gāocháo zuò pūdiàn foreshadowing the climax of the story

铺盖 pūgai bedding

铺排 pūpái to arrange things in order;〈dial.〉extravagant：将一应事宜铺排停当 jiāng yìyīng shìyí pūpái tíngdàng to arrange all the matters satisfactorily

铺张 pūzhāng extravagant：婚事办得过于铺张。
Hūnshì bàn de guòyú pūzhāng. The wedding was
too extravagant.

pù　①a bed

②a shop

③〔a component of place-names〕(signifying a former stag-
ing post)

地铺 dìpù a bed on the ground：打地铺 dǎ dìpù to make
up a bed on the ground

铺子 pùzi a shop

十里铺 Shílǐpù〔a common place-name〕

卧铺 wòpù a sleeping berth (on a train)

# 仆　pú　pū

pú　a servant

仆从 púcóng a footman; a retainer; a lackey

仆人 púrén a (domestic) servant

pū　to fall forward, fall prostrate

前仆后继 qiánpū -hòujì one stepping into the breach as
another falls

# 脯　pú → fǔ

# 朴　pǔ　pò　piáo　pō

pǔ　plain, simple

俭朴 jiǎnpǔ thrifty and simple, economical：生活俭朴
shēnghuó jiǎnpǔ living a thrifty and simple life

朴实 pǔshí simple, plain, sincere, honest：文风朴实

wénfēng pǔshí in a simple writing style // 为人朴实 wéi rén pǔshí having a simple and sincere nature // 朴实的作风 pǔshí de zuòfēng an honest way of doing things

朴素 pǔsù simple, plain: 穿着很朴素 chuānzhuó hěn pǔsù dressed simply

朴质 pǔzhì honest, straightforward, simple and natural (of a person): 朴质的性格 pǔzhì de xìnggé an honest and natural character

pò the Chinese hackberry (*Celtis sinensis*)

朴硝 pòxiāo saltpetre

piáo 〔a surname〕

pō 朴刀 pōdāo a kind of knife

## 堡 pù → bǎo

# Q

## 缉 qī → jī

## 奇 qí jī

qí strange, unusual, unexpected

不足为奇 bùzú wéi qí not at all surprising

奇怪 qíguài strange, odd

奇妙 qímiào marvellous

奇异 qíyì unusual, extraordinary

jī　odd, unpaired

奇数 jīshù an odd number

荞　qí → jì

稽　qǐ → jī

卡　qiǎ → kǎ

纤　qiàn → xiān

强　qiáng　qiǎng　jiàng

qiáng ①strong, energetic：工作能力很强 gōngzuò nénglì hěn qiáng having great capacity for work // 责任心强 zérènxīn qiáng having a strong sense of responsibility

②better, more than：他比我强。Tā bǐ wǒ qiáng. He is better than me. // 百分之十强 bǎi fēn zhī shí qiáng more than ten percent

③by force：强取 qiáng qǔ to take by force

强大 qiángdà big and powerful：力量强大 lìliàng qiángdà having great strength or power

强调 qiángdiào to emphasise：强调学习的重要性 qiángdiào xuéxí de zhòngyàoxìng to emphasise the importance of study

强国 qiángguó a powerful nation

强奸 qiángjiān rape; to rape

强烈 qiángliè very strong; intense：强烈反对 qiángliè

fǎnduì to oppose strongly // 强烈的仇恨 qiángliè de chóuhèn intense hatred // 强烈的情欲 qiángliè de qíngyù very strong (sexual) passion

强壮 qiángzhuàng strong, robust: 强壮的身体 qiángzhuàng de shēntǐ a sturdy body

**qiǎng** to force, insist

勉强 miǎnqiǎng to compel (someone to do something against his will); to manage with effort; reluctantly; inadequate but almost passable; strained or far-fetched: 不要勉强他了。Bú yào miǎnqiǎng tā le. Don't force him to do it. // 病人勉强吃了点儿东西。Bìngrén miǎnqiǎng chīle diǎnr dōngxi. With an effort the patient managed some food. // 他勉强同意了。Tā miǎnqiǎng tóngyì le. He reluctantly agreed. // 你的理由很勉强。Nǐ de lǐyóu hěn miǎnqiǎng. Your reason is very far-fetched. // 这些钱勉强够用。Zhèxiē qián miǎnqiǎng gòu yòng. This money is barely sufficient.

强辩 qiǎngbiàn to defend oneself with sophistry: 不要强辩了! Bú yào qiǎngbiàn le! Stop resorting to sophistry!

强迫 qiǎngpò to compel: 强迫战俘做苦工 qiǎngpò zhànfú zuò kǔgōng to compel prisoners-of-war to do hard labour

**jiàng** inflexible, stubborn: 强脾气 jiàng píqi an obstinate disposition

倔强 juéjiàng stubborn, unbending

强嘴（also 犟嘴）jiàngzuǐ to answer back defiantly and
stubbornly

## 抢 qiǎng   qiāng

qiǎng ①to take by force, grab, snatch：钱被歹徒抢了。Qián
bèi dǎitú qiǎng le. The money was taken with force by
a rogue.

②to vie for, scramble for：抢球 qiǎng qiú to scramble for
a ball // 抢干重活 qiǎng gàn zhòng huó to vie with
one another for the hardest job

③to rush：抢着在暴雨之前把谷子收进仓库 qiǎngzhe
zài bàoyǔ zhī qián bǎ gǔzi shōujìn cāngkù rushing to
get the grain into the granary before the storm

④〈dial.〉to scrape：磨剪子抢菜刀 mó jiǎnzi qiǎng
càidāo to sharpen scissors and knives

qiāng ①（＝戗）to go against, in the opposite direction

②〈lit.〉to knock, hit

呼天抢地 hū tiān qiāng dì to cry out to heaven and beat
one's head on the ground ＝ to lament loudly

抢风 qiāngfēng a head wind; against the wind：小船抢
风行驶，速度很慢。Xiǎo chuán qiāngfēng xíngshǐ,
sùdù hěn màn. The small boat was going against the
wind, so its speed was very slow.

## 呛 qiàng   qiāng

qiàng to irritate（the respiratory organs）：呛鼻子 qiàng bízi to

irritate the nose // 油烟呛人。Yóu yān qiàng rén. The oil fumes are irritating.

**qiāng** to choke; to cough: 他喝呛了。Tā hē qiāng le. He choked on his drink. // 呛了嗓子 qiāngle sǎngzi choked

## 戗　　qiàng　qiāng

**qiàng** ①to prop up: 用木柱把墙戗上 yòng mùzhù bǎ qiáng qiàng shang to prop up a wall with a wooden post

②a prop

戗柱 qiàngzhù a buttress

**qiāng** to break off, oppose: 话说戗了。Huà shuō qiāng le. The talk led to an impasse.

戗风 qiāngfēng against the wind: 戗风行船 qiāngfēng xíng chuán to sail against the wind

## 雀　　qiāo qiǎo → què

## 翘　　qiào　qiáo

**qiào** to project upward: 翘起来 qiào qilai to stick up // 翘辫子 qiào biànzi ⟨coll., humorous or ironic⟩ to die // 翘尾巴 qiào wěiba to raise one's tail = to behave self-importantly or arrogantly

**qiáo** ①⟨lit.⟩ to raise

②upstanding tail feathers

③an ancient women's hair ornament

④outstanding

翠翘 cuìqiáo kingfisher feathers; an ancient hair ornament for women

翘楚 qiáochǔ an outstanding or very talented person

翘首 qiáoshǒu to raise one's head to look up：翘首望天 qiáoshǒu wàng tiān to raise one's head and look up at the sky

## 切 qiē qiè

qiē

to cut：切肉 qiē ròu to cut meat

切磋 qiēcuō to "cut and polish" = to learn by exchanging ideas and comparing experiences：她在工作中经常与同事互相切磋。Tā zài gōngzuò zhōng jīngcháng yǔ tóngshì hùxiāng qiēcuō. She and her colleagues often learn from one another by exchanging ideas at work.

切线 qiēxiàn a tangent

qiè

① to get or stay close to

② to correspond to：不切实际 bú qiè shíjì not corresponding to the facts

③ eager：回乡心切 huí xiāng xīn qiè eager to return to one's home town

④ sincere，firm

⑤ to diagnose by feeling the pulse

⑥ to be sure to . . .：切勿迟延。Qiè wù chíyán. Be sure not to be late. // 切不可自暴自弃。Qiè bù kě zì bào zì qì. Don't on any account lose faith in yourself.

反切 fǎnqiè an ancient system for representing the pronunciation of characters

恳切 kěnqiè sincere：言辞恳切 yáncí kěnqiè sincere in what one says

密切 mìqiè close, intimate：很密切的关系 hěn mìqiè de guānxi a close/intimate relationship

切合 qièhé in accordance with, fitting with：切合实际 qièhé shíjì in accordance with the facts

切脉 qièmài to feel the pulse：给病人切脉 gěi bìngrén qièmài to take a patient's pulse

亲切 qīnqiè sincere, warm：亲切待人 qīnqiè dài rén to treat people with sincerity

一切 yíqiè all

*Polyphonic compound*：

切口 qiēkǒu an incision, cut：手术切口太大，不易愈合。Shǒushù qiēkǒu tài dà, búyì yùhé. The surgical incision was very large and not easy to heal.

qièkǒu argot, cant, cryptic jargon：那黑帮里用的切口太多，外人听不懂。Nà hēibāng lǐ yòng de qiè kǒu tài duō, wàirén tīng bu dǒng. In that gang they speak so much cant that outsiders can't understand them.

茄　qié　jiā

qié the egg-plant

番茄 fānqié the tomato

茄子 qiézi the egg-plant

jiā ①the stalk of the lotus

②〔used in transcribing foreign words〕

雪茄 xuějiā à cigar

# 亲 qīn qìng

**qīn** ① parents

② blood relatives, close kin: 亲兄弟 qīn xiōngdì blood brothers // 亲叔叔 qīn shūshu a blood-related uncle

③ relatives

④ marriage, match: 两家结了亲。Liǎng jiā jiéle qīn. The two families were joined by marriage.

⑤ loving, intimate, close: 亲如一家 qīn rú yì jiā as close as members of the same family

⑥ to kiss: 他在我的脸上亲了一下。Tā zài wǒ de liǎn shang qīn le yíxià. He kissed my cheek.

父亲 fùqīn a father

亲爱 qīn'ài dear, beloved

亲戚 qīnqi relatives

亲事 qīnshì a marriage

亲手 qīnshǒu with one's own hands, in person, oneself: 我亲手把信交给她了。Wǒ qīnshǒu bǎ xìn jiāo gěi tā le. I delivered the letter to her personally.

亲吻 qīnwěn a loving kiss; to kiss lovingly

亲信 qīnxìn a trusted follower

亲自 qīnzì in person, oneself: 张局长亲自到了工地。Zhāng júzhǎng qīnzì dàole gōngdì. Bureau chief Zhang went in person to the work-site.

亲族 qīnzú members of the same clan

双亲 shuāngqīn both parents

沾亲带故 zhānqīn-dàigù to have ties of kinship or

friendship

**qìng** 亲家 qìngjia in-laws

亲家公 qìngjiagōng 〈coll.〉 son's or daughter's father-in-law

亲家母 qìngjiamǔ 〈coll.〉 son's or daughter's mother-in-law

**龟** qiū → guī

**区** qū　ōu

**qū** ①an area, district, region

②an administrative division

③to distinguish, divide

林区 línqū a forest region

区别 qūbié to distinguish, differentiate; a difference: 区别好坏 qūbié hǎohuài to distinguish between good and bad// 这两种药品的疗效区别很大。Zhè liǎng zhǒng yàopǐn de liáoxiào qūbié hěn dà. There is a big difference in the curative effects of these two medications.

区分 qūfēn to distinguish, differentiate: 把质量不同的产品区分开来 bǎ zhìliàng bùtóng de chǎnpǐn qūfēn kāilái to distinguish between products of different quality

区间车 qūjiānchē a train or bus travelling only part of its normal route

区域 qūyù a region, area, district

山区 shānqū a mountain area

商业区 shāngyèqū a business district

自治区 zìzhìqū an autonomous region

ōu 〔a surname〕

# 曲    qǔ    qū

qǔ    ①a piece of music

②a form of classical Chinese verse

歌曲 gēqǔ a song

曲本 qǔběn a libretto

散曲 sǎnqǔ a type of classical Chinese verse

协奏曲 xiézòuqǔ a concerto

qū    ①bent, curved

②wrong, irrational

③a bend (in a road, river, etc.)

④yeast

河曲 héqū a bend in a river

曲解 qūjiě to misinterpret (intentionally), twist: 他曲解了我的意思。Tā qūjiěle wǒ de yìsi. He intentionally misinterpreted my meaning.

曲径 qūjìng a winding path

曲直 qūzhí right and wrong: 曲直不分 qūzhí bù fēn failing to distinguish right from wrong

弯曲 wānqū twisted, curved

心曲 xīnqū one's innermost thoughts

*Polyphonic compound*:

酒曲 jiǔqǔ a drinking song

jiǔqū brewer's yeast

# 圈　quān　juān　juàn

**quān** ①a circle：在地上画个圈 zài dì shang huà ge quān to draw a circle on the ground

②to encircle：圈地 quān dì to encircle a piece of land：用篱笆把鸡圈起来 yòng líba bǎ jī quān qilai to enclose chickens with a bamboo fence

③to mark with a circle：在名册中将他的名字圈了一下 zài míngcè zhōng jiāng tā de míngzi quānle yíxià circled his name on the roll

圈套 quāntào a trap, snare

文化圈 wénhuàquān cultural circles

圆圈 yuánquān a circle

**juān** to pen in, shut up (animals, people)：把牲口圈住 bǎ shēngkou juānzhù to pen in draught animals

**juàn** an enclosure (usually for livestock)

猪圈 zhūjuàn a pig pen

# 雀　què　qiǎo　qiāo

**què** certain types of small birds

黄雀 huángquè the oriole

孔雀 kǒngquè the peacock

麻雀 máquè the common sparrow; mahjong

雀斑 quèbān freckles

雀跃 quèyuè to jump for joy：挤在大街上的人群欢呼雀跃，个个都很激动。Jǐ zài dàjiē shang de rénqún huānhū quèyuè; gègè dōu hěn jīdòng. The crowd filling the streets cheered joyfully; they were all very excited.

qiǎo　雀盲眼 qiǎomángyǎn 〈dial.〉 a person suffering from night blindness

qiāo　雀子 qiāozi 〈dial.〉 freckles

# R

嚷　rǎng　rāng

rǎng　to shout, bawl：别嚷，老人在睡觉呢。Bié rǎng , lǎo rén zài shuìjiào ne. Don't shout. The old people are sleeping. // 你嚷什么? Nǐ rǎng shénme? What are you shouting for?

rāng　嚷嚷 rāngrang 〈coll.〉 to make a noise; to spread the news：别嚷嚷。Bié rāngrang. Don't make a noise. // 门外闹嚷嚷的，是不是出了什么事? Mén wài nào rāngrāng de, shì bu shì chūle shénme shì? There's a lot of noise outside. Could it be that something has happened?

喏　rě → nuò

任　rèn　rén

rèn　①duty

②a position, appointment

③to appoint

④to take up a post or job: 你在哪一期间任该厂厂长？Nǐ zài nǎ yì qījiān rèn gāi chǎng chǎngzhǎng? For what period were you in charge of that factory?

⑤to take on, undertake

⑥〔a measure word for positions or appointments〕: 当过两任总统 dāng guò liǎng rèn zǒngtǒng served two terms as president

⑦to allow, let: 这些衣服任你挑选。Zhè xiē yīfu rèn nǐ tiāoxuǎn. You are allowed to choose freely from among these clothes.

⑧no matter (how, what, ...): 任你怎么说，他也不听。Rèn nǐ zěnme shuō, tā yě bù tīng. No matter what you say, he still won't listen.

就任 jiùrèn to take up a position: 老张昨天就任厂长。Lǎo Zhāng zuótiān jiùrèn chǎngzhǎng. Yesterday Lao Zhang took up the position of factory manager.

离任 lírèn to leave a job, retire: 你爸爸什么时候离任的？Nǐ bàba shénme shíhou lírèn de? When did your father leave the job?

任何 rènhé any: 没有任何理由不去。Méiyǒu rènhé lǐyóu bú qù. There's no reason for not going.

任教 rènjiào to work as a teacher: 她任教多年了。Tā rènjiào duō nián le. She has been teaching for many years.

任劳任怨 rènláo-rènyuàn to work hard regardless of unfair criticism, to bear willingly the burden of office

任其自流 rèn qí zì liú to let things take their course, allow people to act without guidance: 学校里的这些坏现象可不能任其自流。Xuéxiào li de zhè xiē huài xiànxiàng kě bù néng rèn qí zì liú. These bad things going on in the school can't just be allowed to take their course.

任务 rènwù duty, task

任用 rènyòng to appoint, assign to a job: 那老板喜欢任用年轻人。Nà lǎobǎn xǐhuān rènyòng niánqīng rén. That boss likes to appoint young people.

在任 zàirèn to be in a post, hold a position: 他在任期间，工厂管理得很好。Tā zàirèn qījiān, gōngchǎng guǎnlǐ de hěn hǎo. While he was in the job, the factory was well managed.

责任 zérèn responsibility

重任 zhòngrèn a big or important task

rén ①〔component of a place-name〕
②〔a surname〕

任丘 Rénqiū a county in Hebei Province

# S

## 撒   sā   sǎ

sā   ①to let go, let out: 撒网 sā wǎng to cast a net // 撒尿 sā niào 〈coll.〉 to pass urine // 把手撒开 bǎ shǒu sā kāi to let go one's hold (on something)// 撒腿就跑 sā tuǐ jiù pǎo to run in big bounds

②to "let oneself go", throw off all restraint: 撒酒疯 sā jiǔfēng to be roaring drunk

③[used in transcribing foreign words]

撒哈拉 Sāhālā the Sahara

撒娇 sājiāo to act in a spoiled, pouting manner: 那小孩儿在母亲面前撒娇。Nà xiǎohái·r zài mǔqīn miànqián sājiāo. The child was acting spoiled in front of her mother.

sǎ   to scatter, disperse, sprinkle: 撒种 sǎ zhǒng to broadcast seed // 撒农药 sǎ nóngyào to apply agricultural chemicals by scattering

## 塞   sāi   sài   sè

sāi   ①to plug up: 把瓶子塞住 bǎ píngzi sāi zhù to cork a bottle // 把箱子塞满 bǎ xiāngzi sāi mǎn to stuff a box full

②a stopper

塞子 sāizi a stopper, cork

sài    a frontier post

关塞 guānsài a mountain pass

塞外 sàiwài beyond the frontiers

塞翁失马 Sài wēng shī mǎ The old man on the frontier
lost his horse. = a blessing in disguise

sè    ①to block up〔used in compound words〕

②〔used in transcribing foreign words〕

堵塞 dǔsè to block up

塞责 sèzé not to do one's job conscientiously：敷衍塞责
fūyǎn sèzé to do one's job perfunctorily

塞音 sèyīn a stop consonant（in phonology）

# 散    sàn    sǎn

sàn    ①to scatter, disperse

②to divert oneself（from loneliness, boredom, tension,
etc.）：到公园里散散心 dào gōngyuán li sànsàn
xīn to go into the park to relieve one's boredom or depression

分散 fēnsàn to separate, scatter：士兵们分散在树林
里。Shìbīngmen fēnsàn zài shùlín li. The soldiers
scattered into the forest.

散步 sànbù to take a walk, stroll：在河边散步 zài
hébiān sànbù to stroll by the river

散会 sànhuì（of a meeting）to be over：主席宣布散会。
Zhǔxí xuānbù sànhuì. The chairperson declared the
meeting closed. // 晚上九点才散会。Wǎnshang jiǔ
diǎn cái sànhuì. The meeting did not finish until 9

p.m.

sǎn  ①to come loose, fall apart, fail to hold together: 米袋散
了。Mǐ dài sǎn le. The rice bag fell apart. // 麦垛被
风吹散了。Mài duò bèi fēng chuīsǎn le. The wheat
stack was blown about by the wind.

②scattered: 这儿的居民住得很散。Zhèr de jūmín zhù
de hěn sǎn. This is a very scattered community.

③relaxed, lazy

④blank (of verse), not bound by rules of versification

⑤medicinal powder

平胃散 píngwèisǎn  a medicinal powder to settle the
stomach

散漫 sǎnmàn undisciplined, careless, unorganised: 作
风散漫 zuòfēng sǎnmàn working in an undisciplined,
careless manner

散文 sǎnwén prose

散页 sǎnyè loose-leaf

散装 sǎnzhuāng loose (not pre-packaged): 散装饼干
sǎnzhuāng bǐnggān loose biscuits

闲散 xiánsǎn at leisure, at a loose end; not in use, idle:
日子过得很闲散。Rìzi guò de hěn xiánsǎn. The
days pass in leisurely ease.

丧    sāng    sàng

sāng a funeral; a funeral event or matter: 报丧 bào sāng to
announce a death

丧服 sāngfú mourning dress

丧礼 sānglǐ funeral rites

**sàng** to lose: 只开了一枪，就让他丧了命。Zhǐ kāi le yì qiāng, jiù ràng tā sàng le mìng. With just one shot he lost his life.

丧气 sàngqì dejected: 他丢了钱包，丧气得很。Tā diū le qiánbāo, sàngqì de hěn. He lost his wallet, so he's very dejected.

丧失 sàngshī to lose, be deprived of: 丧失勇气 sàngshī yǒngqì to lose courage // 丧失信心 sàngshī xìnxīn to lose confidence

# 臊    sāo    sào

**sāo** a foul smell, stench: 臊气 sāo qì body odour

腥臊 xīngsāo smelling like fish; smelling rancid

**sào** ①shy and embarrassed: 臊得慌 sào de huang very shy and embarrassed

②mincemeat

害臊 hàisào bashful; feeling ashamed

臊子 sàozi 〈dial.〉mincemeat

# 扫    sǎo    sào

**sǎo** ①to sweep: 这房间太脏，得扫一下。Zhè fángjiān tài zāng, děi sǎo yíxià. This room is filthy, and must be swept out. // 扫地 sǎo dì to sweep the floor (also sǎodì; see below)

②to eliminate, wipe out: 扫雷 sǎoléi to clear away mines

打扫 dǎsǎo to sweep, clean up: 打扫教室 dǎsǎo

jiàoshì to clean up the classroom

扫地 sǎodì (of honour, credibility, etc.) to be dragged in the dust, reach rock bottom: 由于那件丑闻，总经理名声扫地。Yóuyú nà jiàn chǒuwén, zǒngjīnglǐ míngshēng sǎodì. Because of that scandal, the general manager's reputation was at rock bottom. (also sǎo dì; see above)

扫数 sǎoshù putting all together, the whole amount

扫兴 sǎoxìng to feel disappointed: 小王的自私表现使得朋友们十分扫兴。Xiǎo Wáng de zìsī biǎoxiàn shǐde péngyoumen shífēn sǎoxìng. Young Wang's display of selfishness thoroughly disappointed his friends.

sào　a broom

扫把 sàoba a broom

扫帚 sàozhou a broom

# 色　sè　shǎi

sè　①colour: 红色 hóng sè red colour // 蓝色 lán sè blue colour

②facial expression, appearance, looks

③scene, scenery

④kind, sort: 各色人等 gè sè rénděng all kinds of people // 各色各样 gè sè gè yàng every sort and variety // 一色一样 yí sè yí yàng the same in every respect

⑤quality (of precious metals, etc.)

⑥woman's (good) looks

成色 chéngsè the percentage of gold or silver in an alloy; quality (e.g. of gold or silver)

和颜悦色 héyán-yuèsè with a kind and pleasant countenance

湖光山色 húguāng-shānsè (beautiful) scenery of lakes and mountains

货色 huòsè goods; stuff

景色 jǐngsè scenery, view

气色 qìsè complexion, facial colour

色鬼 sèguǐ a lecher

色盲 sèmáng colour-blind

神色 shénsè facial expression, look

颜色 yánsè colour

音色 yīnsè tone colour, timbre

姿色 zīsè good looks (of a woman)

shǎi ①〈coll.〉colour

②(= 骰)dice

掉色 diàoshǎi to fade, lose colour

配色 pèishǎi to match colours

色子 shǎizi dice

**塞** sè → sāi

**莎** shā → suō

**厦** shà　xià

shà a tall building, mansion

大厦 dàshà a large building

xià 厦门 Xiàmén a city（Amoy）in Fujian Province

# 嘎 shà á

shà 〈lit.〉hoarse：嘎声地 shà shēng de hoarsely

á （ = 啊 ）〔an interjection expressing interrogation, disbelief, or surprise〕：嘎？什么？ Á？Shénme？Huh？ What's this？

# 煞 shà shā

shà ①a fierce god; an evil spirit

②extremely：煞费苦心 shàfèi-kǔxīn to rack one's brains

煞白 shàbái deathly pale

煞星 shàxīng an unlucky star

凶神恶煞 xiōngshén-èshà demons, fiends

shā ①to stop, check, bring to a close：猛地把汽车煞住 měng de bǎ qìchē shā zhù to brake a car suddenly

②to tighten：煞一煞腰带 shā yi shā yāodài to tighten one's belt

煞笔 shābǐ the final lines of a piece of writing; to write the final lines

煞尾 shāwěi to finish off, round off, wind up：这篇文章不好煞尾。Zhè piān wénzhāng bù hǎo shāwěi. This article is not easy to finish off.

# 色 shǎi → sè

# 钐 shān shàn

shān the element samarium（Sm）

shàn 〈dial.〉to cut with wide swings of a sickle：钐草 shàn

　　　　cǎo to cut grass with a sickle

# 苫　shān　shàn

shān a piece of material (usually of straw) used as a mat, as thatch, or for covering things

草苫子 cǎoshānzi a straw mat

shàn to cover to protect from the weather: 用帆布把货物苫上。Yòng fānbù bǎ huòwù shàn shang. Cover the goods with a tarpaulin. // 把麦子苫起来 bǎ màizi shàn qilai to cover (harvested) wheat

苫布 shànbù a tarpaulin

# 单　shàn → dān

# 扇　shàn　shān

shàn ①a fan

②[a measure word for doors, windows]: 一扇门 yí shàn mén one door

③a flat, plank-like object

电扇 diànshàn an electric fan

隔扇 géshàn a screen for dividing a room or blocking the view

扇子 shànzi a fan

shān ①to fan: 扇风 shān fēng to fan the air // 扇火 shān huǒ to fan a fire

②( = 煽 ) to incite, stir up

③to slap: 扇了他一个耳光 shānle tā yíge ěrguāng gave him a slap in the face

扇动 shāndòng to fan, flap; to incite, instigate: 扇动群众闹事 shāndòng qúnzhòng nàoshì to incite a crowd to make trouble

扇惑 shānhuò to incite, agitate: 扇惑人心 shānhuò rénxīn to stir up people's emotions

**掸** shàn → dǎn

**禅** shàn → chán

**少** shǎo　shào

shǎo ① few, little: 人太少。Rén tài shǎo. There are too few people. // 水太少。Shuǐ tài shǎo. There is too little water.

② short of, lacking: 我们还少一个人手。Wǒmen hái shǎo yíge rénshǒu. We are still one person short (for the task).

③ missing: 屋里少了一把椅子。Wū li shǎole yìbǎ yǐzi. There is one chair missing from the room.

④ a little while: 请少候。Qǐng shǎo hòu. Please wait a little while.

多少 duōshǎo a certain amount, more or less; (read duō shao) how many? how much?: 这点钱多少能解决点问题。Zhè diǎn qián duōshǎo néng jiějué diǎn wèntí. This small amount of money may still help, more or less, to solve a little of the problem.

缺少 quēshǎo lacking

少数 shǎoshù a small number; a minority

shào  young; minor

老少 lǎoshào young and old

少年 shàonián a youth

少尉 shàowèi a second lieutenant

# 折  shé → zhé

# 蛇  shé  yí

shé  a snake

毒蛇 dúshé a venomous snake

蛇行 shéxíng to creep like a snake

蛇足 shézú snake's feet = something superfluous

yí  委蛇 wēiyí 〈lit.〉① ( = 逶迤 ) winding, meandering

② amiable and compliant

虚与委蛇 xūyǔ-wēiyí to treat courteously but without
    sincerity, to pretend politeness and compliance

# 舍  shè  shě

shè  ①a house, inn, shed

②〈lit.〉〔humble reference to one's own home and family〕

③an ancient unit of distance equal to 30 里 lǐ

④〔used in transcribing foreign words〕

寒舍 hánshè 〈lit.〉my humble dwelling

客舍 kèshè an inn

牛舍 niúshè a cowshed

舍弟 shèdì 〈lit.〉my younger brother

舍利弗 Shèlìfú Sāriputra (a prominent disciple of the
    Buddha)

宿舍 sùshè a dormitory

退避三舍 tuìbì-sānshè to retreat a distance of three *she* = to compromise to avoid a conflict

shě ①to discard

②to give away

舍本逐末 shěběn-zhúmò to attend to trifles while neglecting the essentials

舍不得 shěbude reluctant to part with

施舍 shīshě to give in charity; charitable giving: 那庙里的长老常向穷人施舍衣服。Nà miào li de zhǎnglǎo cháng xiàng qióngrén shīshě yīfu. The master of that temple often makes gifts of clothing to the poor. // 她虽穷，却不喜欢接受施舍。Tā suī qióng, què bù xǐhuān jiēshòu shīshě. Although poor, she does not like accepting charity.

参 shēn → cān

什 shén → shí

省 shěng　xǐng

shěng ①a province: 河南省 Hénán Shěng Henan Province

②to economise: 省钱 shěng qián to save money // 省时间 shěng shíjiān to save time

③to omit, leave out: 那个句子可以省掉。Nàge jùzi kěyi shěngdiào. That sentence can be omitted.

省略 shěnglüè to delete, employ ellipsis: 这一段文字不重要，可以省略。Zhè yí duàn wénzì bú zhòngyào, kěyǐ **shěng**lüè. This piece of text is not important, and can be deleted.

省长 **shěng**zhǎng provincial governor

**xǐng** ①to examine critically, consider deeply

②to understand, wake up to

③to visit (esp. an elder)

不省人事 bù **xǐng** rénshì unconscious, in a coma: 他被打得不省人事。Tā bèi dǎ de bù **xǐng** rénshì. He was beaten unconscious.

反省 fǎn**xǐng** to introspect; self-questioning: 你应该认真反省，为什么会犯这样的错误。Nǐ yīnggāi rènzhēn fǎn**xǐng**, wèi shénme huì fàn zhèyàng de cuòwù. You should reflect carefully on how this kind of mistake could have been made.

省察 **xǐng**chá to inspect, examine: 省察事故原因 **xǐng**chá shìgù yuányīn to investigate the cause of an accident

省亲 **xǐng**qīn 〈lit.〉 to visit one's parents

省悟 **xǐng**wù ( = 醒悟 ) to realize: 他省悟了，不再跟那帮人鬼混。Tā **xǐng**wù le, bú zài gēn nà bāng rén guǐhùn. He has come to his senses, and won't be hanging around with that gang any more.

盛 **shèng** **chéng**

**shèng** ①abundant, flourishing, full

②vigorous, energetic: 年轻气盛 niánqīng qì**shèng** young and aggressive

③magnificent, grand

④popular, widespread

⑤〔a surname〕

强盛 qiángshèng (of a country) powerful and prosperous

盛大 shèngdà magnificent：盛大的集会 shèngdà de jíhuì a magnificent gathering

盛服 shèngfú 〈lit.〉formal dress

盛年 shèngnián the more productive years of life (usually 30 to 50)

盛情 shèngqíng great kindness, warm hospitality：盛情款待 shèngqíng kuǎndài lavish hospitality // 盛情难却。Shèngqíng nán què. It would be ungracious to decline your kind invitation.

盛行 shèngxíng widespread, popular：今年这种服装在年轻人中十分盛行。Jīnnián zhè zhǒng fúzhuāng zài niánqīngrén zhōng shífēn shèngxíng. This year this kind of clothing is very popular among young people.

chéng ①to place in a container：盛饭 chéng fàn to ladle cooked rice into a bowl

②〈coll.〉to contain：这间屋盛不下这么多人。Zhè jiān wū chéng bu xià zhème duō rén. This room can't accommodate so many people.

盛器 chéngqì a container, vessel

嘘　shī → xū

# 什　shí　shén

shí　①( ＝ 十 ) ten

②miscellaneous

什锦 shíjǐn assorted, mixed

什一 shíyī one tenth

shén　什么? Shénme? What?

# 石　shí　dàn

shí　①a rock, stone

②[a surname]

石榴 shíliu the pomegranate

石头 shítou a stone

石油 shíyóu petroleum

dàn　①( ＝ 担 , also shí ) ⟨lit.⟩ a unit of weight ( ＝ 50 kilo-
grams)：一石米 yí dàn mǐ one *dan* of rice

②a unit of capacity ( ＝ 1 hectolitre)

# 匙　shi → chí

# 属　shǔ　zhǔ

shǔ　①to belong to, be connected with：属牛的 shǔ niú de
born in the year of the ox

②a class, category, genus：这两种植物同科, 不同属。
Zhè liǎng zhǒng zhíwù tóng kē, bùtóng shǔ. These
two plants belong to the same family but not to the same
genus.

③family members, dependents

④to be：实属无理。Shí shǔ wúlǐ. It is really unreasonable. // 查明属实 chámíng shǔ shí proved to be true through investigation

家属 jiāshǔ family members; dependents

金属 jīnshǔ metals

军属 jūnshǔ a soldier's dependents

亲属 qīnshǔ relatives

属于 shǔyú to belong to: 这房子属于他们家。Zhè fángzi shǔyú tāmen jiā. This house belongs to their family.

zhǔ ①⟨lit.⟩ to concentrate on

②joining, linking, successive

前后相属 qián hòu xiāng zhǔ joining former and latter parts together

属意 zhǔyì ⟨lit.⟩ to fix one's mind on somebody

# 数 shǔ　shù　shuò

shǔ ①to count: 数一数 shǔ yi shǔ to count // 数不过来 shǔ bu guòlái unable to count (because they are so many) // 数数儿 shǔ shùr ⟨coll.⟩ to count the numbers

②to enumerate, list

历数其罪 lì shǔ qí zuì to enumerate someone's crimes

数落 shǔluo to scold by enumerating a person's faults: 他妈妈数落了他一顿。Tā māma shǔluole tā yí dùn. His mother enumerated his faults and gave him a good scolding.

数一数二 shǔyī-shǔ'èr to count as one of the best: 她是全校数一数二的优秀生。Tā shì quán xiào shǔyī-shǔ'èr de yōuxiù shēng. She is one of the top students in the school.

shù ①a number

②several: 仅有数人 jǐn yǒu shù rén only a few people

③fate

单数 dānshù odd numbers; singular number (in grammar)

复数 fùshù plural number (in grammar)

气数 qìshù fate, destiny

数目 shùmù a number

数学 shùxué mathematics

无理数 wúlǐshù an irrational number

无数 wúshù innumerable: 广场上聚集了无数人。 Guǎngchǎng shang jùjí le wúshù rén. Countless people had gathered in the square.

shuò ⟨lit.⟩ frequently

数见不鲜 shuòjiàn-bùxiān a common occurrence, nothing new

# 术 shù zhú

shù ①skill

②tactics

技术 jìshù skill

术语 shùyǔ jargon, technical terminology

艺术 yìshù art

战术 zhànshù military tactics

zhú a type of plant whose roots are used in herbal medicine

白术 báizhú the rhizome of the large-headed atractylodes (used in herbal medicine)

**刷**　shuā　shuà

shuā　①to brush: 刷牙 shuā yá to brush the teeth

②a brush

③to eliminate (e.g. in a competition): 他在上次比赛中被刷下去了。Tā zài shàngcì bǐsài zhōng bèi shuā xiàqù le. He was eliminated in the previous match.

④〔onomatopoeia〕

刷拉 shuālā 〔onomatopoeia for rubbing sounds〕

刷子 shuāzi a brush

牙刷 yáshuā a toothbrush

印刷 yìnshuā printing; to print: 印刷了大量小册子 yìn shuāle dàliàng xiǎo cèzi printed a large number of pamphlets

shuà　刷白 shuàbái 〈dial.〉pale (usually of a face)

**率**　shuài → lǜ

**说**　shuō　shuì

shuō　①to speak, say: 你说什么? Nǐ shuō shénme? What did you say?

②to explain: 这事儿该怎么说? Zhè shìr gāi zěnme shuō? How is this matter to be explained? // 一说就懂 yì shuō jiù dǒng can be understood once it is explained

③to rebuke: 我说了他一顿。Wǒ shuōle tā yí dùn. I

gave him a good talking to.

④a theory, doctrine: 著书立说 zhù shū lì shuō to write books and set up theories

⑤(in matchmaking) to introduce: 给你说个对象 gěi nǐ shuō ge duìxiàng introduce you to a partner

说服 shuōfú to persuade: 她把我说服了。Tā bǎ wǒ shuōfú le. She has persuaded me.

说媒 shuōméi to act as matchmaker: 请她说媒 qǐng tā shuōméi to ask her to act as matchmaker

说明 shuōmíng to explain, show; an explanation, caption: 这种现象说明了什么? Zhè zhǒng xiànxiàng shuōmíngle shénme? What does this phenomenon show? // 这图像附有说明。Zhè túxiàng fùyǒu shuōmíng. There is a caption attached to this picture.

小说 xiǎoshuō a novel

学说 xuéshuō a theory

shuì 〈lit.〉 to persuade

游说 yóushuì 〈lit.〉 to travel around persuading people to adopt one's ideas (as Confucius did)

**数** shuò → shǔ

**伺** sì　cì

sì ①to watch

②to wait

窥伺 kuīsì to be on the watch for: 敌人一直在窥伺我军的动向。Dírén yìzhí zài kuīsì wǒ jūn de dòngxiàng.

The enemy were constantly monitoring the movements of our troops.

伺查 sìchá to spy on：伺查动静 sìchá dòngjing to keep watch on the situation or on someone's movements

伺机 sìjī to watch for a favourable moment：伺机反攻 sìjī fǎngōng to watch for an opportunity to make a counterattack

cì　伺候 cìhou to wait on, serve：那老太太由三个人伺候。Nà lǎo tàitai yóu sān ge rén cìhou. The old lady was being served by three people.

忪　sōng → zhōng

擞　sǒu　sòu

sǒu　to shake

抖擞 dǒusǒu to arouse (spirits, energy)：精神抖擞 jīngshén dǒusǒu full of energy and enthusiasm

sòu　〈dial.〉to poke (a fire)：擞炉灰 sòu lúhuī to shake down the ashes of a fire

宿　sù　xiǔ　xiù

sù　①to lodge for the night, stay overnight

②overnight lodgings

③〈lit.〉old, long-cherished

④〈lit.〉experienced, senior

⑤[a surname]

借宿 jièsù to stay the night at someone's place：在朋友家借宿 zài péngyou jiā jièsù to stay the night at a friend's place

留宿 liúsù to stay the night; to put up a guest for the night: 留宿村中 liúsù cūn zhōng to stay the night in the village

膳宿 shànsù board and lodging: 膳宿费 shànsù fèi the cost of board and lodging // 那学院提供膳宿。Nà xuéyuàn tígōng shànsù. That college provides board and lodging.

宿将 sùjiàng ⟨lit.⟩ an experienced general

宿儒 sùrú ⟨lit.⟩ a learned (old) scholar

宿舍 sùshè a dormitory

宿怨 sùyuàn an old grudge

**xiǔ** night: 三天两宿 sān tiān liǎng xiǔ three days and two nights; a few days // 整宿 zhěng xiǔ all night

**xiù** a constellation

斗宿 Dǒuxiù the Big Dipper

星宿 xīngxiù a constellation

# 缩 sù → suō

# 尿 suī → niào

# 遂 suì　suí

**suì** ①to satisfy, fulfil, succeed: 遂心 suì xīn to one's liking; after one's own heart // 遂愿 suì yuàn to have one's wish fulfilled

②⟨lit.⟩ then, so, thereupon: 此事遂了。Cǐ shì suì le. So the matter is settled.

顺遂 shùnsuì smoothly and well; to go as one wishes: 事情进展得很顺遂。Shìqing jìnzhǎn de hěn shùnsuì. Things developed very smoothly.

suí 半身不遂 bàn shēn bù suí hemiplagia

# 莎 suō shā

suō 莎草 suōcǎo a species of sedge; a medicinal herb

shā 〔used in transcribing foreign words〕

莎士比亚 Shāshìbǐyà Shakespeare

# 缩 suō sù

suō to shrink, shorten, recoil: 布料下水之后缩了不少。Bùliào xià shuǐ zhī hòu suōle bù shǎo. The cloth shrank a lot after being placed in water. // 她吓得缩在屋角发抖。Tā xià de suō zài wūjiǎo fādǒu. She was so frightened she shrank trembling into a corner of the room.

缩本 suōběn an edition in reduced size

缩短 suōduǎn to shorten, cut down, curtail: 距离缩短了。Jùlí suōduǎn le. The distance has been reduced. // 把原计划缩短一半 bǎ yuán jìhuà suōduǎn yí bàn to cut the original plan down to half

畏缩 wèisuō to shrink away from, recoil, flinch: 那孩子畏缩不前。Nà háizi wèisuō bù qián. The child hung back in fear.

sù 缩砂密 sùshāmì a species of medicinal herb

# T

**拓**　tà → tuò

**苔**　tái　tāi

tái　①moss

②any type of bryophyte

青苔 qīngtái moss

苔藓 táixiǎn mosses; bryophytes

tāi　舌苔 shétāi fur on the tongue

**弹**　tán → dàn

**叨**　tāo → dāo

**提**　tí　dī

tí　①to carry or lift (esp. in the hand, with arm hanging):
手里提着一只篮子 shǒu lǐ tízhe yì zhī lánzi carrying
a basket in the hand // 从井里提水 cóng jǐng lǐ tí shuǐ
to draw water from a well

②to lift, raise, bring forward (something abstract): 喝杯
咖啡提提神 hē bēi kāfēi tí tí shén to have a cup of
coffee to revive oneself // 把认识提到一个新的高度
bǎ rènshi tí dào yí ge xīn de gāodù to raise awareness
to a new level // 他们把开会的时间往前提了两个小
时。Tāmen bǎ kāi huì de shíjiān wǎng qián tíle
liǎng ge xiǎoshí. They brought the time of the meeting

forward two hours.

③to bring up, mention, raise, propose: 提问题 tí wèntí to bring up problems; to ask questions // 提意见 tí yìjiàn to make comments or criticisms // 别提它了! Bié tí tā le! Don't mention that! // 提条件 tí tiáojiàn to propose conditions

④to take out, draw out: 提款 tí kuǎn to draw out money (e.g. from a bank) // 提货 tí huò to pick up goods

⑤a dipper (for liquids)

⑥a rising stroke ╱ in Chinese calligraphy

提拔 tíbá to promote: 他被提拔为副局长。Tā bèi tíbá wéi fù júzhǎng. He was promoted to the position of deputy bureau chief.

提高 tígāo to raise, lift: 提高生活水平 tígāo shēnghuó shuǐpíng to raise living standards

提炼 tíliàn to extract and purify; to abstract: 从矿石里提炼金属 cóng kuàngshí lǐ tíliàn jīnshǔ to extract metals from ore

提前 tíqián to give precedence to, bring forward: 提前开会 tíqián kāi huì to bring forward the date or time of a meeting

提议 tíyì to propose, suggest; a proposal, suggestion: 她提议去郊游。Tā tíyì qù jiāoyóu. She suggested going on an excursion. // 大家同意了他的提议。Dàjiā tóngyìle tā de tíyì. Everyone agreed to his proposal.

小提琴 xiǎotíqín the violin

油提 yóutí an oil dipper

**dī**　提防 dīfáng cautious, alert; to be on guard against

提溜 dīliu〈coll.〉to hold lightly in the hand

# 体　tǐ　tī

**tǐ**　①the body

②form, structure

③physical state

④to realise

固体 gùtǐ solid; a solid body

简体字 jiǎntǐzì simplified Chinese characters

身体 shēntǐ the body

体裁 tǐcái types or forms of literature

体会 tǐhuì to know from experience: 我自己干了一天，才体会到那工作有多难。Wǒ zìjǐ gànle yì tiān, cái tǐhuì dào nà gōngzuò yǒu duō nán. Only after I had done it myself for a day did I realise how difficult that job was.

体育 tǐyù physical culture, training

液体 yètǐ liquid; a liquid

**tī**　( = 梯 ) 体己 tījǐ personal, confidential: 体己钱 tījǐ qián secret personal savings

# 挑　tiāo　tiǎo

**tiāo**　①to carry on a pole over the shoulder: 挑水 tiāo shuǐ to carry water // 挑不动 tiāo bu dòng unable to carry (e.g. because it is too heavy)

②a load carried on a pole over the sholder：一挑水 yì tiāo shuǐ a load of water // 从班上挑一个学生去会上发言 cóng bān shang tiāo yí ge xuésheng qù huì shang fāyán to choose a student from the class to go and speak at a meeting // 他老要挑我的短处。Tā lǎo yào tiāo wǒ de duǎnchù. He always picks on my shortcomings.

挑拣 tiāojiǎn to pick and choose

挑选 tiāoxuǎn to choose, select：挑选人才 tiāoxuǎn réncái to select talented persons

tiǎo ①to raise (a curtain etc.)：挑起帘子 tiǎoqi liánzi to raise a curtain

②to poke or pick out：我用针把扎在脚上的小刺挑出来了。Wǒ yòng zhēn bǎ zhā zài jiǎo shàng de xiǎo cì tiǎo chūlai le. I used a needle to pick out the thorn in my foot.

③to provoke, incite

④a rising stroke ╱ in Chinese calligraphy

挑拨 tiǎobō to sow discord, incite：挑拨是非 tiǎobō shìfēi to foment discord // 挑拨双方关系 tiǎobō shuāngfāng guānxi to sow dissention in a relationship

挑动 tiǎodòng to incite to action：挑动群众闹事 tiǎodòng qúnzhòng nàoshì to incite a crowd to make trouble

挑战 tiǎozhàn to pick a fight：向对方挑战 xiàng duìfāng tiǎozhàn to challenge the other party

**调** tiáo → diào

**帖** tiē　tiě tiè

tiē submissive, settled

妥帖 tuǒtiē settled; appropriate, proper, fitting: 所有事务都已安排妥帖。Suǒyǒu shìwù dōu yǐ ānpái tuǒtiē. Everything has been arranged and settled.

tiě ①a card; a note

②〈coll.〉〔a measure word for prescribed doses (in Chinese medicine)〕: 一帖药 yì tiě yào one dose of medicine

春帖 chūntiě inscribed strips of paper pasted on a door at Chinese New Year

请帖 qǐngtiě an invitation card

谢帖 xiètiě a thank-you card

tiè a model for calligraphy or painting

碑帖 bēitiè a book of reproductions of inscriptions, usually serving as models for calligraphy practice

字帖 zìtiè a collection of model calligraphy specimens

**同** tóng　tòng

tóng ①the same, alike: 他们两个的意见不同。Tāmen liǎng ge de yìjiàn bù tóng. The views of those two are not the same.

②together, in common

③with: 有事同大家商量。Yǒu shì tóng dàjiā shāngliang. If there's a problem, discuss it with everyone. //

同那人打交道很不容易。Tóng nà rén dǎ jiāodào hěn bù róngyi. Dealing with that person is very difficult.

同甘共苦 tóng gān gòng kǔ sharing the same joys and sorrows

同时 tóngshí simultaneously

同样 tóngyàng the same, equal, similar: 同样的衣服 tóngyàng de yīfu the same kind of clothes

同意 tóngyì to agree: 大家都同意他的观点。Dàjiā dōu tóngyì tā de guāndiǎn. Everyone agrees with his view.

同志 tóngzhì a comrade

相同 xiāngtóng identical, alike: 志趣相同 zhìqù xiāngtóng having the same aspirations and interests

tòng 胡同 hútòng〈dial.〉a small lane

# 吐　tǔ　tù

tǔ ①to spit: 吐痰 tǔ tán to spit phlegm

②to say, tell, disclose: 她对谁都不吐心思。Tā duì shéi dōu bù tǔ xīnsi. She never discloses her thoughts to anyone.

③to vent, pour out (resentment, grievances): 吐怨气 tǔ yuànqì to give vent to one's grievances // 吐苦水 tǔ kǔshuǐ to give vent to bitterness

④〔used in transcribing foreign words〕

吐鲁番 Tǔlǔfān (the city of) Turfan

吐露 tǔlù to tell, reveal: 吐露心事 tǔlù xīnshì to tell

what is on one's mind // 吐露秘密 tǔlù mìmì to reveal a secret

tù　①to vomit: 吐血 tù xiě to vomit blood

②to hand back unwillingly (ill-gotten gains etc.): 吐出贼赃 tù chū zéizāng to surrender stolen goods

# 囤　tún　dùn

tún　to store: 囤货 tún huò to store goods (also túnhuò; see below) // 仓里囤了许多粮食。Cāng lǐ túnle xǔduō liángshi. There is a lot of grain stored in the warehouse.

囤货 túnhuò stored goods (also tún huò; see above)

囤积 túnjī to store up, hoard: 那仓里的粮食囤积太久，都生虫子了。Nà cāng lǐ de liángshi túnjī tài jiǔ, dōu shēng chóngzi le. The grain in the warehouse has been stored too long, and it's full of insects.

dùn　a storage bin made of bamboo, reeds, etc.: 米囤 mǐ dùn a storage bin for rice

粮食囤子 liángshi dùnzi a storage bin for grain

# 驮　tuó　duò

tuó　to carry on the back, usually of a beast of burden: 驮不动 tuó bu dòng unable to carry // 那马能驮多少斤粮食？Nà mǎ néng tuó duōshao jīn liángshi? How many *jin* of grain can that horse carry?

驮运 tuóyùn to transport on pack-animals: 那山区多用骡子驮运物品。Nà shānqū duō yòng luózi tuóyùn wùpǐn. In that mountainous region they mostly use mules for transporting goods.

duò　驮子 duòzi a load carried by a pack animal；〔measure word for such loads〕：五驮子货 wǔ duòzi huò five loads of goods

## 拓　tuò　tà

tuò　①to expand，open up

②〔used in transcribing foreign words〕

开拓 kāituò to open up（new territory etc.）：开拓出一片新天地 kāituò chū yí piàn xīn tiāndì to open up a new piece of territory

拓朴学 tuòpūxué topology

拓展 tuòzhǎn to expand and develop：研究领域大大拓展了。Yánjiū lǐngyù dà dà tuòzhǎn le. A vast research area has been developed.

tà　to make a rubbing：拓碑 tà bēi to make a rubbing of a stone inscription

拓本 tàběn a stone-rubbing

# W

## 凹　wā → āo

## 瓦　wǎ　wà

**wǎ** ①a tile: 瓦房 **wǎ** fáng a tiled house

②earthenware, pottery: 瓦器 **wǎ** qì an earthenware vessel

③〔used in transcribing foreign words〕

瓦解 **wǎ**jiě to collapse, disintegrate: 整个队伍瓦解了。Zhěng gè duìwu **wǎ**jiě le. The whole battalion fell apart.

瓦特 **wǎ**tè the watt (in physics)

**wà** to tile: 瓦瓦 **wà** **wǎ** to lay tiles

瓦刀 **wà**dāo a trowel used in tiling

**莞** **wǎn → guān**

**蔓** **wàn → màn**

**为** **wéi　wèi**

**wéi** ①to act, do

②to be: 小组以他为领导。Xiǎozǔ yǐ tā **wéi** lǐngdǎo. The group has him as leader. // 在任何情况下他总是以集体利益为重。Zài rènhé qíngkuàng xià tā zǒng shi yǐ jítǐ lìyì **wéi** zhòng. Whatever the circumstances, he always regards the group benefit as paramount.

③〔used in passive constructions〕: 他为坏人所利用 Tā **wéi** huàirén suǒ lìyòng. He is being used by evil people.

④〔suffixed to some monosyllabic adjectives to form adverb of degree〕

大为 dà**wéi** greatly: 大为兴奋 dà**wéi** xīngfèn greatly excited

敢作敢为 gǎnzuò-gǎnwéi decisive and bold in action

极为 jíwéi extremely：极为重要 jíwéi zhòngyào extremely important

事在人为 shìzàirénwéi All depends on human effort.

为止 wéizhǐ until; to end：直到去年年底为止他都住在那儿。Zhí dào qùnián niándǐ wéizhǐ tā dōu zhù zài nàr. He lived there right up until the end of last year. // 今天的讨论到此为止。Jīntiān de tǎolùn dào cǐ wéizhǐ. Today's discussion ends here.

以为 yǐwéi to regard as; to think (usually mistakenly)：我以为她是个学生。Wǒ yǐwéi tā shì ge xuésheng. I thought she was a student.

wèi ①for：为友谊干杯 wèi yǒuyì gānbēi a toast to friendship // 为他说话 wèi tā shuōhuà to speak out for him // 为人民服务 wèi rénmín fúwù to serve the people // 为什么? Wèi shénme? For what? Why?

②because of

为何 wèihé because of what? why?

为了 wèile for the sake of, in order to：为了让学生们都能得到辅导，这学校增聘了好几位辅导员。Wèile ràng xuéshengmen dōu néng dédào fǔdǎo, zhè xuéxiào zēng pìnle hǎo jǐ wèi fúdǎoyuán. To enable all students to get help with their studies, the school has appointed quite a few more tutors.

圩 wéi → xū

## 唯　wéi　wěi

wéi　only, sole

唯心论 wéixīnlùn idealism (the philosophy)

唯一 wéiyī only, sole

wěi　〈lit.〉yes; to affirm

唯唯诺诺 wěiwěinuònuò to be a yes-man, be obsequi-
ous

## 尾　wěi　yǐ

wěi　①the tail, end, rear portion：船尾 chuán wěi the stern
of a ship

②end

③〔a measure word for fish〕：两尾鱼 liǎng wěi yú two
fish

④one of the 28 zodiacal constellations

交尾 jiāowěi to mate：这些牲口在春天交尾。Zhèxiē
shēngkou zài chūntiān jiāowěi. These livestock mate
in the spring.

尾巴 wěiba a tail

尾鳍 wěiqí a tailfin

尾声 wěishēng a coda, end, epilogue

尾随 wěisuí to follow along behind：尾随而来的人相当
多。Wěisuí ér lái de rén xiāngdāng duō. There are
quite a lot of people who have come following along behind.

yǐ　〈dial.〉tail hairs

马尾儿 mǎyǐr the hairs of a horse's tail

# 委　　wěi　wēi

wěi　①to depute, delegate

②a committee member; a committee (short for 委员 or 委员会)

③to push away, shift, shirk (responsibility)

④bent, roundabout, indirect

⑤truly: 委系冤屈。Wěi xì yuānqū. It is really unjust.

⑥( = 萎) weary

常委 chángwěi a member of a standing committee

党委 dǎngwěi a Party committee

委过于人 wěi guò yú rén to shift the blame on to someone else

委靡 ( = 萎靡) wěimí unsuccessful, dispirited; lacking strength of character

委派 wěipài to delegate, depute: 她被委派到小学任教。Tā bèi wěipài dào xiǎoxué rènjiào. She was assigned to teach at a primary school.

委曲 wěiqū winding, tortuous (e.g. road, river)

委实 wěishí really, indeed: 委实不知 wěishí bù zhī really not knowing

委婉 wěiwǎn mild and tactful: 批评得很委婉 pīpíng de hěn wěiwǎn to criticise very tactfully // 口气委婉 kǒuqì wěiwǎn in a mild and tactful tone

wēi　委蛇 wēiyí 〈lit.〉① ( = 逶迤) winding, meandering ② amiable and compliant

虚与委蛇 xūyǔ-wēiyí to treat courteously but without sincerity, to pretend politeness and compliance

# 无 wú mó

wú ①without, lacking, not: 无话可说 wú huà kě shuō speechless, having nothing to say

②regardless of: 事无巨细，一概由她经管。Shì wú jùxì, yígài yóu tā jīngguǎn. All matters, large and small, are managed by her.

③nothing, nil: 从无到有 cóng wú dào yǒu to go from nothing to success

无常 wúcháng variable, changeable: 反复无常 fǎnfù-wúcháng capricious, changeable

无耻 wúchǐ shameless, brazen: 无耻的行为 wúchǐ de xíngwéi shameless behaviour

无妨 wúfáng there's no harm, may as well: 你无妨试一试。Nǐ wúfáng shì yi shì. You may as well have a try.

无非 wúfēi nothing but, only, simply: 那无非是多花点钱，没多大关系。Nà wúfēi shi duō huā diǎn qián, méi duō dà guānxi. It just means spending a little more money, which doesn't matter much.

无论 wúlùn no matter what, regardless of: 无论怎样 wú lùn zěnyàng no matter how

无奈 wúnài cannot help but, have no alternative: 出于无奈 chū yú wúnài to have no choice

无数 wúshù innumerable, countless

无限 wúxiàn limitless

无线电 wúxiàndiàn radio

**mó**  〔used in transcribing Sanskrit words〕

南无 nāmó Hail! (Sanskrit *namo*)

**恶**  wù → è

# X

**洗**  xǐ   xiǎn

**xǐ**  ①to wash, rinse: 洗衣服 xǐ yīfu to wash clothes // 洗碗 xǐ wǎn to wash dishes // 洗脸 xǐ liǎn to wash one's face

②(in photography) to develop or print: 洗胶卷 xǐ jiāojuǎn to develop a film // 洗相片 xǐ xiàngpiàn to print a photograph

③to eliminate, wipe out: 把那段录音洗掉 bǎ nà duàn lùyīn xǐdiào erase that section of the recording

④to baptise: 她昨天受的洗。Tā zuótiān shòu de xǐ. She was baptised yesterday.

⑤to loot and kill extensively

⑥to shuffle: 洗牌 xǐ pái to shuffle cards

洗涤 xǐdí to wash clean: 所有的器皿都已洗涤干净了。Suǒyǒu de qìmǐn dōu yǐ xǐdí gānjìng le. All of the utensils have already been washed clean.

洗劫 xǐjié to pillage: 那些土匪把整个村庄洗劫一空。

Nà xiē tǔfěi bǎ zhěnggè cūnzhuāng xǐjié yìkōng. Those bandits cleaned out the whole village with their pillaging.

洗雪 xǐxuě to wipe out (a disgrace etc.): 洗雪国耻 xǐxuě guóchǐ to wipe out a national disgrace

xiǎn 〔a surname〕

**系** xì jì

xì ①to tie up, fasten, hang, suspend: 他把马系上了。Tā bǎ mǎ xì shàng le. He tied up the horse.

②to connect, contact, relate to, concern, bear on: 性命之所系 xìngmìng zhī suǒ xì something crucially relevant to one's life

③to be (literary equivalent of 是): 其母系山东人。Qí mǔ xì Shāndōng rén. His / her mother is from Shandong.

④a system, series

⑤a department (in a university): 哲学系 zhéxué xì the philosophy department

⑥〈lit.〉to be jailed

联系 liánxì to integrate, link, relate; to contact; a contact, connection, relationship: 请你马上跟他们联系。Qǐng nǐ mǎshàng gēn tāmen liánxì. Please contact them immediately.

太阳系 tàiyángxì the solar system

系恋 xìliàn to be concerned about and miss: 系恋故土 xì liàn gùtǔ to be concerned about one's homeland and miss it

系列 xìliè a series

**jì** to tie：系鞋带 jì xiédài to tie shoelaces // 系扣子 jì kòuzi to tie a knot; to fasten a button

# 吓　xià　hè

**xià** ①to frighten：小心点儿，别把孩子吓着了。Xiǎoxīn diǎnr, bié bǎ háizi xià zháo le. Be careful. Don't frighten the child.

②to be frightened：我吓了一跳。Wǒ xià le yí tiào. I got a fright.

吓唬 xiàhu to frighten：吓唬人 xiàhu rén to frighten people

**hè** ①to intimidate, frighten

②〔an interjection indicating annoyance or amusement〕：吓，好厉害的家伙! Hè, hǎo lìhài de jiāhuo! Wow, what an amazing fellow!

恐吓 kǒnghè to terrify; to blackmail：极端分子不断用恐吓信来威胁他们。Jíduān fènzǐ búduàn yòng kǒnghèxìn lái wēixié tāmen. The extremists continue to use blackmailing letters to threaten them.

# 厦　xià → shà

# 纤　xiān　qiàn

**xiān** fine, minute

纤尘不染 xiān chén bù rǎn spotless, immaculate

纤维 xiānwéi fibres

纤细 xiānxì very fine, slender; tenuous

qiàn a tow-rope, hawser: 拉纤 lā qiàn to tow a boat; to act as
a go-between

纤夫 qiànfū a boat-tracker

# 鲜

xiān　xiǎn

xiān ①fresh, new: 这鱼鲜不鲜? Zhè yú **xiān** bu xiān? Is
this fish fresh?

②bright-coloured

③delicious

④a delicacy

⑤fresh aquatic foods

⑥〔used in transcribing foreign words〕

⑦〔a surname〕

海鲜 hǎixiān fresh seafood

鲜红 xiānhóng bright red

鲜味 xiānwèi a delicious fresh taste or smell

时鲜 shíxiān seasonal delicacies

鲜艳 xiānyàn brightly coloured: 鲜艳的颜色 xiānyàn
de yánsè bright colours

新鲜 xīnxiān fresh

xiǎn 〈lit.〉 rare, few

朝鲜 Cháoxiǎn Korea

鲜见 xiǎnjiàn rarely seen

鲜为人知 xiǎn wéi rén zhī little-known

**洗**    xiǎn → xǐ

**见**    xiàn → jiàn

**相**    xiāng    xiàng

xiāng ①mutually, each other

②〔indicating one party's action or attitude toward the other〕

③to see for oneself (whether someone or something is to one's liking): 那男人她相不中。Nà nánrén tā xiāng bú zhòng. She doesn't like that man (after seeing him for herself).

互相 hùxiāng mutually: 互相帮助 hùxiāng bāngzhù to help each other

相比 xiāngbǐ to compare: 那两件事不能相比。Nà liǎng jiàn shì bù néng xiāngbǐ. Those two matters cannot be compared.

相当 xiāngdāng equal to, to match, balance; suitable, appropriate; rather, quite: 两人年龄相当。Liǎng rén niánlíng xiāngdāng. The two of them are the same age. // 得失相当。Déshī xiāngdāng. The gains balance the losses. // 他的学历相当于硕士。Tā de xuélì xiāngdāng yú shuòshì. His academic qualification is equivalent to a Master's Degree. // 我想不出一个相当的词儿。Wǒ xiǎng bu chū yí ge xiāngdāng de cír. I can't think of an equivalent word. // 那道菜味道相当好。Nà dào cài wèidào xiāngdāng hǎo.

That dish tastes quite good.

相烦 xiāngfán 〈polite.〉 to trouble someone, to ask for a favour: 今天我有事相烦，希望您能帮忙。Jīntiān wǒ yǒu shì xiāngfán, xīwàng nín néng bāngmáng. Today I have to trouble you with something. I hope you can help.

相反 xiāngfǎn opposite, contradictory

相亲 xiāngqīn meeting and appraising a prospective mate

相劝 xiāngquàn to persuade; to offer advice: 我对他好意相劝，但他不听。Wǒ duì tā hǎoyì xiāngquàn, dàn tā bù tīng. I gave him well-intentioned advice, but he wouldn't listen.

相信 xiāngxìn to believe: 他相信鬼神。Tā xiāngxìn guǐshén. He believes in spirits.

xiàng ① a countenance, appearance; a portrait, photograph: 他是个坏人相。Tā shì ge huài rén xiàng. He has the face of a villain. // 照相 zhào xiàng to take photographs

② a prime minister

③ to watch, observe

④ to size up people's appearance, do physiognomy: 你会相面吗？ Nǐ huì xiàng miàn ma? Can you do physiognomy?

⑤ (in physics) phase: 三相发电机 sān xiàng fādiànjī a three-phase generator

⑥ [a surname]

首相 shǒuxiàng a prime minister

相法 xiàngfǎ physiognomy

相机 xiàngjī a camera; to watch for an opportunity：相机行事 xiàngjī xíngshì to watch for an opportunity to act

相貌 xiàngmào looks, appearance

## 降 xiáng → jiàng

## 校 xiào  jiào

xiào ①a school

②certain military and naval ranks

少校 shàoxiào an army major

校长 xiàozhǎng a school principal

学校 xuéxiào a school

jiào ①to revise, collate, check

②( = 较 )〈arch.〉to compare

校场 jiàochǎng a drill ground (in ancient times)

校对 jiàoduì to proof-read

校勘 jiàokān to compare and edit texts, do textual criticism

## 叶 xié → yè

## 血 xiě  xuè

xiě blood〔in colloquial usage, and when as a monosyllabic word referring to actual blood〕：一滴血 yì dī xiě a drop of blood // 流血 liú xiě to bleed

血淋淋 xiělīnlīn dripping with blood

血丝儿 xiěsīr fine capillaries

xuè　blood 〔in literary usage, and when in compounds with technical or figurative reference〕

血汗 xuèhàn blood and sweat = hard toil

血气 xuèqì vigour; courage

血球 xuèqiú blood corpuscles

血统 xuètǒng a blood lineage

# 解　xiè → jiě

# 芯　xīn　xìn

xīn　pith: 铅笔芯 qiānbǐ xīn the graphite in a leadpencil // 玉米芯 yùmǐ xīn a corn cob

xìn　芯子 xìnzi a wick, fuse, or similar object; a snake's forked tongue

# 兴　xīng　xìng

xīng　①to rise

②to raise, start, establish

③to prevail

④prosperous

时兴 shíxīng fashionable: 这种服装今年不时兴。Zhè zhǒng fúzhuāng jīnnián bù shíxīng. This style of clothes is not in fashion this year.

兴兵 xīngbīng to raise an army: 兴兵攻打邻国 xīngbīng gōngdǎ línguó to raise an army to attack a neighbouring country

兴奋 xīngfèn excited: 兴奋得睡不着 xīngfèn de shuì bu zháo too excited to sleep

兴建 xīngjiàn to construct：兴建工厂 xīngjiàn gōngchǎng   to construct a factory

兴盛 xīngshèng thriving, prosperous：国家兴盛。Guó-
jiā xīngshèng. The nation is prosperous.

兴亡 xīngwáng rise and fall

兴旺 xīngwàng thriving：生意兴旺。Shēngyì xīngwàng. Business is thriving.

xìng   joy, happiness, interest

高兴 gāoxìng happy

兴趣 xìngqù interest

兴致 xìngzhì interest, a mood for enjoying

# 行   xíng   háng

xíng   ①to go

②travel; to travel：澳大利亚之行 Àodàlìyà zhī xíng a
trip to Australia

③to do, implement, commit

④ready and able; all right：行不行? Xíng bu xíng? Is it
all right?

⑤current, prevalent

步行 bùxíng to go on foot; a walk：他步行去了杭州。
Tā bùxíng qùle Hángzhōu. He has gone to Hangzhou
on foot. // 步行只要十分钟。Bùxíng zhǐ yào shí
fēnzhōng. It is only a ten-minute walk.

发行 fāxíng to publish, put on sale：发行邮票 fāxíng
yóupiào to issue stamps

简便易行 jiǎnbiàn yì xíng simple and easy to do

流行 liúxíng widely publicised, popular

旅行 lǚxíng to travel: 到非洲旅行 dào Fēizhōu lǚxíng to go for a trip to Africa

行动 xíngdòng to move, act; action, operation: 他们行动起来了。Tāmen xíngdòng qilai le. They have begun taking action. // 军事行动 jūnshì xíngdòng a military operation

行窃 xíngqiè to commit theft: 那人行窃多年，最近才被捕。Nà rén xíngqiè duō nián, zuìjìn cái bèi bǔ. That person has been committing theft for years, and has only recently been arrested.

行书 xíngshū (in Chinese calligraphy) running hand

行为 xíngwéi action, behaviour, conduct

háng ① a row, line [measure word]: 一行字 yì háng zì a line of written characters // 两行树 liǎng háng shù two rows of trees

② a line of business: 各行各业 gè háng gè yè every trade and profession

③ a shop: 珠宝行 zhūbǎo háng a jewellery shop

④ order of seniority

行当 hángdang a trade, profession, line of business; a type of role in Chinese opera

行列 hángliè rows and columns; in rank and file

行业 hángyè a trade, profession, industry

排行 páiháng seniority among brothers and sisters

外行 wàiháng an amateur; a layperson

银行 yínháng a bank

**省**　xǐng → shěng

**宿**　xiǔ xiù → sù

**臭**　xiù → chòu

**圩**　xū　wéi

xū　a country fair: 赶圩 gǎn xū to go to the fair

圩场 xūcháng a country fair; a fairground

wéi　a dike, embankment

圩堤 wéidī a dike to keep water out of low-lying land

圩田 wéitián low-lying fields surrounded by dikes

**嘘**　xū　shī

xū　①to breathe out slowly; to hiss: 嘘气　xū qì to exhale slowly; to blow on（to warm or cool something）

②to scald

吹嘘 chuīxū to "blow someone's trumpet" = to praise: 自我吹嘘 zìwǒ chuīxū to praise oneself

嘘唏 xūxī a deep sigh

shī　[onomatopoeia for hissing, hushing, or shooing sounds]: 嘘！不要说话！Shī！Bú yào shuōhuà! Shhh! Don't talk! // 嘘！滚出去！Shī！Gǔn chūqu! Shoo! Get out!

**畜**　xù → chù

**旋**　xuán　xuàn

xuán ①to turn, circle around; a circle

②to return

③a moment later

凯旋 kǎixuán to return in triumph; a triumphal return: 军队凯旋 jūnduì kǎixuán an army returning in triumph

斡旋 wòxuán to mediate to retrieve or reverse a situation; good offices (in law): 那两家公司能达成谅解，全靠他从中斡旋。Nà liǎng jiā gōngsī néng dáchéng liàngjiě, quán kào tā cóngzhōng wòxuán. That the two companies were able to reach an understanding was entirely due to his mediation.

旋即 xuánjí soon, forthwith: 票旋即卖光了。Piào xuánjí màiguāng le. The tickets were soon sold out.

旋涡 xuánwō a whirlpool

旋转 xuánzhuǎn to revolve; a revolution: 那飞轮旋转得极快。Nà fēilún xuánzhuǎn de jí kuài. The flywheel was rotating at extremely high speed.

xuàn ①circular, cyclonic

②to turn on a lathe; to pare with a circular movement: 把苹果皮旋了 bǎ píngguǒ pí xuàn le peeled off the skin of the apple

③at the time; at the last moment: 饺子最好是旋做旋吃。Jiǎozi zuì hǎo shì xuàn zuò xuàn chī. Dumplings are best eaten as they are made.

旋风 xuànfēng a whirlwind

旋子 xuànzi a whirlwind; a whirlpool; a turning movement in dancing, martial arts, etc.

**血**    xuè → xiě

**窨**    xūn → yìn

**熏**    xūn   xùn

xūn   ①to smoke (meat, fish, etc.): 熏鱼 xūn yú to smoke
       fish (also xūnyú; see below)

②to fumigate: 熏衣服 xūn yīfu to fumigate clothes

③to irritate the nose: 她被烟熏得直流泪。Tā bèi yān
xūn de zhí liúlèi. The smoke made her eyes water continuously.

熏染 xūnrǎn smoking and dyeing = a gradual influence;
to influence gradually: 受不良风气的熏染 shòu
bùliáng fēngqì de xūnrǎn to be gradually affected by
bad influences

熏陶 xūntáo to uplift and edify gradually; an uplifting influence: 经那学院环境的熏陶，那孩子也逐渐养成
了读书的习惯。Jīng nà xuéyuàn huánjìng de
xūntáo, nà háizi yě zhújiàn yǎngchéngle dú shū de
xíguàn. Under the uplifting influence of the college environment, the child gradually became accustomed to
studying.

熏鱼 xūnyú smoked fish (also xūn yú; see above)

xùn   〈dial.〉to asphyxiate: 熏着了 xùn zhao le asphyxiated
       by gas

# Y

哑　　yǎ　yā

yǎ　①dumb, mute

②hoarse, husky: 嗓子哑了，说不出话来 sǎngzi yǎ le, shuō bu chū huà lai become hoarse and unable to speak

沙哑 shāyǎ hoarse

哑巴 yǎba a mute, dumb person

哑谜 yǎmí an enigma

哑炮 yǎpào a dud shell

yā　〔onomatopoeia for various bird cries etc.〕

轧　　yà　zhá　gá

yà　①to apply rolling pressure: 轧死了 yà sǐ le run over and killed // 轧棉花 yà miánhuā to gin cotton

②to jostle for position

③〔onomatopoeia〕

倾轧 qīngyà to jostle against one another; to engage in internal strife: 那帮人表面上和和气气，实际上互相倾轧。Nà bāng rén biǎomiàn shang héhéqìqì, shíjì shang hùxiāng qīngyà. That group appears amiable, but in reality it is full of internal conflict.

zhá　to draw out, or roll (steel) into thin sheets

轧钢厂 zhágāngchǎng a steel-rolling mill

gá 〈dial.〉①to crowd, press against one another: 人多, 轧
得很。Rén duō, gá de hěn. It was packed with people.

②to associate with: 轧朋友 gá péngyou to make friends
with

③to check, audit: 轧账 gá zhàng to check accounts

咽 yān yàn yè

yān the throat
咽喉 yānhóu the throat
咽头 yāntóu the pharynx

yàn to swallow: 咽唾沫 yàn tuòmo to swallow one's saliva
咽气 yànqì to breathe one's last, die: 那老人撑到第三
天才咽气。Nà lǎo rén chēng dào dì sān tiān cái
yànqì. The old man hung on until the third day before
breathing his last.

yè to be choked; to sob
悲咽 bēiyè choking with grief

殷 yān → yīn

燕 yàn yān

yàn ①the swallow
②( = 宴 )〈arch.〉to feast
③( = 宴 )〈arch.〉a feast
燕窝 yànwō edible birds' nests
燕乐 yànyuè 〈arch.〉a traditional type of Chinese music,
originally for court feasts and entertainment
燕子 yànzi the swallow

yān　〔a surname〕; 〔a place-name〕: 燕山 Yān Shān a mountain range in Hebei Province

**约**　yāo → yuē

**疟**　yào → nüè

**要**　yào　yāo

yào　①to want, desire: 他要去。Tā **yào** qù. He wants to go.

②to ask for, beg: 要饭的 **yào**fàn de a beggar

③must, should: 你要小心。Nǐ **yào** xiǎoxīn. You should take care.

④will: 要下雨了。**Yào** xià yǔ le. It's about to rain.

⑤important, necessary

⑥essential points

⑦if: 他要不干，就找别人。Tā **yào** bú gàn, jiù zhǎo bié rén. If he won't do it, then find someone else.

⑧to need, take: 这活儿要用十天才能干完。Zhè huór **yào** yòng shí tiān cái néng gàn wán. This job will take ten days to finish.

⑨〔used before a comparative to indicate an estimate〕: 他的年纪要比你大。Tā de niánjì **yào** bǐ nǐ dà. He must be older than you.

需要 xū**yào** to need: 我需要一个助手来干这事。Wǒ xū**yào** yí ge zhùshǒu lái gàn zhè shì. I need an assistant to attend to this matter.

要价 **yào**jià to ask a price, charge: 他们要价多少? Tāmen **yào**jià duōshao? What price are they asking?

要紧 yàojǐn important

要事 yàoshì an important matter

要是 yàoshi if: 他要是不来，那怎么办呢? Tā yàoshi bù lái, nà zěnme bàn ne? If he doesn't come, what shall we do?

摘要 zhāiyào to make a summary of essential points; a summary, abstract

yāo ①to ask, request, demand

　　②to coerce

要求 yāoqiú to ask, demand; a demand: 要求发言 yāoqiú fāyán to ask to speak // 要求参加组织 yāoqiú cānjiā zǔzhī to ask to become a member of an organisation // 达到质量要求 dádào zhìliàng yāoqiú to meet required quality standards

要挟 yāoxié to coerce with threats: 要挟弱小者 yāoxié ruòxiǎozhě to coerce the small and weak

# 钥　yào　yuè

yào 钥匙 yàoshi a key

yuè 〈fig., lit.〉a key

# 叶　yè　xié

yè ①a leaf, petal

　　②( = 页 ) a page

　　③a historical period

　　④[a surname]

活叶 huóyè loose-leaf: 活叶笔记本 huóyè bǐjìběn a

loose-leaf notebook

树叶 shùyè a tree leaf

叶公好龙 Yègōng-hàolóng Lord Ye's love of dragons = professed love of what one actually fears

叶子 yèzi a leaf

中叶 zhōngyè the middle of a dynasty or era: 20 世纪中叶 èrshí shìjì zhōngyè the middle of the twentieth century

xié 　( = 协 ) to harmonise

叶韵 xiéyùn a change of pronunciation to make words rhyme（when reading classical poetry）

**咽**　yè → yān

**掖**　yè　yē

yè 　①to support by holding by the arms: 我掖住那老人。Wǒ yèzhù nà lǎorén. I supported the old man.

②to help, promote

扶掖 fúyè to uphold, support: 他初到任，还需您大力扶掖。Tā chū dào rèn, hái xū nín dàlì fúyè. He's new in the job and still needs your full support.

奖掖 jiǎngyè〈lit.〉to reward and promote

yē 　to conceal, tuck away: 把上衣下摆掖起来 bǎ shàngyī xiàbǎi yē qilai to tuck in one's shirt tail // 腰里掖着枪 yāo lǐ yēzhe qiāng with a gun in the belt

**蛇**　yí → shé

**尾**　yǐ → wěi

## 迤　　yǐ　yí

yǐ　①〈lit.〉to zigzag, veer

②connected

迤逦 yǐlǐ winding, tortuous

yí　逶迤 wēiyí〈lit.〉winding, meandering

## 椅　　yǐ　yī

yǐ　a chair

交椅 jiāoyǐ an armchair; position, post: 坐第一把交椅 zuò dì yī bǎ jiāoyǐ to occupy the highest post

椅子 yǐzi a chair

yī　椅梓 yīzǐ the catalpa tree, *Idesia polycarpa*

## 艾　　yì → ài

## 荫　　yīn　yìn

yīn　shade: 树荫 shù yīn shade of a tree

荫蔽 yīnbì shaded or hidden by foliage; covered, concealed: 那地方相当荫蔽。Nà dìfang xiāngdāng yīnbì. That spot is rather well concealed.

yìn　shady; cool and damp

荫凉 yìnliáng shady and cool: 大树底下很荫凉。Dà shù dǐxià hěn yìnliáng. Under the big tree it's shady and cool.

## 殷　　yīn　yān

yīn　①abundant, great, rich, substantial

②eager, ardent

③〔a surname〕

④〔an alternative name for〕the Shang Dynasty（c. 16 – 11th century B.C.）

殷富 yīnfù flourishing and rich：殷富之家 yīnfù zhī jiā a rich family

殷切 yīnqiè ardent, eager：殷切的期望 yīnqiè de qīwàng earnest expectations

殷实 yīnshí rich, substantial：殷实人家 yīnshí rénjiā a rich family

yān 〈lit.〉a very dark red colour

殷红 yānhóng dark red

# 饮　yǐn　yìn

yǐn ①to drink：饮茶 yǐn chá to drink tea

②a drink

③to hold, bear, swallow（figuratively）

冷饮 lěngyǐn cool drinks

饮恨 yǐnhèn to bear a grudge; to be regretful

饮食 yǐnshí food and drink

饮水思源 yǐnshuǐ-sīyuán when drinking water, think of its source = be mindful of the source of one's happiness

yìn to cause（an animal or a person）to drink：饮马 yìn mǎ to water a horse

# 窨　yìn　xūn

yìn ①an underground cellar for storage

②to store in such a cellar

地窖子 dìyìnzi a cellar

窨藏 yìncáng to store underground

xūn  ( = 熏 ) to smoke (tea etc. to add flavour to it): 窨茶
叶 xūn cháyè to smoke tea (to add flavour to it)

# 应    yìng    yīng

yìng ① to answer, respond, echo: 应观众要求加演一场 yìng
guānzhòng yāoqiú jiā yǎn yì chǎng to put on an extra
performance in response to audience demand

② to accept (a job offer, military duty, an invitation,
etc.): 应聘 yìng pìn to accept a job offer // 应张小
姐之邀赴宴 yìng Zhāng xiǎojiě zhī yāo fùyàn at-
tending the banquet in acceptance of Miss Zhang's invitation

③ to cope with, deal with

④ to suit, be suitable

答应 dāying to assent, promise, answer: 答应要求 dāying yāoqiú to accede to a request

得心应手 déxīn-yìngshǒu able to handle with ease, "in
one's element"

响应 xiǎngyìng to respond: 响应号召 xiǎngyìng hào-
zhào to answer a call

应酬 yìngchou social engagements; to socialise

应付 yìngfu to deal with, cope: 他一个人应付不过来，
你去帮帮吧。Tā yí ge rén yìngfu bú guòlái, nǐ qù
bāngbang ba. He can't cope on his own. Why don't
you go and help out.

应用 yìngyòng to apply, use, utilise: 应用一种新方法 yìng yòng yì zhǒng xīn fāngfǎ to apply a new method

有求必应 yǒuqiú-bìyìng always acceding to requests

照应 zhàoyìng to look after: 请帮我照应一下店面。 Qǐng bāng wǒ zhàoyìng yíxià diànmiàn. Please look after the shop for me for a while.

yīng ①ought to, should

②to answer, respond: 我喊她，她不应。 Wǒ hǎn tā, tā bù yīng. I called her but she didn't answer.

③to consent, promise

④[a surname]

应该 yīnggāi ought to

应允 yīngyǔn to consent and promise, permit: 应允一件事 yīngyǔn yí jiàn shì to give consent and a promise regarding a matter

# 佣　yōng　yòng

yōng ①a servant

②to hire (a labourer)

女佣 nǚyōng a female servant, maid

佣工 yōnggōng hired labour; a servant

yòng commission

佣金 yòngjīn a commission, middleman's fee

# 柚　yòu　yóu

yòu the grapefruit tree or its fruit

柚子 yòuzi the grapefruit or pomelo

**yóu** 柚木 yóumù the teak tree, teak wood

## 与    yǔ    yù

**yǔ**

①and, with: 我与他 wǒ yǔ tā he and I

②to give: 与人方便 yǔ rén fāngbiàn to be of help to people

③〈lit.〉to get along with: 此人难与。 Cǐ rén nán yǔ. This person is hard to get on with.

④〔a preposition introducing the recipient of an action〕: 与人为善 yǔ rén wéi shàn sincere in helping others

给与 jǐyǔ to give: 给与关怀 jǐyǔ guānhuái to give concern and attention

相与 xiāngyǔ〈lit.〉to get along with: 二人相与甚洽。 Èr rén xiāngyǔ shèn qià. The two of them got along really well.

**yù**

to participate: 与闻其事 yù wén qí shì in the know, in on a secret

参与 cānyù to participate in: 参与管理 cānyù guǎnlǐ to participate in management

与会 yùhuì to participate in a meeting or conference: 与会代表共三百人。 Yùhuì dàibiǎo gòng sān bǎi rén. Altogether three hundred delegates participated in the conference.

## 熨    yù → yùn

## 约    yuē    yāo

**yuē**    ①a treaty, agreement, appointment

②to make an appointment, invite：我们约好明天见面。Wǒmen yuē hǎo míngtiān jiànmiàn. We agreed to meet tomorrow. // 他约我去郊游。Tā yuē wǒ qù jiāoyóu. He invited me to go on an excursion.

③to restrain

④simple, brief

⑤approximately

⑥thrifty

⑦（in mathematics）to reduce a fraction：六分之二可以约成三分之一。Liù fēn zhī èr kěyǐ yuē chéng sān fēn zhī yī. Two sixths can be reduced to one third.

⑧〔used in transcribing foreign words〕

大约 dàyuē approximately, roughly：这项任务大约一个星期能完成。Zhè xiàng rènwù dàyuē yí ge xīngqī néng wánchéng. This task can be finished in about a week.

简约 jiǎnyuē brief, concise：简约的报告 jiǎnyuē de bàogào a brief report

节约 jiéyuē to economise, practise thrift：节约用电 jiéyuē yòng diàn to economise on electricity

条约 tiáoyuē a treaty

约旦 Yuēdàn Jordan

约定 yuēdìng to agree on（a date, time, appointment）：约定日期 yuēdìng rìqī to agree on a date

约会 yuēhuì an appointment

约束 yuēshù to restrain, control; restraint, restriction：

他被纪律约束，不能自由行动。Tā bèi jìlǜ yuēshù, bù néng zìyóu xíngdòng. He is under disciplinary restraint, and can't move about freely.

yāo ⟨dial.⟩ to weigh: 约一约多重。Yāo yi yāo duō zhòng. Weigh it and see how heavy it is.

# 乐    yuè    lè

yuè ①music

②〔a surname〕

音乐 yīnyuè music

乐队 yuèduì an orchestra, ensemble, band

乐器 yuèqì a musical instrument

lè ①happy, pleased

②pleasant

快乐 kuàilè happy

乐观 lèguān optimistic

乐园 lèyuán a paradise

# 钥    yuè → yào

# 晕    yūn    yùn

yūn ①to faint: 他晕过去了。Tā yūn guoqu le. He fainted.

②giddy: 我晕得很。Wǒ yūn de hěn. I feel very giddy.

晕倒 yūndǎo to swoon: 老太太晕倒了。Lǎo tàitai yūndǎo le. The old lady swooned.

晕头转向 yūntóu-zhuànxiàng confused and disoriented

yùn ①vapour

②a halo

③faint, dizzy: 晕船 yùn chuán seasick

血晕 xuèyùn dizziness in women due to anaemia following childbirth; a bruise

月晕 yuèyùn a halo around the moon

**熨**　yùn　yù

yùn　to iron clothes: 熨衣服 yùn yīfu to iron clothes

熨斗 yùndǒu a smoothing iron

yù　熨帖 yùtiē smoothed out, settled (of affairs, problems); calm (of the mind); appropriate (of wording)

# Z

**扎**　zā → zhā

**咋**　ză → zhā

**仔**　zǎi → zǐ

**载**　zài　zǎi

zài　①to carry loads on a vehicle: 载货 zài huò to load goods // 这卡车能载几吨? Zhè kǎchē néng zài jǐ dūn? How many tonnes can this truck carry?

②filling, spread everywhere

③and, as well as

④[a surname]

怨声载道 yuànshēng-zàidào complaints are heard everywhere

载歌载舞 zàigē-zàiwǔ singing and dancing festively

**zǎi** ①a year：一年半载 yì nián bàn zǎi a year or half a year; in a year or so

②to record, publish：载入史册 zǎi rù shǐcè recorded in the history books

登载 dēngzǎi to publish：地方报登载了她的故事。Dìfāng bào dēngzǎile tā de gùshi. The local newspaper published her story.

记载 jìzǎi to write down, record; a record

## 攒 zǎn cuán

**zǎn** to hoard, save up：攒钱 zǎn qián to save up money // 他攒了不少邮票。Tā zǎnle bùshǎo yóupiào. He has collected many stamps.

积攒 jīzǎn to save up, hoard：积攒钱财 jīzǎn qiáncái to save up money

**cuán** to collect, assemble, surround

攒聚 cuánjù to crowd together：那些人常攒聚一处，通宵赌钱。Nà xiē rén cháng cuánjù yí chù, tōngxiāo dǔqián. Those people often get together and gamble the night away.

## 脏 zāng zàng

**zāng** dirty, unclean：这屋太脏，需要清扫。Zhè wū tài zāng, xūyào qīngsǎo. This room is very dirty. It needs cleaning. // 脏东西 zāng dōngxi filthy stuff // 脏字 zāng zì a dirty word, a swearword

肮脏 āngzāng dirty: 肮脏衣服 āngzāng yīfu dirty clothes

zàng　internal body organs, viscera

肝脏 gānzàng the liver

内脏 nèizàng the internal organs, viscera

藏　zàng → cáng

奘　zàng → zhuǎng

咋　zé → zhā

择　zé　zhái

zé　to select, choose: 请你任择一件。Qǐng nǐ rèn zé yí jiàn. Please choose whichever one you like.

选择 xuǎnzé to select: 选择合身的衣服 xuǎnzé héshēn de yīfu to choose clothes that fit // 选择工作 xuǎnzé gōngzuò to choose a job

择配 zépèi to choose and match (a spouse): 他那对象是由父母择配的。Tā nà duìxiàng shì yóu fùmǔ zépèi de. His fiancee was chosen by his parents.

zhái　〈dial.〉 to select, choose: 择毛儿 zhái máor to pluck out hair // 择菜 zhái cài to trim vegetables for cooking

曾　zēng → céng

扎　zhā　zhá　zā

zhā　①to pierce: 在耳朵上扎一个洞 zài ěrduo shang zhā

yí ge dòng to pierce a hole in the ear

② to prick: 手被花刺扎了 shǒu bèi huācì zhā le pricked in the hand by a thorn

③ to stick (a needle etc.) into: 把针扎进皮肤 bǎ zhēn zhā jìn pífu to stick needles into the skin // 扎花儿 zhā huār 〈coll.〉 to embroider

④ to station: 部队在村里扎下来了。Bùduì zài cūn li zhā xiàlái le. The army has been stationed in the village.

扎耳 zhā'ěr grating on the ear, ear-piercing (of a sound): 那声音太扎耳, 我受不了。Nà shēngyīn tài zhā'ěr, wǒ shòu bu liǎo. That sound is so piercing that I can't stand it.

扎根 zhāgēn to take root: 她在乡下扎根了。Tā zài xiāngxià zhāgēn le. She has settled in the countryside.

扎心 zhāxīn heart-rending: 这么惨的事儿, 听了扎心。Zhème cǎn de shìr, tīngle zhāxīn. Such a tragic affair, it's heart-rending to hear about.

扎营 zhāyíng to pitch camp: 我们在小溪边扎营。Wǒmen zài xiǎo xī biān zhāyíng. We pitched camp beside a small mountain stream.

驻扎 zhùzhā to station: 边境上驻扎了一支大部队。Biānjìng shang zhùzhāle yì zhī dà bùduì. A large army is stationed on the border.

zhá　挣扎 zhēngzhá to struggle (e.g. to get free): 那溺水

者挣扎着爬上了岸。Nà nìshuǐzhě zhēngzházhe pá shàng le àn. The drowning person struggled to get up the bank.

**zā** to tie, bind: 扎裤脚 zā kùjiǎo to tie up one's trouser legs // 扎皮带 zā pídài to do up one's belt

**查** zhā → chá

**楂** zhā → chá

**咋** zhā  zǎ  zé

**zhā** 咋呼 zhāhu to shout or talk blusteringly: 你咋呼什么呢? Nǐ zhāhu shénme ne? What are you blustering about?

**zǎ** 〈dial.〉〔a fusion of zěnme, 怎么〕How? Why?
咋样? Zǎyàng? How about …? How is …?

**zé** 〈lit.〉to bite
咋舌 zéshé biting one's tongue = speechless with fear or surprise: 那杂技演员的惊险表演令人咋舌。Nà zájì yǎnyuán de jīngxiǎn biǎoyǎn lìng rén zéshé. The acrobat's thrilling performance left the audience speechless.

**轧** zhá → yà

**炸** zhá  zhà

**zhá** to deep-fry in oil: 炸鸡 zhá jī to deep-fry chicken meat (also zhájī; see below) // 炸丸子 zhá wánzi to deep-fry meatballs (also zháwánzi; see below)

炸鸡 zhájī deep-fried chicken（also zhá jī; see above）

炸丸子 zháwánzi deep-fried meatballs（also zhá wán-zi; see above）

zhà ①to explode, burst：那堤岸被炸了一个大洞。Nà dī'àn bèi zhàle yí ge dà dòng. A big hole was blown in the embankment by the explosion.

②〈coll.〉to fly into a rage：气炸了 qì zhà le flew into a rage

③〈dial.〉to flee in terror：炸了窝 zhàle wō fled from the nest

爆炸 bàozhà to explode：厂里锅炉爆炸，工人死伤惨重。Chǎng lǐ guōlú bàozhà, gōngrén sǐshāng cǎnzhòng. The factory boiler exploded, killing and injuring many workers.

轰炸机 hōngzhàjī a bomber（aircraft）

炸弹 zhàdàn a bomb

炸药 zhàyào dynamite

蜡　zhà → là

择　zhái → zé

占　zhān　zhàn

zhān to divine, foretell, observe omens

占卜 zhānbǔ to divine; divination：她会占卜。Tā huì zhānbǔ. She practises divination.

zhàn to take possession of, occupy（territory, status）：这个班男生占三分之二。Zhège bān nánshēng zhàn sān fēn zhī èr. Male students make up two-thirds of this class.

占领 zhànlǐng to occupy (territory): 敌军占领了 302 高地。Díjūn zhànlǐng le sān líng èr gāodì. The enemy have occupied mountain post 302.

占有 zhànyǒu to possess; to occupy: 他一人占有三幢 楼房。Tā yì rén zhànyǒu sān zhuàng lóufáng. He alone owns three buildings.

**粘**　zhān → nián

**长**　zhǎng → cháng

**涨**　zhǎng　zhàng

zhǎng to rise, swell (e.g. water, prices): 河水涨得很高。 Hé shuǐ zhǎng de hěn gāo. The water level in the river has risen very high.

高涨 gāozhǎng a rise, upsurge: 情绪高涨 qíngxù gāo zhǎng emotions running high

涨潮 zhǎngcháo the flood tide

涨价 zhǎngjià to increase in price: 市面上大幅度涨 价，弄得人心惶惶。Shìmiàn shang dà fúdù zhǎng jià, nòng de rénxīn huánghuáng. Market prices increased greatly, causing people to become alarmed and anxious.

涨落 zhǎngluò rise and fall (e.g. of prices, water level): 潮水涨落是有规律的。Cháoshuǐ zhǎngluò shì yǒu guīlǜ de. The rise and fall of the tide follows a certain pattern.

**zhàng** to swell （through absorbing liquid）：种子泡涨了。
Zhǒngzi pàozhàng le. The seeds swelled after soaking.
// 他的脸涨得通红。Tā de liǎn zhàng de
tōnghóng. His face flushed red all over. // 头昏脑涨
tóu hūn nǎo zhàng with head swimming

涨大 zhàngdà to increase in size：那物质因受潮而涨
大。Nà wùzhì yīn shòu cháo ér zhàngdà. That
substance has expanded because it became moist.

## 着　zhāo zháo → zhuó

## 朝　zhāo　cháo

**zhāo** morning, day

今朝 jīnzhāo today

朝夕 zhāoxī day and night, constantly

朝阳 zhāoyáng the early morning sun

**cháo** ①a dynasty：唐朝 Táng cháo the Tang Dynasty

②a court：上朝 shàng cháo to approach the emperor in
court；（of the sovereign）to hold court

③to have audience with royalty

④to face toward：朝西 cháo xī facing west

⑤〔used in transcribing foreign words〕

朝代 cháodài a dynastic period

朝见 cháojiàn to have audience with royalty：朝见皇帝
cháojiàn huángdì to have audience with the emperor

朝廷 cháotíng the royal court

朝鲜 Cháoxiǎn Korea

在朝党 zàicháodǎng the party in power

**爪** zhǎo  zhuǎ

zhǎo  a nail, claw: 鸡爪 jīzhǎo chickens' feet

爪牙 zhǎoyá nails and teeth = lackeys

zhuǎ  〔always with suffixed 儿 or 子〕〈coll.〉a nail, claw:

三爪儿锅 sān zhuǎr guō a three-legged pot

爪子 zhuǎzi a claw

**折** zhé  shé  zhē

zhé  ①to break: 折断 zhé duàn to break off, break in two //

折一根树枝 zhé yì gēn shùzhī to break off a tree

branch

②to fold: 把纸折起来 bǎ zhǐ zhé qilai to fold paper

③to bend, bow down

④to change direction: 他才走出没多远，就折回来

了。Tā cái zǒu chū méi duō yuǎn, jiù zhé huílái

le. He had not gone far before he turned and headed

back.

⑤to suffer setbacks

⑥a discount, rebate: 打八折 dǎ bā zhé to give a 20%

discount

⑦a booklet

⑧(in traditional Chinese drama) a scene: 一折戏 yì

zhé xì one scene of a drama

百 折 不 挠 bǎizhé -bùnáo undaunted by repeated

setbacks

存折 cúnzhé a bank deposit book

曲折 qūzhé winding, tortuous：河道曲折。Hédào qūzhé. The river's course is tortuous. // 曲折的故事 qūzhé de gùshi a convoluted tale

折光 zhéguāng refracted light

折扣 zhékòu a discount：打折扣 dǎ zhékòu to give a discount

折寿 zhéshòu to shorten one's lifespan：纵欲过度会使人折寿。Zòngyù guòdù huì shǐ rén zhéshòu. Too much sensual indulgence can shorten one's lifespan.

折子 zhézi a booklet in accordion form

折子戏 zhézixì performance of selected scenes from a drama

shé ①to lose money (in business)：生意不好，本钱折了。Shēngyi bù hǎo, běnqián shé le. Business is so bad that the capital has been lost.
②broken：棍子折了。Gùnzi shé le. The rod broke.

折本 shéběn to lose money in business：今年他们折本了。Jīnnián tāmen shéběn le. This year they lost money in business. // 折本买卖 shéběn mǎimai a bad bargain

zhē to turn upside-down：折跟头 zhē gēntou to turn somersaults

# 着

着 zhe → zhuó

# 挣  zhēng  zhèng

**zhēng**  挣扎 **zhēng**zhá to struggle: 那老虎在笼中挣扎。Nà lǎohǔ zài lóng zhōng **zhēng**zhá. The tiger struggled in the cage.

**zhèng**  ①to earn: 挣钱 **zhèng** qián to earn money

②to struggle to get free (from bonds): 他挣开了身上捆着的绳索。Tā **zhèng**kāile shēn shang kǔnzhe de shéngsuǒ. He struggled free from the ropes that bound him.

挣脱 **zhèng**tuō to break free: 挣脱锁链 **zhèng**tuō suǒliàn to break free from chains

# 正  zhèng  zhēng

**zhèng**  ①straight, upright, standard, exact; proper, correct, right: 这镜框没挂正。Zhè jìngkuàng méi guà **zhèng**. This picture frame has not been hung straight. // 正南 **zhèng** nán due south // 正前方 **zhèng** qiánfāng right in front // 那人心术不正。Nà rén xīnshù bú **zhèng**. That person harbours evil intentions.

②to correct, rectify, set right, straighten: 正一正领带 **zhèng** yi **zhèng** lǐngdài to straighten one's tie // 正音 **zhèng** yīn to correct pronunciation (also **zhèng**yīn; see below)

③just right, precisely, exactly: 正合心意 **zhèng** hé xīnyì just in keeping with one's intentions // 这衣服正

合适。Zhè yīfu zhèng héshì. This garment is just right. // 正八点 zhèng bā diǎn eight o'clock exactly

④situated in the middle; principal, chief, main：正主席 zhèng zhǔxí the principal chairperson // 正驾驶员 zhèng jiàshǐyuán the chief (or first) pilot

⑤〔indicating continuing or concurrent action〕：我正吃饭呢。Wǒ zhèng chī fàn ne. I'm in the middle of having a meal. // 外面正下大雨。Wàimiàn zhèng xià dà yǔ. It's raining hard outside.

⑥(in geometry) regular：正多面体 zhèng duōmiàntǐ a regular polyhedron // 正三角形 zhèng sānjiǎoxíng an equilateral triangle

⑦(in physics, mathematics) positive：负负得正。Fù fù dé zhèng. A negative times a negative gives a positive.

⑧the obverse side：哪一面是正的？Nǎ yí miàn shì zhèng de? Which is the front side?

⑨(of smell, taste, colour) pure, original, authentic：这酱油味儿不正。Zhè jiàngyóu wèir bú zhèng. The taste of this soy sauce is not authentic. // 颜色不正。Yánsè bú zhèng. The colour is not pure.

纯正 chúnzhèng pure and original

公正 gōngzhèng fair, fair-minded, impartial

正本 zhèngběn the original copy (of a document, manuscript, etc.)

正当 zhèngdàng proper, legitimate, appropriate：正当

的理由 zhèngdàng de lǐyóu a legitimate excuse

正房 zhèngfáng the principal room(s); a legal wife (as contrasted with a concubine)

正好 zhènghǎo just right, perfectly fitting: 他来的时候正好我在。Tā lái de shíhou zhènghǎo wǒ zài. When he came I just happened to be in.

正极 zhèngjí (in physics) the positive pole or electrode

正经 zhèngjing sincere, honest: 正经人 zhèngjing rén a sincere person

正楷 zhèngkǎi (in Chinese calligraphy) standard regular script

正门 zhèngmén the main door or entrance

正面 zhèngmiàn the front, obverse side

正确 zhèngquè accurate: 正确的答案 zhèngquè de dá'àn the correct answer

正数 zhèngshù (in mathematics) a positive number

正厅 zhèngtīng the main hall

正午 zhèngwǔ midday

正音 zhèngyīn standard pronunciation (also zhèng yīn; see P.277)

正直 zhèngzhí honest and upright

正宗 zhèngzōng an orthodox doctrine; authentic: 正宗四川风味 zhèngzōng Sìchuān fēngwèi authentic Sichuan flavour

zhēng first in the lunar calendar

正月 zhēngyuè the first month in the lunar calendar

*Polyphonic compound* :

正旦 zhèngdàn the main female role in Chinese operas

zhēngdàn Chinese New Year's Day

# 症    zhèng    zhēng

zhèng disease

不治之症 búzhì-zhīzhèng an incurable disease

症状 zhèngzhuàng symptoms

zhēng a lump in the abdomen

症结 zhēngjié a lump in the abdomen; a crux, crucial reason, key problem

# 只    zhǐ    zhī

zhǐ only, merely: 他只给了我三块钱。Tā zhǐ gěile wǒ sān kuài qián. He gave me only three dollars.// 我只说了他一句，他就生气了。Wǒ zhǐ shuōle tā yí jù, tā jiù shēngqì le. I'd said just one word of criticism to him, and he got angry.

只好 zhǐhǎo to have to, to have no alternative: 我们只好走回家。Wǒmen zhǐhǎo zǒu huí jiā. We had to walk home.

只怕 zhǐpà only fear

只是 zhǐshì merely, only, simply; however

zhī ①single, one only

②〔a measure word for one member of a pair, and for birds and certain other animals and objects〕: 这只手 zhè zhī shǒu this hand // 三只鸟 sān zhī niǎo three birds

只身 zhīshēn alone, by oneself: 他只身在外，一定感到孤单。Tā zhīshēn zài wài, yídìng gǎndào gūdān. He's outside by himself; he must be feeling lonely.

## 中 zhōng zhòng

zhōng ① the centre, middle: 闽中 Mǐn zhōng central Fujian

② in, among, amidst: 跳入水中 tiàorù shuǐ zhōng to jump into the water // 家中 jiā zhōng among one's family

③ mid: 年中 nián zhōng mid-year // 在途中 zài tú zhōng midway, en route

④ [abbreviation for] China; Chinese: 澳中关系 Ào Zhōng guānxi Australia-China relations

⑤ midway between extremes, moderate

⑥ intermediary: 请人作中 qǐng rén zuò zhōng invited someone to act as intermediary

⑦ in the process of: 在进行中 zài jìnxíng zhōng in the process of being implemented // 发展中国家 fāzhǎn zhōng guójiā developing nations

⑧ fit for, good for

居中 jūzhōng located in the middle: 那房居中。Nà fáng jūzhōng. The room is located in the middle.

适中 shìzhōng moderate; in a moderately suitable location: 位置适中 wèizhi shìzhōng in a suitable position

折中 ( = 折衷 ) zhézhōng to compromise ( by seeking the middle ground ): 折中的办法 zhézhōng de bànfǎ a way of compromise ( by seeking the middle ground )

正中 zhèngzhōng right in the centre: 主席坐在台上正中。Zhǔxí zuò zài tái shang zhèngzhōng. The chairperson was seated right in the centre of the stage.

中等 zhōngděng medium, moderate, intermediate: 中等身材 zhōngděng shēncái of medium build

中国 Zhōngguó China

中人 zhōngrén a go-between, intermediary

中途 zhōngtú mid-way, on the way: 她在中途下车。Tā zài zhōngtú xià chē. She disembarked half-way.

中心 zhōngxīn a centre

中医 Zhōngyī traditional Chinese medicine; a practitioner of traditional Chinese medicine

中用 zhōngyòng useful, helpful: 那人不中用。Nà rén bù zhōngyòng. That person is useless.

zhòng ① to hit the mark: 射中靶心 shè zhòng bǎxīn to hit the bull's-eye // 她猜中了。Tā cāi zhòng le. She guessed right. // 中奖 zhòng jiǎng to win a prize ( in a lottery etc. )

② to fit exactly

③ to be hit by, be affected by, fall into: 中了一枪 zhòngle yì qiāng hit by a bullet // 中了埋伏

zhòngle máifu caught in an ambush

中毒 zhòngdú to be poisoned

中肯 zhòngkěn sincere and pertinent（of remarks）：说话很中肯 shuō huà hěn zhòngkěn to speak sincerely and to the point

中伤 zhòngshāng to vilify, slander：中伤他人 zhòngshāng tārén to vilify others

中意 zhòngyì to find to one's liking：那几个女人他一个也不中意。Nà jǐ ge nǚrén tā yí ge yě bú zhòngyì. Not one of those women is to his liking.

# 忪　zhōng　sōng

zhōng　怔忪 zhēngzhōng〈lit.〉terrified

sōng　惺忪 xīngsōng bleary-eyed from sleep：睡眼惺忪 shuì yǎn xīngsōng with eyes still bleary from sleep

# 种　zhǒng　zhòng

zhǒng　①a seed

②a race, species, kind, breed：这种人 zhè zhǒng rén this sort of person // 几种食品 jǐ zhǒng shípǐn several kinds of food

③guts, grit：这人真没种。Zhè rén zhēn méi zhǒng. This person is really gutless. // 有种的过来打呀！Yǒu zhǒng de guòlái dǎ ya! Whoever has the guts come forward and fight!

品种 pǐnzhǒng a breed, type, variety; an assortment

种类 zhǒnglèi a class, variety, type

种子 zhǒngzi seed for planting

zhòng　to plant, cultivate：种地 zhòng dì to farm the land // 种
痘 zhòng dòu to vaccinate // 老王家今年种了十亩棉
花。Lǎo Wáng jiā jīnnián zhòngle shí mǔ miánhuā.
This year Lao Wang's family have planted ten *mu* of
cotton.

# 重　　zhòng　chóng

zhòng　①heavy：箱子很重。Xiāngzi hěn zhòng. The boxes are
heavy.

②important：老板把她看得很重。Lǎobǎn bǎ tā kàn
de hěn zhòng. The boss regards her as important.

③weight：这只猪有一百斤重。Zhè zhī zhū yǒu yì bǎi
jīn zhòng. This pig weighs one hundred *jin*.

④gravely, seriously：她病得很重。Tā bìng de hěn
zhòng. She is seriously ill.

⑤discreet

慎重 shènzhòng careful and discreet

重量 zhòngliàng weight

重伤 zhòngshāng serious injury

重视 zhòngshì to regard as important：警方对这一案
件很重视。Jǐng fāng duì zhè yí ànjiàn hěn
zhòngshì. The police regard this case as important.

重要 zhòngyào important：重要文件 zhòngyào wén-
jiàn important documents

chóng　①to repeat：这两本书买重了。Zhè liǎng běn shū mǎi
chóng le. A second copy of this book was bought (by

mistake）.

②again, once more: 旧地重游 jiù dì **chóng** yóu to revisit a familiar place

③layers: 九重天 jiǔ **chóng** tiān the nine layers of heaven // 越过万重山 yuè guò wàn **chóng** shān crossing range after range of mountains

重版 **chóng**bǎn a reprint; to reprint

重迭 **chóng**dié piled layer on layer

重复 **chóng**fù to repeat, duplicate: 重复一句话 chóng-fù yí jù huà to repeat a sentence

重新 **chóng**xīn again, anew, afresh: 重新开始 chóng-xīn kāishǐ to start afresh, begin anew

*Polyphonic compound*:

重犯 **zhòng**fàn a person guilty of a serious crime: 他是一个重犯。Tā shì yí ge zhòngfàn. He is a serious offender.

重犯 **chóng**fàn to repeat a crime or mistake: 重犯同一错误 chóngfàn tóng yí cuòwù to commit the same mistake again

# 轴 zhóu zhòu

zhóu ①an axle

②an axis

③〔a measure word for scrolls〕: 一轴画 yì zhóu huà one scroll-painting

车轴 chē**zhóu** an axle

地轴 dì**zhóu** the earth's axis

线轴 xiànzhóu a bobbin, reel for thread

zhòu    大轴子 dàzhòuzi (in Chinese drama) the last act

压轴子 yāzhòuzi (in Chinese drama) the second last act; the climactic act

## 术    zhú → shù

## 属    zhǔ → shǔ

## 爪    zhuǎ → zhǎo

## 拽    zhuài    zhuāi

zhuài    to pull: 把门拽上 bǎ mén zhuài shàng to pull a door shut // 拽住门把手 zhuài zhù mén bǎshǒu to hold tight to a door handle // 生拉硬拽 shēng lā yìng zhuài to force (someone) to do (something) against his will; to stretch the meaning, to give a strained interpretation

zhuāi    ① ⟨dial.⟩ to throw with force: 把缆索拽过去 bǎ lǎnsuǒ zhuāi guoqu to toss a cable across

② ⟨dial.⟩ a defect of the arm causing awkward movement

## 转    zhuǎn    zhuàn

zhuǎn    ① to change direction, position, situation, etc.: 向右转 xiàng yòu zhuǎn to make a right-hand turn // 一转弯就看到车站。Yí zhuǎn wān jiù kàndào chēzhàn. On turning the corner, one sees the station. // 转向 zhuǎn xiàng to change direction or stance (also zhuànxiàng; see below)

② to transfer, forward: 转到另一所学校读书 zhuǎn

dào lìng yì suǒ xuéxiào dú shū (of a student) to transfer to another school

转变 zhuǎnbiàn to change; a change: 转变立场 zhuǎnbiàn lìchǎng to change one's stance // 立场的转变 lìchǎng de zhuǎnbiàn a change in stance

转交 zhuǎnjiāo to forward: 转交信件 zhuǎnjiāo xìnjiàn to forward mail

转学 zhuǎnxué (of a student) to transfer to another school

转载 zhuǎnzǎi to reprint material elsewhere: 那文章被三家报纸转载。Nà wénzhāng bèi sān jiā bàozhǐ zhuǎnzǎi. The article was reprinted in three newspapers.

zhuàn ① to turn, rotate, revolve (on own axis, or around another object): 轮子转了。Lúnzi zhuàn le. The wheel is turning.

② a revolution or turn (of a wheel, etc.): 这飞轮每分钟转一千转。Zhè fēilún měi fēnzhōng zhuàn yì qiān zhuàn. This flywheel spins at 1000 revolutions per minute. // 他绕着大树跑了三转。Tā ràozhe dà shù pǎole sān zhuàn. He ran round the big tree three times.

公转 gōngzhuàn (in astronomy) to revolve

转向 zhuànxiàng to lose one's bearings: 在密林里绕了这么久，我早已转向了。Zài mìlín li ràole zhème jiǔ, wǒ zǎo yǐ zhuànxiàng le. I had been walking round in the dense forest for so long that I soon lost my bearings. (also zhuǎn xiàng; see above)

转椅 zhuànyǐ a swivel chair

自转 zìzhuàn (in astronomy) to rotate

## 传　zhuàn → chuán

## 赚　zhuàn　zuàn

zhuàn　to earn, gain: 赚钱 zhuàn qián to earn money

赚头 zhuàntou a profit

zuàn　〈dial.〉to cheat, deceive: 他叫人赚了。Tā jiào rén zuàn le. He was cheated.

## 奘　zhuǎng　zàng

zhuǎng　〈dial.〉thick, solid: 这棵树很奘。Zhè kē shù hěn zhuǎng. This tree is big and solid.// 身高腰奘 shēn gāo yāo zhuǎng of tall and solid build

zàng　玄奘 Xuán Zàng [monastic name of] a great Buddhist pilgrim and translator (A.D. 602 – 664)

## 幢　zhuàng　chuáng

zhuàng　[a measure word for buildings, houses]: 一幢房屋 yí zhuàng fángwū one house

chuáng　①a stone pillar bearing a Buddhist inscription

②a pennant, streamer, war standard

幢幡 chuángfān silk streamers

经幢 jīngchuáng a stone pillar inscribed with a Buddhist scripture

# 着

zhuó zháo zhāo zhe

zhuó　①to wear: 穿红着绿 chuān hóng zhuó lǜ colourfully dressed

②to touch, come into contact with

③to apply, use

④whereabouts: 经费无着。Jīngfèi wú zhuó. Funding cannot be found anywhere.

⑤to depute, send (someone) to do (something): 着人来取 zhuó rén lái qǔ to get someone to come and fetch (something) // 着你去办 zhuó nǐ qù bàn to depute you to go and do it

穿着 chuānzhuó clothes, apparel (also chuānzhe; see below)

着力 zhuólì to put forth effort: 着力办理那件事 zhuólì bànlǐ nà jiàn shì to make an effort to attend to the matter

着陆 zhuólù to land, touch down: 飞机着陆。Fēijī zhuólù. The plane is touching down.

着色 zhuósè to apply colour; the colours in a painting: 那幅画着色清淡。Nà fú huà zhuósè qīngdàn. The colours in that painting are delicate.

着眼 zhuóyǎn to fix attention, concentrate: 办事要从大处着眼。Bàn shì yào cóng dà chù zhuóyǎn. In doing a task, one should fix attention on the essentials.

zháo　①to feel, be affected by, catch (fire, a sickness, etc.): 她着了凉。Tā zháole liáng. She caught cold. // 干草着了火。Gān cǎo zháole huǒ. The dry grass caught fire. // 别着急。Bié zháo jí. Don't worry.

②〔verbal complement signifying success〕：她找着了。Tā zhǎo zháo le. She's found it. // 猜着了 cāi zháo le guessed right // 见不着 jiàn bu zháo unable to get to see

③to reach (a place)：上不着天下不着地 shàng bù zháo tiān, xià bù zháo dì having reached neither heaven nor earth = suspended in mid-air

zhāo ①( = 招 ) a stratagem

②( = 招 ) a move (in chess)

③〈dial.〉 All right!：着！就这么办。Zhāo! Jiù zhème bàn. All right! Let's do it. ( or So, do it this way.)

高着 gāozhāo a clever move / idea

绝着 juézhāo a unique skill or unexpected tricky move (usually one employed as a last resort)

zhe 〔a verbal suffix indicating a continuing action or state〕：坐着等 zuòzhe děng to sit waiting // 站着 zhànzhe standing // 开着 kāizhe open (of a door, box, etc.) // 穿着 chuānzhe wearing, dressed in (also chuānzhuó; see above)

# 仔　zǐ　zǎi

zǐ the young of domestic animals or fowl

仔鸡 zǐjī a chick

仔细 zǐxì careful, minute

仔猪 zǐzhū a piglet

zǎi ①( = 崽 ) the young of animals

②〈dial.〉a son or boy

鲸仔 jīngzǎi a whale calf

牛仔裤 niúzǎikù cowboy pants, jeans

# 钻 zuān zuàn

zuān ①to pierce, bore, drill: 钻孔 zuān kǒng to drill a hole // 钻木取火 zuān mù qǔ huǒ to make fire by friction

②to penetrate deeply: 钻进密林里 zuān jìn mìlín li to penetrate into dense forest

③to dig into, study intensively: 钻业务 zuān yèwù to study intensively in one's field

钻研 zuānyán to study intensively: 刻苦钻研 kèkǔ zuānyán make great effort to study intensively

钻营 zuānyíng to curry favour for personal gain: 他善于钻营，不久便发了财。Tā shànyú zuānyíng, bùjiǔ biàn fāle cái. He's good at currying favour, and it wasn't long before he'd grown rich.

zuàn ①a borer, drill, awl

②a diamond; a jewel: 18 钻的手表 shíbā zuàn de shǒubiǎo an 18-jewel watch

③to pierce, bore, drill

电钻 diànzuàn an electric drill

钻石 zuànshí diamond

钻头 zuàntóu a drill, awl

**赚** zuàn → zhuàn

**作** zuò   zuō

zuò  ①to do, make: 作功课 zuò gōngkè to do homework //
作出结论 zuòchū jiélùn to draw a conclusion

②to act as: 作保 zuò bǎo to act as guarantor

③to write, compose: 作一篇文章 zuò yì piān wénzhāng to write an article // 作了两首曲子 zuòle
liǎng shǒu qǔzi wrote two musical pieces // 作画 zuò
huà to do a painting

④a composition

⑤to break out, start up: 枪声大作。Qiāng shēng dà
zuò. Heavy gunfire broke out.

⑥as: 我们把那只猫叫作咪咪。Wǒmen bǎ nà zhī
māo jiào zuò Mīmī. We call that cat Mimi.

发作 fāzuò to break out, start up: 老张的心脏病发作
了。Lǎo Zhāng de xīnzàngbìng fāzuò le. Lao Zhang
had a heart attack.

工作 gōngzuò a job, work

杰作 jiézuò a masterpiece

名作 míngzuò a famous piece of work

认贼作父 rènzéi-zuòfù to take a thief as one's father =
to become a committed follower of an evil person

作家 zuòjiā an author, writer

作料 zuòliào (coll. also zuóliào) condiments

zuō  a workshop

洗衣作 xǐyīzuō a laundry shop
作坊 zuōfang a workshop

撖　　　zuǒ → cuō

# STROKE-COUNT INDEX

| | | | | | | | | |
|---|---|---|---|---|---|---|---|---|
| 鲜 | xiān | 245 | 撒 | sā | 208 | 臊 | sāo | 211 |
| 嘘 | xū | 252 | 熨 | yùn | 267 | | | |
| 熏 | xūn | 254 | 幢 | zhuàng | 288 | **19 strokes** | | |
| 窨 | yìn | 261 | | | | 簸 | bò | 17 |
| 赚 | zhuàn | 288 | **16 strokes** | | | 蹶 | jué | 134 |
| | | | 薄 | báo | 8 | 靡 | mǐ | 168 |
| **15 strokes** | | | 擂 | léi | 143 | 攒 | zǎn | 268 |
| 磅 | bàng | 8 | 燎 | liáo | 147 | | | |
| 澄 | chéng | 28 | 磨 | mó | 170 | **20 strokes** | | |
| 撮 | cuō | 36 | 擞 | sǒu | 226 | 嚼 | jiáo | 121 |
| 横 | héng | 94 | 燕 | yàn | 256 | 嚷 | rǎng | 205 |
| 糊 | hú | 97 | | | | | | |
| 稽 | jī | 108 | **17 strokes** | | | **21 strokes** | | |
| 撩 | liāo | 147 | 藏 | cáng | 20 | 蠡 | lí | 144 |
| 澎 | péng | 185 | 豁 | huō | 106 | 露 | lù | 154 |
| 劈 | pī | 186 | 縻 | mí | 168 | | | |

责任编辑　贾寅淮　郁　苓
封面设计　安洪民

**图书在版编目(CIP)数据**

多音多义字汉英字典/(澳)白瑞德,杨沐编,—北京:华语教学出版
社,1998.10

ISBN 7 – 80052 – 634 – 8

Ⅰ. 多…　Ⅱ.①白…　②杨…　Ⅲ.①汉语—字典　②字典—汉、英
Ⅳ.H195 – 61

中国版本图书馆 CIP 数据核字(98)第 17290 号

**多音多义字汉英字典**
白瑞德　杨　沐　编
＊

ⓒ华语教学出版社
华语教学出版社出版
(中国北京百万庄路 24 号)
邮政编码 100037
电话:86 – 010 – 68326333 / 68994599
传真:86 – 010 – 68326642
电子信箱:sinolingua@ihw.com.cn

北京外文印刷厂印刷
中国国际图书贸易总公司海外发行
(中国北京车公庄西路 35 号)
北京邮政信箱第 399 号　邮政编码 100044
新华书店国内发行
1999 年(32 开)第一版
(汉英)
ISBN 7-80052-634-8/H·733(外)
定价:22.00 元
9-CE-3297P